STRATEGIC PLANNING IN ACTION

Dedicated to the memory of Hugh T. MacCalman (1905-1973)

First Chairman of the Clyde Valley Regional Planning

Advisory Committee

Strategic Planning in Action

The Impact of the Clyde Valley Regional Plan 1946-1982

Edited by
ROGER SMITH
Reader in Town and Country Planning
Trent Polytechnic
and
URLAN WANNOP
Professor of Urban and Regional Planning
University of Strathclyde

Gower

Published by
Gower Publishing Company Limited,
Gower House, Croft Road, Aldershot, Hampshire, England.

Gower Publishing Company,
Old Post Road, Brookfield, Vermont 05036, USA.

HT
395
.G73
C557
1985

British Library Cataloguing in Publication Data

Strategic planning in action : the impact of the
  Clyde Valley Regional Plan 1946-1982.
  1. Regional planning——Scotland——Clyde, River,
  Region   2. Clyde, River, Region (Scotland)——
  Economic policy
  I. Smith, Roger, *1941-*   II. Wannop, Urlan
  338.9414'1   HC257.Z7C5/

115 99470

Library of Congress Cataloging in Publication Data

Strategic planning in action.

  Bibliography: p.
  Includes index. 1. Regional planning--Scotland--
Clyde River Valley--History--Addresses, essays, lectures.
2. Metropolitan areas--Scotland--Planning--History--Addresses,
essays, lectures. I. Smith, Roger, 1941-   . II. Wannop,
Urlan, 1931-   .
HT395.G73C557 1985   307'.12'094141   84-29044

ISBN 0-566-00782-7

3-25-91

Printed and bound in Great Britain by
Biddles Ltd, Guildford and Kings Lynn.

Contents

Figures and Tables

Contributors

Miller Allan Lecturer in the Department of Town and Regional Planning, University of Glasgow.

Veronica Burbridge Formerly Senior Research Officer, Scottish Development Department and Consultant to the Ford Foundation in Indonesia.

Elspeth Farmer Formerly Lecturer in the Department of Town and Regional Planning, University of Glasgow.

John R. Firn Managing Director, Firn, Crighton, Roberts, Ltd., Economic Consultants. Formerly Head of Industrial Programmes Development, Scottish Development Agency.

Sir Robert Grieve Formerly Chief Planner, Scottish Office, Chairman of the Highlands and Islands Development Board, and Emeritus Professor of Town and Regional Planning, University of Glasgow.

Fred Hay Lecturer in the Department of Political Economy, University of Glasgow.

Shiela McDonald Senior Lecturer in the Department of Town and Regional Planning, University of Glasgow.

Roger Smith Reader in the Department of Town and Country Planning, Trent Polytechnic.

Urlan Wannop Professor of Urban and Regional Planning, University of Strathclyde.

Acknowledgements

The financial support given by the British Academy small grants fund and the Trent Polytechnic Research Committee to enable Roger Smith to visit Scotland and to defray other expenses is gratefully acknowledged.

We also wish to thank Ian Lumsden for his assistance with Chapter 8, Francis Hadden for cartographical assistance and John Close for searching for and preparing illustrations. Anne Lockhart processed and printed the text, with patience. Permission to quote extensively and to reproduce illustrations from the Clyde Valley Regional Plan has been given by HMSO. Permission to draw on Table 7 of James G. Kellas, The Scottish Political System, 1973, has been given by Cambridge University Press.

For photographs, acknowledgements are due to:

Annan, Photographer, Glasgow	118 High Street, Glasgow, 1868
Cumbernauld Development Corporation	Cumbernauld Town Centre Housing for the Elderly, Kildrum
Glasgow District Council Department of Planning	Custom House Quay
Glasgow Herald	Upper Clyde Shipyard Work-in, 1971
Shiela McDonald	Various Buildings
George Oliver, Photographer, Glasgow	Gable Painting, Govanhill
W. Ralston, Photographers, Glasgow	Clydeside Conurbation Strathclyde Park

Introduction

The first industrial society was created in Europe in the nineteenth century. It set in motion a dynamic process which over almost two hundred years stimulated growth in the conurbations of Britain, many of which are now in decline. This decline has often followed the exhaustion of local raw materials such as coal and iron ore which once encouraged growth. New technologies have also brought decline to communities unable to innovate or readapt older practices. The emergence of multi-national economic activities has redeployed capital investment from the advanced nations to the Third World where unit costs are lower. Thus, although industrialisation has provided many with growing access to a wide range of consumer goods, high quality housing, wholesome environments, mobility and a wide range of social facilities, others have suffered the harsh consequences of economic adaptation. As Britain entered the war of 1939-45, obsolescent industrialisation and the unbalanced distribution of the products of economic expansion left a legacy of poor quality housing and an impoverished social and physical environment, compounded by concentrated social problems in the country's large towns and cities. Economic historians have extensively documented the social pain of the long ·process of industrialisation in Britain. Then, between the mid 1950s and mid 1960s, nearly full employment coincided with rapidly improving housing and environmental conditions. Subsequently key areas have fallen into either absolute or relative decline.

Figure 1

Looking west over the Clydeside Conurbation from the
City Centre of Glasgow to the Lower Clyde, 1981

Some observers have detected a process of rapid de-industrialisation.

There have been significant political responses within Western Europe to these international trends. Governments have attempted to direct and control industrialisation and have attempted to ameliorate many of its worst consequences. All Western governments now have a major say in national economic management, although various political parties and factions may dispute the optimum level of intervention. Most Western governments have regional policies, while the European Economic Community recognises that the benefits of industrialisation are not distributed on a spatially even basis within nation states. Recently, however, urban policy has become a distinctive feature in several countries and is now a more vigorous subject of debate and concern than is regional policy. On a non-spatial basis, governments also accept some degree of responsibility to redistribute wealth by taxation from the most to the least prosperous members of society, imperfect as the results are.

This book is an attempt to explore how public agencies and bodies have attempted to deal with metropolitan planning and development in one of the most distinctive regions in Britain - Scotland's Clyde Valley - over the course of thirty five years, spanning the period in which industrialisation rallied and then entered its decline. From this experience, there are historic lessons of policy formulation and implementation for other regions and other countries. With Glasgow at its heart, the Clyde Valley is a classic case of a metropolitan area which grew to industrial greatness during the nineteenth century and which then fell into economic decline during the twentieth century. The region became characterised by the social ills of an appalling housing environment, chronic overcrowding and congestion and the industrial ills of a collapsing manufacturing base. The region also became - together with South-East England - a classic case of comprehensive strategic planning, sustained and reviewed more determinedly than in other regions of Britain. This book uses the Clyde Valley Regional Plan as a pioneering and classic case through which to examine the history and influence of a great plan together with some wider issues in regional planning and governance. Of all the regional plans made in Britain during the 1940s the Clyde Valley Regional Plan has arguably exercised the greatest influence. The book traces the history of the Plan's recommendations and shows how extensively they have been realised. Other recommendations have been implemented in modified forms. It is certain that the urban environment and metropolitan landscape of Glasgow and West Central Scotland would have evolved very differently since 1950 had it not been for the proposals of the Plan. Elsewhere in Scotland, ideas carried forward from the Plan were to be translated into national or regional initiatives which contributed to the special Scottish experience of regional planning and development. This raises a crucial question. How did the Plan exercise its influence? Intimately associated with an answer must be assessments of why some recommendations were fulfilled and others were not, and of why some recommendations were subsequently modified and readapted to meet changing circumstances.

The book assesses the scale of the impact of the Plan since its completion in 1946. Having done that, it examines -

(i)   How and why the Plan generated new ideas or acted as a filter for planning ideas then enjoying a general currency;

(ii) The institutional framework, through which the ideas could be implemented;

(iii) The wider influence of social and economic change in the Clyde Valley as well as throughout Britain in the post-war years;

(iv) The influence of significant personalities involved in preparing and implementing the Plan.

The book contributes to an understanding of planning issues in West Central Scotland but, because these are in many respects now shared with other mature industrial regions in countries with advanced economies, we believe that the analyses present here have much more than a local interest. A retrospective reflection on the Clyde Valley Regional Plan has insights to offer on the overall scope, limits and nature of regional and strategic planning.

Roger Smith
Urlan Wannop

Prologue

SIR ROBERT GRIEVE

In the Spectator of January 27, 1950, Sir Frederic Osborn, a pioneer of the new towns movement, the leader for so long of the Town & Country Planning Association and a most shrewd commentator on the planning process, wrote a review of the Clyde Valley Regional Plan, 1946. The Plan had taken 2 years to prepare and issue in type, and over 3 years for its full publication, which was only effected eventually through the agency, and editing, of the Scottish Office.

Among other comments, Osborn wrote: 'This superb report - the masterpiece of the Abercrombie series .... is at once a geography of the region, a history of its development, an analysis of its economy, a study of the ways and works of its people, an appreciation of its beauties and ugliness, and a philosophy of physical planning ... it is magnificently illustrated .... I am tempted to say that it would come into the class of fine literature but for the fact that it displays statistical sense as well as sensitivity ...' He was obviously impressed, although he stood closer to its twin, the Greater London Plan, 1944, produced just before it. And his eulogy has to be seen against the prewar practice of planning, with its severe limitations in law, practice and professional capacity.

The Clyde Valley Regional Plan was produced by a staff of a dozen or so professional people (apart from part-time draughting staff for publication); a small number by comparison with later regional plans. Of the senior team of five people,

1

two had worked in local planning authorities at the cutting-edge of a primitive planning machine. Not all local authorities had planning departments; and the planning being carried out under the current 1932 Town & Country Planning Act, immediately before the Second World War, largely dealt with the problems raised by suburban speculative private building, and consisted of simple zoning arrangements to ensure minimum provision of public necessities e.g., school sites, open spaces (very few), shopping sites and roads and services. There was the minimum of collaboration between adjoining authorities. In the whole of Scotland, when the Clyde Valley planning team was set up in 1944, there were no more than a dozen or two qualified planners; that is, planners who had professional planning qualifications or had gone through planning courses in advanced educational institutions which taught the subject. In short, the challenge presented by the tackling of such a regional plan was a very big one. One can only describe it as an enormous leap in thought and action from the preceding process; and the creative opening that this Plan represented to us can be appreciated.

This book shows that its authors have gone a long way ahead of the 1946 Plan in almost all manner of statistical material and methods of analysis: we were looking forward from a narrow base of available material. The social-industrial picture had been distorted almost incalculably by a terrible World War, not yet at an end when we began. But we were, of course, supported (or dominated, if one chooses that word) by a mass of statistical material and theory from special commissions and committees set up around the period of the War. In effect, they dealt with the future handling of Industrial Revolution Britain; and the principal one was the Barlow Commission on the Distribution of the Industrial Population, published in 1940 and overshadowed by the War's beginning. But its influence was very great - a kind of foundation for strategic planning. Fundamentally, it argued on a number of important grounds that the million-mark conurbation was too big. The other committees, between them, laid the foundations for the future town and country planning system; the justification for, and building of, new towns; and the handling of rural areas (but not such rural areas as the Highlands and Islands of Scotland). So, we were operating within certain socio-political constraints; the general shape of national policies were forming around us as we worked; and there was a genuine idealism which engaged us all, in greater or lesser degree.

But our idealism must not be exaggerated. In our innumerable staff and individual discussions we went over almost all the practical considerations that were likely to take hold of, distort, and even destroy the base of the Plan. I might give

2

one example of this: the question of the principal theme of the Barlow Commission Report. Two of our number had served on that body, Professor Abercrombie, himself, and the Clerk to the Regional Committee, Sir William E. Whyte. I was asked by Abercrombie to apply to Greater Glasgow the Barlow argument that the million-mark conurbation was too big; this for our Final Report. I was obliged, therefore, to read the Barlow Commission's arguments much more carefully than any of us had done. I found myself not convinced and said so. He said the detailed arguments would be in the Evidence to the Commission. From Sir William - who had kept his papers - I got the material. I read that carefully and came back still not convinced. The matter was dropped; the weight of general conviction was too great, and mine only a personal opinion. Years later, in a review of the Plan (1954), I pointed out that there might have been other options in general strategy, but that the balance of considerations made for the line taken in the published Plan.

Also, for a number of reasons, not least because some of us knew the way of pragmatic politics, and all of us the lack of a highly-trained planning administration (and therefore, education), the Plan had to be rather a preceptive plan than a phased economics-based one. Future legislation could not be assessed, nor local government administration. Above all, it was a long-term plan, and the precepts or desiderata above fitted that. The inimitable Sydney Smith, 200 years before, however, gave this advice to Lady Morpeth (among his own 20 'rules of life' and in answer to her letter of depression)....'Short views of human life - not further than dinner or tea...' Smith's genial exhortation is, and always has been, well understood by the normal pragmatic politician who might say that the whole art of the thing is in keeping the ground just before the planner (say, downwards, at 45°) particularly in view - with an occasional, preferably intelligent, look upwards at the distance. We, who worked on the Plan, wrote it up and illustrated it, were certainly aware of all that, even within the somewhat euphoric atmosphere we then lived in. We were also aware of the need for a greater economic and 'social input' to the Plan; and recorded that at the time. But the simple fact is that those two on the staff who had some knowledge of these subjects could not appear to see their role in such a planning team of actual practitioners, and the latter were hardly in a position (or with the knowledge) to tell them; there was no real junction between the practitioners of various skills and the academics. That kind of fruitful coming-together did not occur till much later in the early 60's; but, in the 40's, their reaction was essentially ... 'you make it, we break it ...' There was no sense of a collective responsibility for the essential

3

component of planning - a projection into the future upon which serious and extensive action could be taken administratively and physically. It is rather different today; but, again, I am conveying the atmosphere and constraints of that time.

And this leads me finally to action on the <u>Plan</u>. I was quoted by Derek Senior, that former doyen of planning journalists, as having once said in a conference speech that 'planning without implementation is just doodling.' Patrick Geddes expressed the thing rather more felicitously, a long time ago, when he said that planning without the corrective of action is ... 'simply playing into the puzzles of the maze ...' J.H. McGuinness, who held a key administrative position in the Scottish Office on regional planning and development work for many years, is on record in a paper given to the Royal Town Planning Institute as saying that the policy of the Scottish Office in the immediate postwar period was to bring into the planning department as many of the Clyde Valley Plan staff as possible. This, he said, was to use their skills and experience for advancing action on various proposals in the <u>Plan</u>. There was, of course, much more central government dirigisme then, than now.

To finish: we, 40 years ago, rolling along on a great wave of postwar reform, believed passionately in a better, more socially equitable, more beautiful future than is now the fashion and expectation. So, therefore, the <u>Plan</u> is written with more warmth and colour than its grandchildren of today. Those who have written this book are the heirs of a better statistical and analytical system. I, myself, have overlapped their careers and times and some of them were my later colleagues. I fully understand them, with some regret for the loss of the underlying passion. I am absolutely aware of the need for a closely analytical book of this sort; and recognise that it, too, will endure analysis in manners and knowledges as yet unknown.

1 The Industrialisation of the Clyde Valley

ROGER SMITH

The Clyde Valley Regional Plan analysed and offered solutions to a complex range of land-use, economic and social issues and problems in West Central Scotland, most of which were the product of a long historical process. Arguably, public land-use planning as it is practised in Britain derived from responses to many of the adverse consequences of the Industrial Revolution. But it was not simply that the Industrial Revolution bequeathed overcrowded and unhygienic dwellings, set within a chaotic mix of noxious factories and workshops, thereby creating an environment which was ugly, 'inefficient' and sometimes dangerous. All this is true. But in addition, out of the Industrial Revolution grew a new system of social relationships and novel approaches to government, as well as different awareness of the very essence of man. These social and philosophic changes have probably been more enduring and of greater significance than the legacy of bricks and mortar. It is therefore important to see the Plan within the context of the features which have shaped the physical environment, the economic and industrial structure and social and political attitudes in the Clyde Valley.

In few areas was the impact of the Industrial Revolution more dramatic or more profound than in the watershed of the River Clyde. Before the mid eighteenth century, the region's economy was based predominantly on agriculture buttressed by a little fishing and trading, and serviced by a number of market towns. At that point where the Clyde could be forded, lay Glasgow, a small Cathedral and University town (Gilfillan 1958, 82-95).

The first stirrings which transformed that diminutive settlement into the heart of one of the world's great industrial regions can be detected during the first quarter of the eighteenth century when a small group of Glasgow merchants began to engage, with increasing success, in the lucrative American tobacco trade, which by 1735 they had monopolised. This trade collapsed, never to be revitalised, when the American War of Independence broke out in 1776. The infrastructure these merchants provided, such as bridges, the widening of the Clyde, and the docks, encouraged in no small measure the next stage in the region's economic growth. It also seems that the demand for goods, needed for barter when the tobacco trade was at its zenith, created a generation of small manufacturers who had by the last quarter of the century become sufficiently viable to withstand the shock of the collapse of the Atlantic trade (Price 1967).

Meanwhile, the European demand for textiles increased. The technical developments in spinning and weaving cotton enabled Britain to exploit that demand and a number of production centres quickly developed, one of which was in the Clyde Valley. Several factors account for this. Glasgow's past history enabled links with America, the supplier of the raw cotton, to be re-established. The region's damp climate was advantageous to spinning, there was an abundance of fast flowing streams to power the mills, and there was the expertise provided by the local linen manufacture - stimulated earlier by the tobacco trade - upon which to build this new industry.

During the last quarter of the eighteenth century, therefore, mechanised spinning in isolated mills and hand loom weaving in villages adjoining or in the vicinity of Glasgow, progressed apace. By the early nineteenth century, however, the textile industry was passing through a further technical phase. The invention of the power loom transformed weaving from a domestic to a factory system, and steam power freed both the spinning and weaving process from the dependence on fast flowing streams. As a consequence, steam powered spinning and weaving mills came to be established in Glasgow as well as other towns within the region, but notably in Paisley.

The demand for labour to man the new factories drew workers and their families into these emergent urban centres, not only from the nearby rural areas but from further afield. Substantial numbers came from the Highlands and Islands to the Clyde Valley and, especially during the 1840's, many also came from Ireland driven out by the potato famine. Glasgow grew from a population of some 30,000 in 1770 to 359,000 in 1851,

6

and from the 1780's onwards the building of tenements – that most distinctive form of Scottish domestic architecture – proceeded rapidly to accommodate the newcomers. During the early nineteenth century tenements had been built at considerable densities, wedged between the main east-west thoroughfare of the city and the northern bank of the Clyde.

The Clyde Valley tenement of this era tended to be four storeys high and each floor contained eight dwellings, four of two rooms and four of one. Each dwelling led off narrow staircases and passages. This, combined with the large number of tenement blocks per acre, was enough to create horrifically high residential densities with all the attendant public health problems.

The growth of Glasgow also created new social groupings and new social pressures and divisions. Scots drawn into the urban areas from the Lowlands and the Borders had some familiarity with the new productive processes and the new work disciplines that were demanded. Many also had the advantages deriving from the rural educational system which owed its origins to Knox and the Scottish Reformation. Obviously, the new urban environment into which they moved must have presented them with unforeseen traumas as well as opportunities, but their earlier social experience and heritage had prepared them for many of the demands that their new life was to make on them. From this stock came many of the apprentices and skilled craftsmen.

These migrants can be contrasted with those from a peasant background in Ireland and the Highlands and Islands. The 'culture shock' for these immigrants must have been immeasurably greater than those coming from nearer parts. The agricultural worker – the product of an embryonic capitalist farming system – is nearer to the industrial worker than is the peasant. The transition of the former into industrial man is in many respects more fundamental than the transition of the latter. Consequently, it was to the non-skilled and considerable less secure jobs – accepting that all work was accompanied by a larger measure of insecurity – that such peasants gravitated. They were to become the poorest of the urban society of the Clyde Valley and it was they who brought with them major social ills. They were also segregated from their fellow immigrants by religious divisions. The peasants tended to be Roman Catholics, the agricultural workers were Presbyterians.

The growing application of steam power in the Clyde Valley encouraged a rapid exploitation of the region's coal seams and iron ore deposits, and a number of 'iron' and later 'steel' towns began to be established on the upper reaches of the

Figure 1.1 Lobnitz and Co. shipyard, Renfrew, mid 1880's

8

Clyde. By the middle of the nineteenth century, Airdrie, Coatbridge and Motherwell had all mushroomed into considerable population centres, mirroring, although on a smaller scale, the housing and other social problems which were beginning to develop in Glasgow.

Partly because the mercantile element remained strong in Glasgow during the first half of the nineteenth century, the city's craftsmen turned to making wooden ships. This was at a time when engineering concerns, manufacturing steam engines to power the textile mills and work the pumps in the mines, were also becoming established in the city. These factors, combined with the ready supply of coal and iron in the region, made it almost inevitable that Clydeside should pioneer and then lead the world in the building of marine engines and iron and then steel made ships. As these new industries became established in Glasgow so a second generation of industrial towns in the region, based on shipbuilding, began to establish themselves from the 1850's on the lower reaches of the Clyde, where the river was broader and deeper. (Robb 1958, 181; Lenman 1977, 116-121).

For the Clyde Valley the rise of heavy engineering heralded the second phase of its industrial revolution and came at an opportune time. By the second half of the nineteenth century the Scottish cotton industry found itself unable to compete effectively with Lancashire. Serious unemployment was prevented, however, as labour moved into the new heavy engineering sector. The growth in the number of jobs in the region, therefore, continued to remain a major feature of the second half of the nineteenth century and the flow of immigrants and their families to fill the vacancies continued. Largely as a result of this, Glasgow's population grew from 329,000 to 784,000 between 1841 and 1911,

The rise of the industrialised middle class during the first half of the nineteenth century brought about major changes in the political structures and institutions of Britain. In Scotland the 1833 Burgh Reform Act effectively brought the control of the urban areas like Glasgow into the hands of the middle class voters. In the long term it enabled the middle classes to direct their concerns towards the amelioration of some of the worst consequences of rapid industrialisation when they took seats on the new council and drew on a growing body of professional and technical expertise, as a distinct body of competent and uncorrupt local government officers began to emerge.

This can be seen in Glasgow. The great industrialists of the city tended to avoid local politics (Checkland 1976). Within

Figure 1.2   118 High Street, Glasgow, 1868

the lower middle classes, however, a concern with civic affairs grew and during this second half of the century, Glasgow Corporation adopted a more interventionist role in housing in an attempt to prevent the repetition of past mistakes. In order to reduce the incidence of overcrowding, a series of local Police Acts and by-laws from 1866 onwards fixed minimum room sizes and effectively minimum densities of tenements per acre for all subsequent building and the number of persons per room in all working class dwellings was at least theoretically regulated.

In order to improve conditions in the worst areas, in 1866 Glasgow Corporation also embarked on an ambitious slum clearance programme, and over the course of the next half century, eighty-eight acres of slums were demolished and replaced by 1,546 improved tenements (Allan 1965). Yet despite the marginal improvement in the urban environment brought about in Glasgow during these years, many of the evils associated with the tenement were still very evident at the outbreak of the Great War. The Report of the Royal Commission on Housing in Scotland made it clear that even by 1917 the majority of Glaswegians were compelled to live under conditions of extreme deprivation, and it would be difficult to over-exaggerate the misery engendered by overcrowding and congestion (Royal Commission 1917).

The inter-war period witnessed the near collapse of the Clyde Valley economy. Coal was the first of the region's industries to be adversely affected once the Great War had ceased, partly because other fuels had become cheaper and partly because the local seams were becoming exhausted. The local iron ores, too, were running out (Scottish Home Department 1944, Chap III; Oakley 1937, Chaps. VII and VIII).

Shipbuilding and marine engineering remained relatively buoyant during the 1920's and whilst the tonnage output never reached the prewar figure, the industry was nonetheless able to remain competitive (see Slavon 1975, Chap. 8). But shipbuilding and marine engineering suffered equally with the other staple industries of the Clyde Valley in 1929 when international trade virtually came to a halt. It had not been uncommon in the 1920's for unemployment rates in various parts of the Clyde Valley to reach fifteen per cent. As a result of the 1929 crisis, rates rose generally to over thirty per cent and in some areas they were as high as sixty per cent (Board of Trade 1932).

It was during the first World War and the inter-war period that the images of 'Red Clydeside' and Glasgow gang warfare became established. The political reputation preceded the

11

Depression and its earlier history was related to the nature of late nineteenth century Clydeside trade unionism, which tended to be concerned with issues which were seen in a more doctrinaire way than was general throughout Britain. It was within this atmosphere that the Independent Labour Party in the region developed, and within which a generation of politicians were produced who, as M.P.s, made a major impact on the two inter-war minority Labour governments. The names of Maxton, Johnston and Wheatley were prominent. The 1915 Rent Strike and the 1919 'Forty Hours' strike for reduced hours helped stamp the region as one of left wing militancy. The other reaction to unemployment and poverty was gang warfare in Bridgeton and the Gorbals. This was the apolitical side of industrial collapse. But more insidious and a much more enduring legacy were the demonstrations and open conflicts between the Catholics and the Orange Lodges.

Central Government responded to the industrial problems of the region by designating much of the Clyde Valley – excluding Glasgow for reasons of civic pride rather than purely economic considerations – as a special area under the 1931 Special Areas Act. The power of the Scottish Commissioner, however, like his colleague in England and Wales, was limited, and it was not until 1937 that the Special Area Amendment Act allowed him to give Treasury grants to profit-making organisations. The Commissioner was now enabled to introduce trading estates – run by non-profit making companies – into the Clyde Valley. Through this Act, it was hoped that subsidised factory floor space could be made available to attract light industry to the region and so replace jobs lost in the traditional sectors. By 1939, four industrial estates had been established in the Clyde Valley in which 5,000 new jobs had been created (Trotman – Dickenson 1961; Kirkwood 1948).

Yet during the 1930's, if it is possible to write of a coherent Government strategy for the Clyde Valley at all, it was one of revitalising the shipbuilding industry whose
    'influence extends backwards to steel, the iron and
    coal trades, and forward first and obviously to
    marine engineering and then to a very great number of
    other industries' (Board of Trade 1932).
Even so, it was recognised that because of recapitalisation the basic industries would no longer require labour forces of former size. Extra work for some 60,000 persons would, it was calculated, be required. (Ministry of Labour 1934, para. 3).

Despite the privations which were inflicted on the Clyde Valley during the 1920's and 1930's, some improvement was made in the region's housing environment. This was especially so in the case of Glasgow. The combination of the condemnation of

12

tenements made in the Housing Commission Report of 1917 and the powers and requirements made under the 1919 Housing and Town Planning (Scotland) Act, resulted in the building of low density local authority estates on the periphery of Glasgow in the 1920's and 1930's.

The controlling political party in the City was, as it had been for two generations, in the hands of the Moderates, described by one historian as 'traditional, unstructured, middle class kind of rule' (Checkland 1975, 37). By carefully vetting tenants they were able to ensure that only the 'better type' of working class families were given these new council houses. Effectively, this meant that few from the worst housing areas experienced any housing improvement.

The low density inter-war estates were developed on land which Glasgow acquired through boundary extensions in 1891, 1926 and 1938, and the schemes which approximated most closely to the semi-detached ideal of 12 houses to the acre were built during the early and mid 1920's at Mosspark and Knightswood. But by the early 1930's this ideal had become somewhat tarnished. Nationally, local authority housing fell from the high standards of 1919 as building costs rose and as higher proportions of these costs were borne by the local authorities. The coming to power of the Labour Party in Glasgow in 1933 accentuated this trend. The Glasgow local councillors saw the rehousing of the working class of their city as a major priority. Consequently, there was a strong desire to provide the maximum number of council houses at the lowest cost to the authority and to the tenant. This marked the beginning of a policy which was to have a profound impact on the planning of Glasgow during the post 1945 period.

Thus, during the 1930's many of the local authority dwellings in Glasgow were stylistically modified versions of the old tenements. True, they were usually no more than three storeys high and their design would have met with the approval of those who had sat on the Royal Commission. Yet they were still below what many at the time regarded as desirable housing standards. Further, little regard was paid to community facilities on the new housing estates. Shopping centres, community buildings and recreational provisions were all seen as expensive luxuries that had to be dispensed with in face of the more pressing problem of providing houses. This policy only added to the tensions in areas where people moved away from their places of work - if they were in employment - and from the tight knit communities in which they were brought up. It is hardly to be wondered at that during the late 1930's social problems, measured in crude terms like violence and crime, spread from the Gorbals to the new housing estates such as Blackhill.

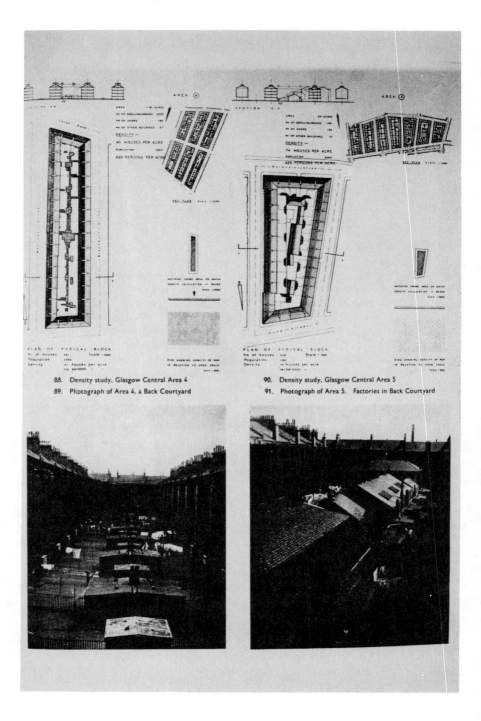

88. Density study, Glasgow Central Area 4
89. Photograph of Area 4, a Back Courtyard

90. Density study, Glasgow Central Area 5
91. Photograph of Area 5. Factories in Back Courtyard

Figure 1.3 The Plan's density study of Glasgow Central Area

14

Glasgow Corporation, now given powers under national legislation, began its policy of heavily subsidising council housing rents from the rate funds. Even in the private rented sector, Glasgow rent levels had been low. This situation stretched back into the nineteenth century, despite the fact that wage levels in the region were not notably depressed. It has been argued that Clydesiders preferred to limit their rent budgets to what they could pay in times of depression rather than prosperity. Whatever the reason, local authority housing in Glasgow in the 1930's was relatively cheap. This, combined with the high levels of unemployment, may help to explain why the level of owner occupation was much lower in Glasgow than in comparable English cities during the 1930's. Having said this, the new houses provided in Glasgow were a marked improvement on their nineteenth century predecessors. As a result of the implementation of a battery of housing and public health legislation, Glasgow was also able to press ahead with slum clearance, so that between 1919 and 1939 15,000 unfit properties were cleared. Many of those displaced as a result of these operations found themselves living in the post 1930 schemes (Jury 1966, 4).

By the end of the 1930's the economy of the Clyde Valley had to a large extent recovered, and the launching of the Queen Elizabeth and the Queen Mary did much to retrieve the region's self confidence. The government's industrial policy helped marginally in this recovery, although the national rearmament drive did much more and unemployment rates began to fall. This did not, however, mean that all was now well with the Clyde Valley economy. The lower unemployment rates were dependant on a continued out-migration from the region and nothing could be done to replenish its exhausted coalfields and iron deposits. The removal of Stewart and Lloyds from Lanarkshire to Corby in England to be nearer to the source of the right kind of ore encapsulated the whole problem.

As for housing, on the eve of the Second World War and despite the overcrowding that had been relieved as a result of the slum clearance and municipal housing schemes, chronic overcrowding remained in the older tenements, especially in Glasgow where three quarters of the city's population still lived. Indeed, the 1935 Overcrowding Survey demonstrated that nearly thirty per cent of all Glasgow families had less than one room for every two members (Jury 1952, 4). Furthermore, most of those families also had to live in dwellings which had damp rising from the ground as well as seeping down from faulty plumbing higher in the block. There was little wonder that infant and child mortality rates at this time were amongst the worst in Britain.

On the eve of the Second World War the Clyde Valley was one of stark and bold contrast. There was degradation and there was sublimity. The skills of the artist, as well as the technical sociologist, are needed to reveal the full strength and creativeness of its people as well as their pitiful weaknesses.

The rural lowland character of many of its inhabitants remained with their attachment to the Kirk and to rigorous education standards and to scholarship. From their neat and well ordered towns these hardy people looked with respect to the ancient University of Glasgow which had contributed so much to the scientific revolution and to the applied sciences which were so necessary to the progress of the Industrial Revolution.

At the heart of the region lay the greatest self-contradiction of all - the city of Glasgow. In the 1930's it was still a city of international renown. In the long passage of history, it has its place of honour along with some of the major cities of the classical world - if not Athens then certainly Corinth - and the medieval world - if not Venice then certainly Genoa. It generated great wealth during the nineteenth century. Echoes of the self esteem that went with it remained even in the harsh years of the 1930's. The great neo-classical buildings that came of its years of prosperity - and especially those associated with the architect 'Greek' Thompson - stood proud alongside the Victorian tenements. On the periphery of the city the well designed garden suburbs built by the council in the 1920's lay adjacent to this more cost conscious counterparts of the 1930's with their dominant and depressing neo-tenement habitations.

The effect of the decay of the region's economic base manifested itself in many ways on the people of the region. For some there was simple dispair. For some there was street violence, opening up old religious and ethnic divides. For some their was left wing political and industrial aggitation. It was against this background that bi-partisan approaches to government intervention and planning were deliberated and out of that background the region was planned and systems were forged to implement those plans.

2 The Setting Up of the Clyde Valley Regional Planning Team and Agencies for Implementation

ROGER SMITH

THE POLITICAL CONTEXT

In order to appreciate the interaction between the plan making and plan implementation processes in the Clyde Valley, it is necessary to appreciate something of the departments, agencies and other administrative bodies which were capable of realising, modifying or thwarting planning ideas and concepts set down in the Clyde Valley Regional Plan. In doing this, we have to discuss those distinctive features of the political and social culture which had and have a bearing on attitudes towards planning in Scotland.

At least since the mid 1940's, planning had become an acceptable element in Scotland's political culture. In this respect, there is and has been a contrast with England. This situation may largely derive from many of the urban and regional problems in Scotland after 1918 which were so acute as to demand substantial treatment through the intervention of public agencies. This consensual view of planning, shared by the major political parties within Scotland, has been nurtured within the Scottish Office. Certainly, the impact of the Clyde Valley Plan was to a very large degree determined by a positive response to planning linked to the executive powers available within that office.

The Scottish Office dates from 1885 but only in 1939 did the Office move to St. Andrews House in Edinburgh. At that time, the Secretary of State had responsibility for the departments of Agriculture, Education, Health and Home Affairs. Since then, the composition of the Ministerial team has changed. In 1939 there was at the political level, in addition to the Secretary of State himself, one Under-Secretary. By 1974 this complement had grown to include one Minister of State and three Under-Secretaries. The departmental structure was also changed so that by the end of the 1970's there were five Departments in the Office, those of Agriculture and Fisheries, Development, Home and Health, Education and Economic Development. The Scottish Office thus provides a considerable leverage for Scotland within the content of the British governmental system, and may be seen to represent something of a state within a state (Kellas 1975, 26-6).

The power of the Scottish Office is, of course, by no means absolute. Many other central governmental ministries, apart from the Scottish Office, have powers which not only extend into Scotland but also relate closely to some of the powers of the departments in the Scottish Office. This having been said, the Scottish Office is capable of taking a corporate view of Scottish affairs. Outside of Cabinet, there is no comparable institutional framework for England. Furthermore, the Scottish Office is capable of exerting influence to the extent that it can be argued that, compared with those regions in England experiencing economic decline, Scotland has gained a disproportionate volume of public resources.

The Scottish Office can also be seen - de facto although not de jure as an intermediary agency lying between the local authorities and central government (Kellas 1975, 3). Because of this it can be argued that the relationship between the local authorities in Scotland and the Scottish Office can be closer - and by the same token more turbulent - than the relationship between the English local authorities and the ministries responsible for them.

It was within the Scottish Office that the idea to undertake a regional plan in the Clyde Valley germinated, but drawing on initiatives which were underway south of the border. The publication of the report in 1940 of the Royal Commission on the Distribution of the Industrial Population (the Barlow Report) marks a watershed in British regional planning (Hall 1975, Chap. 4). There was growing concern during the 1930's about the high unemployment in northern Britain and South Wales, and about problems of urban congestion in the Midlands and South-East of England in particular, including what appeared to be a relentless and largely uncontrolled suburban growth despite a series of Town Planning Acts since 1909. The Royal Commission was thus appointed to examine the underlying causes of the geographical distribution of population and to pronounce on likely future trends. The committee was to examine the social, economic and, with the possible advent of large scale air attack, the strategic disadvantages of such concentration of populations in the industrial cities (Smith 1980). In terms of land-use planning, the report brought together a number of strands of policy that were already becoming accepted into what appeared to have been a coherent and readily understandable strategy. An important element in this strategy was that many of the major problems of cities could only be solved within the context of regional planning.

The report concluded that massive concentrations of population were economically, socially and strategically undesirable. Associated with this was the major shift of population from the depressed regions of northern Britain and South Wales to the more prosperous cities of the South East and Midlands, thereby adding to their problems of congestion. The Barlow solutions to these problems were (1) to strengthen the regional economic policies of the 1930's, whereby a proportion of the jobs created by the new and growing light industries of the South East and the Midlands were to be transferred to the depressed regions (2) to contain the outward growth of the industrial cities and (3) to ease inner city congestion and facilitate redevelopment by transferring population and jobs into industrially self-contained satellite new towns and expanded smaller towns.

The publication of the Barlow Report in 1940 marked a new stage in government's concern about planning. This was reflected in the publication in 1942 of two major and related reports; one - the Uthwatt Report - on the issue of compensation and betterment (coming out in favour of the very radical measure of nationalising development rights in land) and the other - the Scott Report - on land utilization in rural areas. Then, in 1943, a separate Ministry of Town and Country Planning was set up to oversee land-use planning in England and Wales. A Town and Country Planning Act was passed in 1944, effectively to deal with the blitzed and blighted urban areas (Cullingworth 1975), the forerunner of the great 1947 Town and Country Planning Act.

One specific area of concern during the early years of the 1940's was that of regional planning and, because of the history of prewar regional planning in the London region, it was there that a new initiative was taken. The Ministry of Town and Country Planning commissioned Sir Patrick Abercrombie to prepare a plan for Greater London. It was published in 1944. Following on broadly from the Barlow proposals - Abercrombie was a prominent member of the commission - he

19

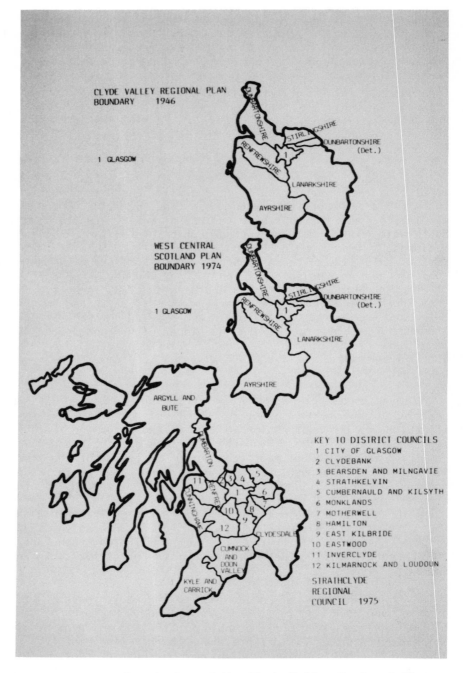

CLYDE VALLEY REGIONAL PLAN
BOUNDARY   1946

1 GLASGOW

DUNBARTONSHIRE
STIRLINGSHIRE
DUNBARTONSHIRE
(Det.)
RENFREWSHIRE
1
LANARKSHIRE
AYRSHIRE

WEST CENTRAL
SCOTLAND PLAN
BOUNDARY 1974

1 GLASGOW

DUNBARTONSHIRE
STIRLINGSHIRE
DUNBARTONSHIRE
(Det.)
RENFREWSHIRE
1
LANARKSHIRE
AYRSHIRE

ARGYLL AND
BUTE

DUMBARTON
RENFREW
CUNNINGHAME
11
3
4
5
1
6
10
8
7
12
9
CLYDESDALE
CUMNOCK
AND
DOON
VALLEY
KYLE AND
CARRICK

KEY TO DISTRICT COUNCILS
1 CITY OF GLASGOW
2 CLYDEBANK
3 BEARSDEN AND MILNGAVIE
4 STRATHKELVIN
5 CUMBERNAULD AND KILSYTH
6 MONKLANDS
7 MOTHERWELL
8 HAMILTON
9 EAST KILBRIDE
10 EASTWOOD
11 INVERCLYDE
12 KILMARNOCK AND LOUDOUN

STRATHCLYDE
REGIONAL
COUNCIL 1975

Figure 2.1   The Boundaries of the Clyde Valley Regional Plan
1946, the West Central Scotland Plan 1974 and of Strathclyde
Regional Council 1975

assumed that the number of jobs in the capital would remain constant as industrial expansion was syphoned off into the depressed regions, and also that there would be virtually no demographic growth within the country as a whole. Planning within the London area would thus be a matter of redistributing existing population and industry. The London green belt was to be strengthened, thereby containing the growth of the city. Beyond the green belt were to be eight industrially self-contained new towns. Within the inner parts of London the slums and blighted areas were to be redeveloped.

THE ORIGINS OF THE CLYDE VALLEY REGIONAL PLAN

The Barlow Report was as influential in the Scottish Office as it was in the English Ministries. During the war-time coalition government, Scotland was headed by one of its most outstanding Secretaries of State, Rt. Hon. Thomas Johnston. Although committed to national planning, Johnston claimed to be uninterested in the technicalities at the sub-national scale. Nonetheless, by 1943 he had set up three regional committees for Scotland, which according to his autobiography (Johnston 1952, 166) he had done for purely political considerations. It had become apparent during the early 1940's that a new ministry responsible exclusively for town and country planning would be set up in Whitehall. Johnston was anxious that the powers of such a ministry should stop at the English border. In order to do that, he believed that he had to demonstrate that Scotland was at least as advanced as England in matters relating to land use planning - hence the setting up of the regional planning committees. These tactics appear to have met with some success, for when in 1943 the first minister of Town and Country Planning was appointed his powers were restricted to England and Wales. In Scotland, the Secretary of State retained his powers over town and country planning matters.

The three regional committees that Johnston convened were for the Clyde Valley, Central and South East Scotland and for East Central Scotland. But his own estimation of the reasons why they were set up should not be accepted without question. The Scottish Office had already had some experience of regional planning and, as a consequence of the 1919 Housing and Town Planning legislation, a number of joint schemes had been prepared including one for the Clyde Valley in 1927. This plan was, however, limited in scope, dealing largely with roads and other transport matters. But by 1936 the then Secretary of State noted that regional planning in Scotland was a matter of urgency, and this theme was explored further towards the end of the inter-war period by the Scottish Department of Health - responsible until 1962 for the administration of the various

Town and Country Planning Acts and associated planning matters. The influence of the assistant secretary in the planning division of that department, J.H. McGuinness, was especially strong here and he played an important role in introducing Barlow-type regional planning concepts into the Scottish Office.

Reasons for choosing the Clyde Valley for one of those planning exercises are obvious enough. The region, as was noted in the previous chapter, was suffering from severe social and economic problems and remedies were urgently needed. Furthermore, the watershed of the River Clyde was seen as an integrated economic unit, in which the extractive industries of the upper reaches of the valley were associated with manufacturing enterprises in Glasgow and the other towns in the lower reaches. The urban areas of the Clyde Valley depended upon the region's farms, market gardens and smallholdings for fresh fruit, vegetables and milk, whilst the region's industrial workers and their families depended to a large extent on the nearby seaside resorts, countryside, mountains, lochs, and wild moorlands for recreation. These factors help to explain why the Scottish Office came to see the basin of the River Clyde and that part of it which spilled over into the agricultural and recreational parts of Ayrshire, as a coherent unit which would benefit from having an overall regional strategy.

The Clyde Valley region was thus one of considerable variety. There was a rich diversity in scenery and land use and a markedly uneven spatial distribution of population, industry and types of community. As was noted in the Plan,

'whilst over two fifths of the whole population of Scotland live and work in the region, half of its area is moorland and heath, and the wild slopes of Ben Lomond are only 25 miles from the heart of Glasgow, where, in the dockside tenements over 700,000 people crowd together into an area of less than three square miles' (para. 7).

The Clyde Valley Regional Planning Advisory Committee, which Johnston assembled in 1943, consisted of representatives from seventeen local authorities in the region. Bailie Hugh T. MacCalman, one of the Glasgow Labour representatives and the convener of the City's Highways and Planning Committee (1942-45), was elected chairman. The Clerk was Sir William E. Whyte. The cost of the exercise was to be shared between the Scottish Department of Health and the constituent authorities. A technical committee was appointed to prepare the plan, although the ultimate responsibility for any recommendations was with the advisory committee. Sir Patrick Abercrombie, at the time

22

still working on the regional plan for Greater London, was invited, as a consultant, to lead the technical team. Closer to the day to day operation was Abercrombie's deputy, R.H. Matthew, an architect from the Scottish Department of Health. The rest of the technical team consisted of five senior technical officers. They were backed up by a small staff of academics, draughtsmen and clerical workers.

THE PLAN'S RECOMMENDATIONS

One of the remarkable features of the regional planning exercises of the 1940's was the speed with which those involved completed their work. The <u>Clyde Valley Regional Plan</u> was no exception and the first edition, of 1946, was produced after only two year's work.

The <u>Plan's</u> Summary of Conclusions and Recommendations is reproduced in the Appendix. It is important that they should be seen as they were originally presented. A glance at the appendix will show that broader strategic policy recommendations were apparently given the same emphasis as detailed local policies. However, over the course of thirty years the proposals were re-packaged in the minds of those involved in planning in the region. Indeed, the passage of time has meant that the ideas of <u>the Plan</u> have been distilled into broad and synchronised areas of policy. One can be less certain as to whether such coherent strategies were apparent to all those involved in preparing <u>the Plan</u>.

The most significant recommendations were concerned with the containment of Glasgow and the dispersal of upwards of a quarter of a million of its population beyond the city boundaries. The containment of Glasgow was to be done by means of a green belt, which was seen also as a means of providing for recreation, fresh air and fresh foods and milk (recommendations 21, 22, 23 and 25). The twin objectives of urban containment and the reduction of residential densities in Glasgow and other industrial towns of the region (recommendations 29 and 30) meant that overspill outlets had to be found. These were to take the form of up to four new towns and the expansion of smaller towns in the region (recommendations 5, 6 and 31-36).

The other major concern of <u>the Plan</u> was the need to see the whole region as an economic unit and to replace the declining traditional industries with the newer light industries (recommendations 1-3 and 7-12). This was to be done within the context of a national redistribution of industry policy, but at the regional level this could be assisted by the provision of

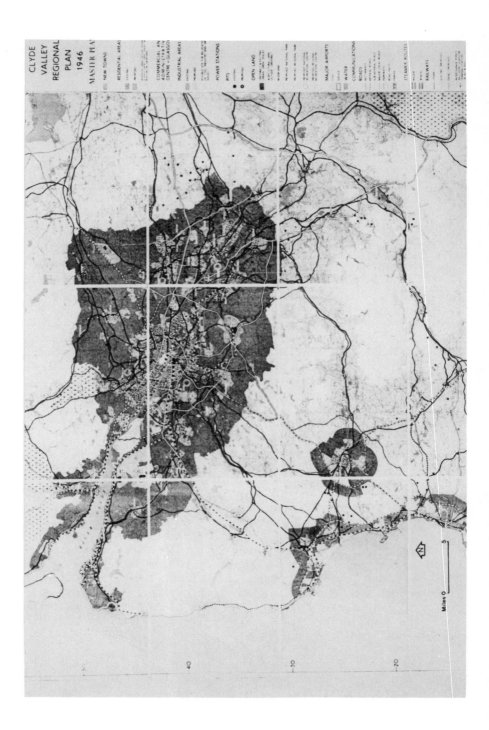

Figure 2.2   Clyde Valley Regional Plan 1946.   Master Plan

24

industrial estates, the zoning of individual areas for industry by local authorities and a comprehensive programme for the physical rehabilitation of derelict areas (recommendations 10, 13, 18 and 19). The industrial recommendations were associated with the proposals for the decentralization of population. New industry must be steered away from the congested urban centres into the new towns, thereby providing jobs for the incoming population (recommendations 14-17).

Obviously the industrial and decentralisation proposals had to mesh in with coordinated transportation planning concepts (recommendation 38). Main roads or motorways were needed to connect the region with England and Edinburgh and the east of Scotland. These would be associated with tunnels and bridges crossing the Clyde (recommendations 44, 45 and 46). The new road patterns would be related to a carefully thought out hierarchy of service roads and intersections (recommendations 39-43). Attention would also have to be paid to landscaping the roads (recommendation 47). As far as the railways were concerned, a programme of electrification should be embarked upon as well as the redevelopment of the Glasgow stations and the linking in of rail and road services for haulage purposes (recommendations 48-51).

The air transport recommendations centred on Prestwick as an international airport linked in with the new rail and road network. It was thought that there was also a case for a regional airport near Glasgow as well as Renfrew, linked into a network of helicopter flights (recommendations 52-54). The Glasgow docks were to be improved and the Forth and Clyde, Monklands and Mid-Scotland Ship Canals should be closed (recommendations 55-60).

Stress was put on the agricultural aspects of the region. Urban development should not impede farming, especially dairy farming. Fruit growing should also be protected. This could be done by providing stability of tenure of farms in the green belt. Associated with this should be good village planning, with sufficient houses, social, educational and shopping facilities for agricultural workers (recommendations 61-64).

The well-being of the region's population was seen to depend upon the provision of recreational facilities. This included protecting the coastline and the provision of holiday towns. Furthermore, two National Parks at Loch Lomond and St. Mary's Loch were recommended. Then there were to be Regional Parks and Regional Recreational Centres. All urban areas should be provided with adequate public open spaces (recommendations 25-28).

Community planning was seen to be important and standards for residential shops, schools and community facilities were recommended. Similarly, architectural design standards for new building and conservation were provided (recommendations 65-70). The overall development of the region would be dependent upon the provision of water, gas and electricity to match the development of communities, and appropriate recommendations were made (recommendations 71-74).

One indication that the regional plan was only a starting point in the development of the Clyde Valley was the recommendation (4) that a University Chair of Town and Regional Planning should be established in Scotland. This would enable detailed social studies to be made throughout the region and so make its planning more effective.

IMPLEMENTING THE PLAN: THE PRELIMINARY RESPONSE

The plan produced by the technical committee was expected to be presented to the full advisory committee for ratification. It was then up to the constituent local authorities - as far as they had the powers - to implement those parts which applied to their own areas. Other of the recommendations, however, could only be implemented by central government. A number of the industrial proposals, for example, could only be implemented by the Board of Trade, using the powers under the 1945 Distribution of Industry Act, and it was only after the Plan had been completed that the Scottish Office had powers, under the 1946 New Towns Act, to designate new towns. Many of the transportation proposals and recreational proposals could not be implemented without new legislation.

The regional planners were very much aware of the problems of implementation. Consequently, they recommended setting up a regional authority with statutory powers to implement some of the wider planning strategies. The green belt proposals, it was argued, could only be implemented within the context of a regional authority. The recommendation here was that the land should actually be purchased and controlled by such a body. At the time of preparing the Plan, a regional authority was also seen as the only vehicle through which new towns and regional parks could be provided. Furthermore, a regional authority would also be needed to monitor and regulate the purely local plans that would be produced by the local authorities within the Clyde Valley.

In examining the territorial jurisdiction of the proposed regional authority, the regional planners believed that it should not encompass the whole region. Although the industrial

Clyde Basin was dependant upon Ayrshire for agricultural products and recreational facilities, they were not regarded as forming 'outstanding common interests' requiring a common administrative system. The recommendation was, therefore, that the proposed Regional Authority should be restricted to the Glasgow conurbation. The bulk of the region's population fell within the conurbation and it was there that the great changes and movement of industry and population were expected to take place.

A regional authority for the Glasgow conurbation with a lower tier of existing local authorities, including the ancient city of Glasgow, was a radical proposal, although only sketchily thought out. The legal administrative and political complexities were not considered. Broadly the regional authority was to be made up of representatives nominated by the constituent local authorities, and its budget was to come from allocation from each of those authorities' rate funds. How would such a relationship work? What were the implications of a non-representative body controlling democratically elected local authorities? How would the regional authority relate to central government departments? These matters went undiscussed.

The proposals for a regional authority made little headway. Despite the many radical policies which the first postwar Labour government implemented, there was no serious attempt to reform the structure of local government, and what enthusiasm there had been in the mid 1940's for regional government had all but evaporated by the latter years of the decade. Together with this waning interest in regional government, there was a corresponding decline in commitment to regional planning. Paradoxically, the 1947 Town and Country Planning (Scotland) Act was partly responsible for this. Those local authorities which were given the status of planning authorities had new and exclusive plan making and plan implementation powers. They were jealous of them and were disinclined to share responsibilities with higher authorities lying between themselves and central government. And central government for its part, especially after the return of the Conservatives in 1951 elected partly on an 'anti-planning' platform, saw little justification for commissioning further regional plans (Grieve 1954, 18).

In addition to this, within the Clyde Valley there were purely extraneous factors working against regional planning, the most significant of which was the objection that the Glasgow Corporation had to the overspill recommendations made by the Plan. Glasgow did not want to lose population and believed that it could undertake all the rehousing necessary substantially within its boundaries, provided that the green belt recommendations were subject to major modifications. Consequently, the regional advisory committee was unable to give its approval to the Plan because the unanimous support of the constituent members was required and, of course, with Glasgow's objection to a major area of recommendations, this was impossible. Indeed, Glasgow withdrew from the committee and this led to its dissolution. Thus, by the late 1940's, all the indications were that the preparation of the Clyde Valley Regional Plan was an abortive exercise and that regional planning in West Central Scotland would not be realised.

THE GOVERNMENT'S BACKING

Despite Glasgow's objections, the Clyde Valley Regional Plan had a powerful ally in the Scottish Department of Health. By 1946 the New Towns Act was on the statute book, and the powers were now available for the Scottish Office to designate new towns. Based on the arguments of the Plan and against the opposition of Glasgow, the first of the new towns for the region, East Kilbride, was designated in 1947. Even so, Glasgow was an influential local authority if only judged on the number of parliamentary constituencies it contained. Life could be made difficult for the Scottish Office if it attempted to exercise too great a pressure on an unwilling city.

Yet, within the Department of Health were men who were committed to the proposals in the Plan. Some, like McGuinness, had been instrumental in setting up the exercise, some like Robert Grieve had worked on it as one of the senior technicians, whilst others had been involved in the early attempts at implementation. By 1949 this informal group had seen the Plan given a wider readership when it was published in 1949 by HMSO. A re-assessment of the Plan was then undertaken by the Department, only to conclude that the basic principles upon which it was based were sound. There was certainly some enthusiasm for the Plan in the press. A review by F.J. Osborn in the Spectator lauded the Plan on publication as Abercrombie's crowning achievement. Other commentators, however, were less enthusiastic. Angus McIntosh writing in the Town Planning Review (1949/50, 288-93) argued that irrespective of the merits of the Plan, and they were deemed to be many, by 1949, time had run out. The new planning climate was such that the Plan could not be implemented. In retrospect this was an unfortunate judgment.

The recommendations on regional economic planning in the Clyde Valley certainly dovetailed into the more general national policies being devised by the Board of Trade. The

Board's powers extended into Scotland and it was expected to work closely with the Home Department in the Scottish Office. The 1945 Distribution of Industry Act established development areas into which growth industries were to be steered. West Central Scotland was one. The 1945 Act made provision for building subsidized factories in the development areas, and through the powers that the government had in granting licences - an administrative legacy left over from the war - industrial building could be restricted in the prosperous parts of Britain and encouraged in the development areas. Such powers were extended by the Board of Trade through the 1947 Town and Country Planning Act and its Scottish equivalent, which set up the industrial development certificate (IDC) system.

The transport proposals in the Clyde Valley Regional Plan were less contentious than those relating to overspill. Certainly there was no great debate at the local authority level. Many of the transport proposals were drawn from a number of contemporary plans and reports. And then, of course, there was the 1947 Transport Act which introduced, amongst other matters, the nationalisation of the railway companies. This was part of a general package that gave the Ministry of Transport direct powers to implement, if it so chose, many of the proposals in the Clyde Valley Regional Plan.

As far as recreational provision was concerned, whilst the local authorities had increased powers after 1947 to implement many of the Clyde Valley Regional Plan recommendations over the protection of coastal and scenic areas and agricultural land, there was little that could be done as far as national parks were concerned. The 1949 National Parks and Access to the Countryside Act permitted the setting up of National Parks in England and Wales, but those aspects of the Act did not apply to Scotland. Nonetheless, the Ministry of Agriculture and the Scottish Agriculture Department were in a position to act upon some of the proposals concerned with the farming industry.

THE REVIVAL OF PLANNING IN THE 1960'S

Even before the Labour government went out of office in 1951, governmental commitment to regional planning had waned and there was little expectation that regional planning would revive with the incoming Conservative government. Indeed, during the early years of Conservative govermment there was some dismantling of the land-use planning system that had been erected during the previous years. Those parts of the 1947 Town and Country Planning Act which effectively nationalised the development rights in land were repealed. The Ministry of Housing and Local Government, which replaced the Ministry of

Town and Country Planning, made it known that within the foreseeable future no more new towns would be designated. As far as England was concerned overspill would be handled by town expansion schemes, made possible through the 1952 Town Development Act. In terms of regional economic planning there was now little real attempt to use IDC's to steer industry northwards.

It was not until the late 1950's that regional planning was revived in Britain (Hall 1975, Chaps. 6 and 7). This was partly because of a new drive to overspill populations from the great industrial cities, and partly because of a disquieting decline in the older industrial sectors. The Conservative government initiated a series of regional studies, a massive slum clearance programme, and work began on designating more new towns. New legislation affecting the distribution of industry was also passed. The Labour government which came into office in 1964 extended these initiatives.

Although this renaissance of regional planning partly stemmed from an increasing concern with problems created by growth in the South East and economic decline in North East England, developments within West Central Scotland were of considerable significance. Indeed, it might be argued that regional planning never completely died in the Clyde Valley. The designation of Cumbernauld new town in 1955 was one example of this. Furthermore, a number of important studies into industrial regional planning in Scotland were also initiated in the late 1950s.

In order to more adequately deal with changing policies for Scotland, a major reorganisation of the Scottish Office was undertaken in 1962. All the functions associated with physical, economic and transport planning, and which hitherto had been divided between the Scottish Health and Home Departments, were brought together in the new Scottish Development Department. An early task of this new department was to prepare a White Paper on the economy of Central Scotland which was published in 1963. In this document, the whole central belt of Scotland was seen as the wider region within which the economic problems of the Clydeside conurbation were to be solved.

The thinking which lay behind the White Paper had considerable repercussions in many areas of planning. It was as if the determination to reduce rising unemployment released new energies and new hopes. Glasgow was beginning one of Europe's most extensive urban renewal programmes. The birth rate had been rising and there was no longer the concern about the 'over-saturation' of population in the Clyde Valley which the Plan had shown. To handle the growth and overspill, the target populations of East Kilbride and Cumbernauld were increased and a further new town was designated - Livingston in the Lothians. Irvine was designated soon after, and at the end of the 1960's moves began towards yet another new town within the Clyde Valley, at Stonehouse, to absorb those not accommodated in the recently started 'new community' at Erskine.

During the 1960's, it was argued that overspill and industrial regeneration were two faces on the same coin. Industry would come to the growth centres and overspill would provide the labour. The logic of this was that the new towns should become industrial growth centres. And, of course, the growth centres needed good communications with each other, with Glasgow and Edinburgh, and with England. This resulted in a programme of motorways and other road building programmes and, specifically within the Clyde Valley, Glasgow started upon an urban motorway system. To co-ordinate the region's traffic flow, the Glasgow Highway Plan and then the Greater Glasgow Transportation Study was set up.

Recreation was not to be left out of this vigorous plan-making activity. This area of planning had been virtually neglected since the Clyde Valley Regional Plan had been prepared, but with the emergence of the Countryside Commission earlier ideas were once more revived and explored. A range of plans were prepared for country parks, open spaces, walkways and especially on the recreational and tourist potential of Loch Lomond.

The range and number of plans relevant to the Clyde Valley produced in the 1960's was extended as the number of working party reports produced jointly by local authorities in the region increased. The Clyde Valley Advisory Committee, which had been reconvened when Glasgow reversed its earlier policy and now agreed to a formal overspill programme in the mid 1950's, realised that it could not alone undertake the work of co-ordination. Matters came to a head in 1969. New outlets, it was believed, had to be found to maintain the housing programme for Glasgow overspill. The redeployment of population was still seen as an important factor in planning the region. Furthermore, at that time the deep water potential of the Clyde Estuary was being seriously considered and was expected to give rise to a new complex of industrial and commercial activities. However, serious difficulties were being found in local oil-related industries. The Murco company failed to obtain permission for a refinery at Longhaugh in Renfrewshire as did Chevron at Hunterston in Ayrshire. The S.D.D. and the local authorities (reluctantly) saw the need for a new regional study (Scottish Development Department 1970, para. 2).

The Scottish Development Department proposed that the preparation of a new plan for West Central Scotland should be a collaborative exercise. In September 1970, therefore, the Secretary of State announced the setting up of the West Central Scotland Plan Steering Committee, consisting of 48 representatives from the Clyde Valley Advisory Committee, central government and industry and commerce. Early in 1971, the Steering Committee set up a study team composed of seconded staff from the Scottish Development Department and the Regional Development Division of the Scottish Office. Then, early in 1972 Colin Buchanan and Partners and Professor K.J.W. Alexander were appointed as Consultants to the Steering Committee. A study team was then appointed, under the direction of Urlan Wannop. The study team produced a consultative draft report which was received by the Steering Committee in 1974.

The boundaries of the West Central Study, embracing an even larger area than the old Clyde Valley region, encompassed most of Ayrshire, the whole of Bute, the whole of Dunbartonshire, the whole of Lanarkshire including Glasgow, the whole of Renfrewshire and a little of Stirlingshire. This area was chosen because it was almost coterminous with the Glasgow Planning Region as defined in 1970.

The recommendations of the West Central team associated with open spaces, recreational planning and aspects of transportation, reveal a direct or indirect lineage with the Clyde Valley Regional Plan. However, whilst all the other planning documents mentioned in this chapter, including the Clyde Valley Regional Plan, were shot through with economic optimism, this cannot be said for the West Central Study. During the period between the setting up of the team and the production of the draft report it was recognised that the economic future of the region was far from optimistic. Attempts at stimulating economic growth had failed to provide jobs for the natural increase of population and, despite the now falling birth rate, it was very likely that these conditions would persist. Indeed unemployment rates were rising, productivity was low and enterprise was lacking. Against the background of a worsening British economy, salvation could no longer be expected from outside firms migrating into the region. Consequently recommendations had to revolve around the revitalisation of local resources. Related to this, the relationship between economic recovery, Glasgow overspill and new towns was reassessed. The argument was now put that because of the unassisted movement of population away from the City, the established new towns had an excess of potential for growth. Resources were being drained from the older areas themselves, where there was an underdeveloped potential for economic recovery. No longer should solutions to the economic and social plight in the older areas be linked so significantly with decentralisation. The emphasis should be redirected to solutions within the inner parts of the urban areas.

LOCAL GOVERNMENT REFORM

With the revival of regional planning in the 1960's, attention was also directed to local government reform (Scottish Development Department 1963a, para. 37). Consequently, a Royal Commission headed by Lord Wheatley was set up in 1966 to examine Scottish Local Government. A parallel exercise had already been started for England under the chairmanship of Lord Redcliffe Maud. The Scottish report, when it was published in 1969, clearly appreciated the link between local government reform and regional planning. Partly to accommodate this, Wheatley recommended a two-tier structure of local government for Scotland, with regional authorities forming the top tier taking the responsibility, amongst other matters, for strategic planning.

In considering the boundaries for the new regional authorities, the West Central part of Scotland, consisting of Ayr, Bute, Dunbarton, Lanark, Renfrew and the City of Glasgow, as well as parts of Argyll and Stirling, gave the greatest concern, if only because of its size: 3,200 square miles in all with a population in excess of 2,500,000. The Commission opted to see it as one region, calling in justification on the Clyde Regional Valley Plan which was used in evidence to argue that such an area represented a 'community of interest'. But on that point the Plan was being abused. The Plan had recommended the Clyde Basin as the optimum size for a regional administration and not the whole of the Clyde Valley. Furthermore, the Commissioners added in a substantial proportion of Argyll to the area covered by the Clyde Valley Regional Plan. In some respects there was valid enough reason. The regional planners of 1946 had argued that once recreational and farming considerations were taken into account, the links between the Glasgow conurbation and Argyll were as strong as those between the conurbation and Ayr. But, it had been insisted, such links were not strong enough to warrant other counties being administered by the same authority carrying the responsibility for the Clyde Basin. Lord Wheatley and his fellow commissioners thought otherwise. Starting with the proposition that,
'We are in no doubt ... that the lack of a single

unit for the entire Clyde Valley area is one of the
greatest impediments to the economic and social
regeneration of the west of Scotland today' (Royal
Commission 1969, para. 759),

they went on to argue that the influence of Glasgow extended
well beyond the Clyde Valley.

In a White Paper on the Reform of Local Government in
Scotland issued in 1971 the Scottish Office, in general,
accepted the Wheatley recommendations for the Clyde Valley.
The government, however, was anxious to include the whole of
Argyll in the Western region - subsequently to be named
Strathclyde. This intention was incorporated into the 1973
Local Government (Scotland) Act.

DEVELOPMENTS IN THE 1970'S

The reform of local government structure in Scotland itself
demonstrated a greater commitment to regional government and
planning than was present in England and Wales, where the
reforms in local government were based upon much less radical
proposals. South of the border, the recommendations of the
Royal Commission on Local Government (the Redcliffe Maud
Report) which argued for a regional tier were ignored.

Indeed, this greater concern for the regional dimension in
Scotland was demonstrated in the Report of the Select Committee
on Scottish Affairs on Land Resource Use in Scotland, published
in 1972. The origins of the report lay in a concern to improve
the planning system to help industrial development in Scotland,
the impact of the entry into Europe, Scotland's potential for
tourism, the need for port facilities and related needs for
infrastructure. The Committee proposed a top-level working
party, within the context of a structure plan for Scotland
(McDonald 1977). Within the structure of the Scottish Office,
this mode of thinking could be seen in the decision in 1973 to
promote the Regional Development Division to a full Department.
The new Scottish Development Department retained responsibility
for local government, town and country planning, housing and
building control, roads and local transport planning, North Sea
oil infrastructure, ancient monuments and historic buildings,
the Scottish Special Housing Association, the Countryside
Commission for Scotland and the Historic Buildings Council for
Scotland. The new Scottish Economic Planning Department became
responsible for industrial and economic development, North Sea
Oil, selective regional assistance to industry and factory
building, electricity, Highland and rural development,
passenger road and sea transport and tourism and various
industrial bodies, including the new town development

corporations.

This commitment on the part of the Scottish Office to economic and physical planning has to be understood in order to appreciate the planning implications of the 1973 Local Government (Scotland) Act. Each regional authority was required to submit a Regional Report to the Secretary of State for his observations and tacit approval. Significantly, the reports were concerned with the formulation of economic strategies for the regions relating to patterns of settlement, the development of communications and centres of population and the use of resources, particularly of land and finance. Significantly also, the Clyde Valley Regional Plan had described itself as a Regional Report (para. 42) thirty years before.

In the Strathclyde Region, the West Central Scotland Plan formed the basis of the Council's Regional Report, which was prepared by the Strathclyde Policy and Physical Planning departments and submitted to the Secretary of State in 1976. This report itself was then drawn upon to form the basis of the region's structure plan, a requirement of the 1972 Town and Country Planning (Scotland) Act and the 1973 Local Government (Scotland) Act. The Strathclyde Structure Plan was approved - with modifications - by the Secretary of State in 1980. The first Review of the Plan was completed in 1981. Related to the Structure Plan, the Council produced a number of annual studies. Transport Policies and Programmes and the Financial Plan Budgets were prepared annually as was the Regional Planning Survey.

But much in the Structure Plan, like the Clyde Valley Regional Plan, could only be implemented through central government departments, a listing of whose responsibilities is given in the Table. Associated with these departments were the various appointed bodies and boards which had plan making or implementation powers. And these boards and departments had to work in collaboration with the local authorities.

Before reorganisation, the local authorities on occasion met in ad hoc committees or working parties set up by the Scottish Office or in the reconvened Clyde Valley Regional Advisory Committee. After reorganisation collective and individual liaison Committees were established to coordinate the work of the Strathclyde Regional Council with that of the nineteen lower tier districts. The council instituted a Policy and Resources Committee to develop a corporate strategy for its responsibilities and to guide and coordinate its various service and resource committees. On the service side, these committees included highways and transportation, leisure and

Table 2.1

Functions of Central Government in Scotland 1975
relating to those activities relating to regional plan
implementation in West Central Scotland

British Departments

Department of Trade
  British Airports Authority
  British Airways Board

Department of Industry
  Relations with shipbuilding,
  engineering, vehicles and
  aerospace industries
  National Enterprise Board,
  British Steel Corporation,
  Scottish Telecommunications
  Board

Department of Energy
  Energy production,
  Offshore Supplies Office for
  Scotland, British National
  Oil Corporation, British Gas
  Corporation, National Coal
  Board, Atomic Energy
  Authority

Department of Employment
  Industrial training and
  employment offices. Regional
  employment premium

Department of Environment

  Ports, Docks, Waterways,
  Freight, Public Buildings
  and Works, British Rail,
  National Freight Corporation

Scottish Departments

Department of Agriculture
and Fisheries
  Estate Management,
  Agricultural Education

Scottish Development Department
  Local Government, Town and
  Country Planning, Housing and
  Building Control, Roads and
  Local Transport Planning,
  Ancient Monuments and Historic
  Buildings, Scottish Special
  Housing Association, Countryside
  Commission for Scotland
  Historic Buildings Council for
  Scotland

Scottish Economic Planning Dept.
  Industrial and economic
  development, selective regional
  assistance to industry and
  factory building, direction and
  support of industry, New Towns,
  Electricity, Passenger Road and
  Sea Transport
  Scottish Development Agency and
  Scottish Industrial Estate
  Corporation, Small Industries
  Council, Scottish Transport
  Group, Scottish Tourist Board.

The Scottish Economic Planning Board is a Civil Service Inter Department
Committee which includes members of British and Scottish Departments

Taken from Kellas (1974) Table 2.

36

recreation and water and sewage. On the resources side, the committees included planning and development and economic and industrial development (Strathclyde Regional Council 1978). An Industrial Development Committee was set up to induce industrial growth in the region and a sub-committee of the Policy and Resources Committee on multiple deprivation was established; these two committees reflected the twin priorities emerging from the Council's Regional Report.

A major factor in the development of contemporary planning in the region has been the setting up of the Scottish Development Agency. The West Central Team had recommended setting up SEDCOR, the Strathclyde Economic Development Corporation, to help improve industrial efficiency with advice on marketing, staff recruitment, internal organisation, industrial relations, financial planning, diversification and exporting, backed by financial aid. In the event, a body embracing wider functions was set up for the whole of Scotland - the Scottish Development Agency - under the 1975 Scottish Development Agency Act, aimed at regenerating the Scottish Economy by (a) encouraging further economic development (b) providing, maintaining and safeguarding employment (c) promoting industrial efficiency and international competitiveness and (d) furthering the improvement of the environment. Two hundred million pounds were to be made available to do this, which could be increased by the Secretary of State for Scotland to £300 million (Scottish Development Agency 1977). As far as Strathclyde was concerned, the Agency noted:
    'The industrial West of Scotland, with about half the population, contains at least half the needs, whether in terms of employment or in terms of industrial problems; the Agency takes this into account, and gives it proper attention' (Scottish Development Agency 1977, p.7).
Taken into the responsibility of the Scottish Development Agency in 1976 was the Glasgow Eastern Area Redevelopment Project - GEAR.

The 1975 White Paper Policy for Inner Cities had demonstrated central government's concern for the inner cities. It was put that economic decline, physical decay and social disadvantages had created what was seen to be a new problem of 'urban deserts', characterised by acute deprivation caused by large numbers of people being forced to live in a poor physical environment where unemployment was high. As far as Glasgow was concerned new approaches had to be found. The termination of Stonehouse new town in 1976 was quickly followed by the Government's initiation of the coordinated GEAR project to revive the eastern part of the central area of the City (i.e. Calton, Bridgeton, Dalmarnock, Parkhead, Shettleston,

37

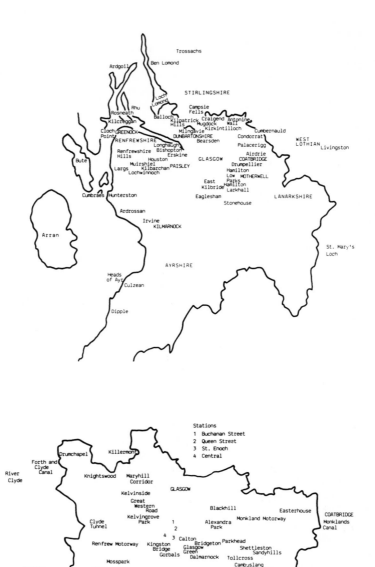

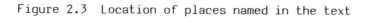

Figure 2.3 Location of places named in the text

38

Tollcross, Sandyhills and the Cambuslang Recovery Area), where the SDA had started a major industrial recovery and building programme on land made available by the British Steel Corporation where the obsolescent Clyde Iron Works and the Clydebridge Steel Works were located. A steering group was formed under the chairmanship of the Minister of State in the Scottish Office with responsibility for housing, comprising the political leaders of Glasgow and Strathclyde and representatives of the Scottish Development Agency, Scottish Special Housing Association and the Scottish Development Department. Over a period, it was expected that the parties to this committee would invest some £120 million in regenerating and rehabilitating the East End of Glasgow.

The executive role of SDA was to invest in industrial and environmental improvement work in the area and to act as coordinator of public investment by the Strathclyde Regional Council, Glasgow District Council, the Greater Glasgow Health Board, the Housing Corporation and Housing Associations involved in the GEAR project. With this example preceding it, the Maryhill Corridor project was launched by the City District Council in cooperation with the Regional Council. This second project reached from the periphery of the City centre to the north-west boundary of Glasgow, where the initial investment programme amounted to £54 million.

LOCAL PARTY POLITICS

The combined representation of Socialists and the Independent Labour Party first took control of the old Glasgow Corporation in the 1933, and would be re-elected to control the city for 50 years apart from very short intervals. The right wing in the guise of the Progressive Party took control between 1949 and 1952. Then again in 1968, the Progressives and Conservatives took control only to be swept out of office in 1971. With the setting up of the City of Glasgow District Council in 1975, Labour continued to control the City, but in the 1977 elections the Conservatives won twenty-five seats and the Scottish National Party won sixteen, compared with Labour's thirty and the Liberal's one. Conservatives took over minority control, depending upon support from Scottish National Party members. Labour, however, was returned to power in 1980 when all the Nationalist seats were lost and half those of the Conservatives. This more recent interchange of power was not paralleled as far as the Regional Council was concerned, where Labour has been in control since 1975.

The role of the Scottish National Party makes a significant footnote, to the politics of West Central Scotland during the late 1960's and throughout the 1970's. The rallying of Scottish nationalism was demonstrated when Mrs. Ewing won a notable by-election at Hamilton in 1967 for the SNP. The Wilson Government (1964-1970) responded by setting up the Royal Commission on the Constitution - chaired initially by Lord Crowther and then by Lord Kilbrandon - which was published in 1973. Based on the report, the Government issued a White Paper in 1975, Our Changing Democracy, in which it argued for setting up a Scottish Assembly, without power to raise money but with responsibility for local government, health, education, development agencies (except for the SDA) and natural resources. The Government was encouraged in this path by what it saw as the need to bring back into the fold that substantial volume of traditional Labour voters who were switching their votes to the Scottish National Party.

The proposals for the Assembly had potential ramifications for Strathclyde. What was the logic behind having an Assembly for the whole of Scotland and a local authority which administered half the country's population? Would not the Strathclyde region be able in many issues to dominate the Assembly rather than the other way round? On these grounds the Scottish National Party was especially concerned to see the dismantling of the Strathclyde Region. But in the event, the plans for the Assembly were abandoned following the referendum in 1978, when its supporters failed to register the required minimum number of votes.

3 Housing, Population and Decentralisation

ROGER SMITH AND ELSPETH FARMER

THE PLAN'S DOMINANT THEME

Housing and Population

The Clyde Valley Regional planning team saw housing as an urgent issue and a special report on housing sites in Glasgow was produced within months of it starting work (Regional Planning Committee 1944). The Plan took a wider view, of course, expressing concern over accommodation for agricultural workers and miners, as well as over the general provision of dwellings in the smaller townships of the outer parts of the region, but the crucial problem was in Glasgow where, it was noted, living conditions

'with regard to density of building, overcrowding and obsolescence have ... reached a degree hardly touched elsewhere in the country' (para. 4).

A dominant theme in the Plan, therefore, was the resolution of this housing problem within a broad regional strategy. It was this recognition, drawing heavily on concepts hammered out at national level in the 1920's and then more vigorously in the 1930's, that was the bedrock of the invigorated - even visionary - approach to regional planning which was so apparent in the Clyde Valley and other regional plans of the period. Yet, unlike Abercrombie's Greater London Plan, there was no specific chapter in the Clyde Valley Regional Plan on housing. This omission was fortuitous; the intended housing chapter had

41

to be abandoned because of the inability of the technical officer responsible to write up his researches. Other authors had to incorporate aspects of housing within their own chapters. This accident strengthened the resolve of the regional planners to integrate housing with other areas of planning.

Nationally, demographers were in general agreement that despite the increase in the birth rate immediately after the war, there was an underlying low level of fertility. The Royal Commission on Population in Britain which published its findings in 1949 concluded that 'no further large increases in our population are probable' (para. 638). The Barlow Commission had taken a similar line nine years earlier and argued that the need was for the redistribution of population within Britain for social, economic and strategic reasons. There was no discussion about how to handle a growing population. Working within this climate of ideas, the Clyde Valley regional planners too assumed that they would be dealing with a generally static population. The demographic studies undertaken as a part of the regional planning exercise to a large extent mirrored the national situation. Certainly, the planners believed that the region had reached saturation point as far as population numbers were concerned and that any inflow should be counteracted. The crucial problem was to bring about a more equitable balance of population not only within the region but within Scotland as a whole. As matters stood at the time, 36 per cent of Scotland's population was concentrated within the region, 22 per cent being in Glasgow alone. There was, it was noted, a process of 'automatic decentralisation' underway with the middle classes moving out from the city to the suburbs and county and coastal towns. A major question was how could public action encourage decentralisation on a broader social basis?

The Plan's Recommendations to Relieve the Housing Problem

Studies undertaken by the Glasgow Corporation's City Engineer and Master of Works during the war had revealed densities as high as 400-500 persons net per acre in many of the older districts of Glasgow like Hutchesontown and the Gorbals. By 1944, both the Scottish Department of Health and the English Ministry of Town and Country Planning had come to accept that densities in the central areas of cities should be no higher than 120 persons per acre (net), whilst on the outskirts that figure should ideally be no higher than 60 persons (Ministry of Health 1944, 60, Scottish Housing Advisory Committee 1943, 60). Calculations based on these standards revealed that over half of Glasgow's population of 1,127,948 would have to be decanted from redevelopment areas.

Table 3.1
The Plan's Estimated Population to be Decentralised
from Re-Development Areas

Location	Estimated Population	Decentralised Population from Redevelopment Areas (Approximate figures)
City of Glasgow -	1,127,948	550,000
Large Burghs		
Airdrie - - -	27,860	3,500
Clydebank - -	47,912	17,500
Coatbridge - -	45,045	10,000
Dumbarton - -	22,214	10,000
Greenock - -	81,297	39,000
Hamilton - -	39,315	11,000
Motherwell & Wishaw	67,693	11,500
Paisley - - -	91,167	28,500
Port Glasgow - -	19,785	9,500
Rutherglen - -	25,441	9,000
Small Burghs		
Barrhead - - -	12,265	6,000
Johnstone - -	13,882	4,000
Milngavie - - -	6,400	nil
Renfrew - - -	16,509	7,000

Since the nineteenth century there had been an outward movement of population from inner Glasgow. In the 1920's and 1930's, the local authority intensified the movement when it provided peripheral municipal estates. But by the mid 1940's there were serious questions raised about the expediency of peripheral expansion as a means of rehousing those from the most overcrowded areas. The Barlow report was not alone in stressing that uncontrolled peripheral expansion could result in lengthy journeys to work, could absorb good agricultural or high amenity land and could run the risk of physically fusing a conurbation like Glasgow with surrounding towns. In order to guard against these potential dangers, therefore, the Clyde Valley planners recommended a regional green belt. Green belt theory, checking urban peripheral growth, was one with a long history, although in the hands of the Clyde Valley planners it was subject to a major innovation. The London green belt, with which Abercrombie himself had been involved and which had been established by Act of Parliament in 1938, was conceived simply to surround London with a collar that would contain the outward spread of the capital and syphon off any growth generated there to places beyond the restrictive limits (Abercrombie 1944, chap. 12). The terrain and distribution of settlements within the Clyde Valley, however, meant that a London type of green belt could not be adopted. Instead, and after considerable deliberations, the Clyde Valley planners recommended that their green belt was to envelop much of the Midland Valley and the towns which stood in it, so creating a region composed of what were described as 'polynucleated settlements'. The outer limits of the belt were set by the high moorland hills which encircled the Clyde Basin (paras. 568-9), but strictly speaking within this system, there could be no inner limits. The Glasgow conurbation and the other towns of the region would simply be engulfed in a green 'envelope', and in this way their growth too could be contained and regulated. Much of the green belt, consisting of good agricultural land, could then be preserved, and so continue to provide the conurbation with supplies of fresh milk and vegetables (paras. 570-2).

As far as Glasgow was concerned, the regional planners recommended that the green belt should engulf the city in such a way that it would be prevented from merging with surrounding towns and that a further interlinking where it had already occurred should be stopped. Furthermore, the regional planners were also anxious to preserve high amenity open land, especially along the river valleys which penetrated Glasgow. On those criteria, 13,000 acres which lay within the Glasgow municipal boundaries were recommended as green belt. It was this recommendation which, if implemented, would have profound repercussions on the redistribution of the 500,000 persons who were to be moved from the overcrowded central areas. There

44

would be room for only 250,000 of them within the municipal boundaries.

The sieve map which the planners used to survey the region revealed - after taking into account areas of good agricultural land, possible mining subsidence and difficult terrain - that there were only four sites on which it would be possible to build free standing new towns (Grieve 1954, 15-6). A solution, therefore, suggested itself. Four new towns should be built to accommodate a substantial proportion of that exodus. It was proposed that in all some 150,000 persons should be dispersed in new towns at East Kilbride, in Lanarkshire, Cumbernauld-Condorrat in Dunbartonshire and Bishopton and Houston in Renfrewshire (paras. 897-922). This still left 100,000 of those required to leave Glasgow unaccounted for. Some were expected to leave the region altogether - a proportion perhaps making their way to Fife where new coal mines were planned - some to the towns on the outer periphery of the Clyde Valley which could be allowed to grow without contravening any basic planning principles (paras. 759, 770). The green belt was so drawn that the congestion in most of the industrial towns near to Glasgow could be relieved by allowing them to expand peripherally provided that it was away from the city rather than towards it. The congestion in North Lanarkshire and Greenock could, however, only be relieved through 'overspill' and the new towns of East Kilbride and Bishopton were, in addition to their roles of acting as reception areas for the Glasgow population, expected to assist in this (paras. 898, 916).

Decentralisation and new towns policies were associated in the minds of the regional planners with their industrial recommendations. As was shown in an earlier chapter, 60,000 new jobs were expected to be required in the region during the immediate post-war years to replace those lost through the contraction of the traditional heavy industries. These new jobs would have to be attracted, in the main, from the more prosperous regions of England. As far as the Clyde Valley planners were concerned, what better magnet could such firms have to draw them into the west of Scotland than new towns equipped with their own industrial estates (para. 482)? Even so, there were additional sources of employment that the regional planners were also anxious to tap for the new towns. The congested state of Glasgow, it was thought, was a major impediment to the expansion of firms located in the central areas. By moving them out to the new towns such an impediment would be removed whilst at the same time jobs would be provided for the overspill population (para. 483).

Figure 3.1   The Plan's Negative Building Map

46

DECENTRALISATION IN ACTION

The Impact of the Decentralisation Recommendations, 1946-50

There was a close liaison between the regional planners and the
Scottish Office - and more particularly the planning division
of the Scottish Department of Health - in the production of the
Clyde Valley Regional Plan. This helped to clarify at an early
stage the thinking of the new Secretary of State for Scotland
in the first postwar Labour government, Rt. Hon. Joseph
Westwood, who had long been anxious to see Glasgow's
overcrowding reduced. As a result, in only a matter of weeks
after the initial publication of the Plan in June 1946, and
before the representative local authorities had the chance to
pass judgement on it, Westwood announced plans for implementing
the first part of the decentralisation strategy (Smith 1974b).

The New Towns Act of 1946 was one of the first major pieces
of legislation in the new Labour government's programme. The
act enabled the Minister of Town and Country Planning in
England and the Secretary of State in Scotland to designate new
towns subject to Cabinet approval. Each was to be built and
run largely independently of the local authority by a
development corporation appointed by the relevant Minister.
Money was to be provided through Treasury loans, repayable from
revenues - primarily rents - that the towns would ultimately
yield. So eager was Westwood to utilise the Act in the Clyde
Valley, that even before the Bill's final reading he had
convened a meeting of the region's local authorities to discuss
the possibility of designating Scotland's first new town at
East Kilbride. As a result, in 1947 the designation order was
confirmed, the Development Corporation was appointed and the
town was started, but only after major objections had been
faced (Department of Health for Scotland 1947).

Glasgow Corporation strenuously disapproved of the
designation of East Kilbride and voiced its objections at a
public inquiry. The City's case was that there was no need to
disperse population beyond the municipal limits. Land would be
available to undertake all the rehousing necessary at
acceptable densities, provided that the green belt did not
encroach into Glasgow territory (Bruce 1946, Notes of
Proceedings 1947, esp. 242 ff.) The Secretary of State,
however, re-affirmed the regional planners strategy for a green
belt and the need for a new town at East Kilbride.

Westwood was anxious to have at least two more new towns
designated in the Clyde Valley as soon as possible but, in view
of the precarious state of the national economy, by 1947 he was
fortunate to be allowed to continue with the one already

Figure 3.2 Staking the foundations of East Kilbride, designated 1947.
L to R. Elizabeth Mitchell, Joe Westwood and Sir Patrick Dollan

Figure 3.3 Cumbernauld Town Centre. Fourth Shopping Phase under construction

designated. Arguably the Treasury was persuaded to allow the scheme to continue because, apart from its role as a reception area for an overcrowded population, the town could also be justified in terms of the jobs that it could be expected to attract into North Lanarkshire, an area of potential high unemployment (Treasury 1947, para. 11). Within the Clyde Valley, North West Lanarkshire gave special cause for concern. The seams of the central coalfields were nearing exhaustion and the county's steel works had fallen into difficulty (Scottish Home Department 1944, para. 15 ff., Ministry of Supply 1946, 19). The importance of pressing ahead with the new town there to act as a magnet drawing in new jobs was obvious.

Yet even at that stage, the green belt recommendations were far from established, the Scottish Office showed no impetus to create a statutory green belt. Westwood, had he stayed at the Scottish Office, may have retained his strong personal commitment to a Clyde Valley green belt. But he was soon replaced by Rt. Hon. Arthur Woodburn, one of whose first moves was to give Glasgow permission to extend their building operation at Castlemilk, to the south of the City, on land intended as green belt by the regional planners.

The number of good sites for public housing schemes in Glasgow was limited and plans for the development of Castlemilk had been drawn up during the war, but permission to build had been refused by Westwood on the grounds that East Kilbride could provide all the necessary houses. But by 1948 it was apparent that, in the short run at least, Westwood had been over optimistic. In view of this, whilst still retaining general support for a regional green belt, Woodburn decided that necessity dictated that some Glasgow building should be on land designated as open spaces.

By 1950, however, Woodburn turned his attention to providing a second new town for the Clyde Valley, at Houston, an indication that by that date the Scottish Office was renewing a commitment, no matter how tenuous, to the principles of green belt. But this project came to nought, largely as a result of the general election that was called in that year. The Labour government was returned, albeit with a substantially reduced majority. In the Cabinet changes that followed, Woodburn moved from the Scottish Office and was replaced by Rt. Hon. Hector McNeil, the M.P. for Greenock. Had the Houston project been allowed to continue then, it would have taken some of its population and jobs from McNeil's constituency. The new Secretary of State did not want that to happen, and the Houston project was quietly dropped.

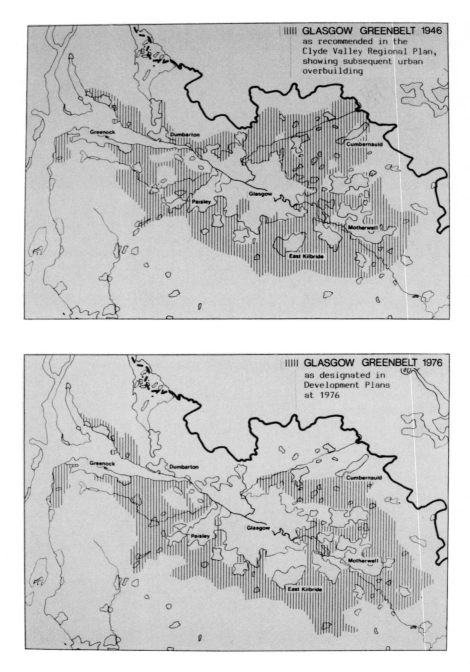

Figure 3.4 Glasgow Greenbelt as proposed by the Plan in 1946 and as designated in Development Plans in 1976 (Skinner, 1976)

The Return of a Conservative Government
and the Designation of Cumbernauld

The life of the second postwar Labour government was short,
and the return of a Conservative administration in 1951, with
the Rt. Hon. James Stuart as the Scottish Secretary of State,
was greeted with some apprehension by regional planners in the
Scottish Office. The new Minister of Housing and Local
Government, Rt. Hon. Harold MacMillan, let it be known that no
more new towns would be designed in England (MacMillan 1969,
418-9). As far as Scotland was concerned, there were fears
that if such a decision were also taken there, what little
regional planning had so far been undertaken to ease Glasgow's
congestion would be terminated forthwith. In the event,
although progress in that direction was far from rapid during
the 1950's, the expectations were unduly pessimistic.

That group of able civil servants who were working to keep
the Clyde Valley Regional Plan alive were especially interested
in seeing its decentralisation recommendations implemented.
The overspill proposals in the plan were retested by this
group, only to confirm the massive exodus needed if Glasgow's
housing environment was to be substantially improved (Grieve
1960, 3). The results of the retesting process did much to
influence Commander Galbraith, the new Minister in the Scottish
Office responsible for planning and housing. He in turn was
able to impress on Stuart the urgency of continuing to
implement a regional strategy aimed at reducing overcrowding in
Glasgow, whilst preserving the spirit of the green belt. Even
so, due to the continued pressure for housing in Glasgow, which
could not wait upon further implementation of overspill policy,
a major erosion of the green belt occurred when Glasgow was
given permission to build to the north west at Drumchapel, and
at Easterhouse to the east.

Yet, despite this compromise it was clear that the new
administration in the Scottish Office was anxious to contain
the peripheral growth of Glasgow. Against such a background,
Glasgow Corporation, too, gradually found itself during the
late 1940's and early 1950's accepting the necessity of an
overspill policy. By 1950 the Labour Party, which had
controlled Glasgow during the period when the East Kilbride
designation order was being opposed, had fallen from office
and, for a brief period, was replaced by the Progressive Party.
The new chairman of the housing committee, Bailie Patterson,
was thus unencumbered by former postures, and was able to
reappraise the need for overspill. Patterson believed that the
Scottish Office was reluctant to grant further permission to
build on the green belt. Further, because only non-traditional
materials had been available, house building during the

immediate postwar years had been undertaken at much lower densities than had originally been anticipated. The land that the Scottish Office was willing to approve for development was thus being rapidly utilised; so much so that if the City was to meet its housing commitments an overspill policy was essential. A newly appointed architect and planning officer, A.G. Jury, was able to quantify this in a report on the City's housing published in 1952 (Jury 1952).

The need for overspill was further reinforced by the publication of the 1951 Census results. For the first time it was possible to compare the degree of overcrowding in the seven conurbations of Great Britain. The most damning figure was the one which showed that over 43.4 per cent of the Clydeside conurbation lived at residential densities in excess of $1\frac{1}{2}$ persons per room (Census 1951, 1952, Section II). The nearest other conurbation was Tyneside with 19.8 per cent. The case for dispersal was clear, and by the early 1950's a Conservative Scottish Office and a Labour Glasgow Corporation were in agreement with the Clyde Valley planners that a considerable planned exodus of population from the City would have to be undertaken.

The Glasgow Development Plan, which had to be submitted to the Secretary of State in accordance with the 1947 Town and Country Planning (Scotland) Act, was approved by the Corporation in December 1951. It was prepared at a time when Glasgow was reassessing its overspill position. Not unexpectedly, the Clyde Valley green belt recommendations were largely incorporated into the plan (Corporation of Glasgow 1954, 10) - the Secretary of State's approval would obviously not be given otherwise - but there was no overt recognition of the overspill question. It was this which caused considerable concern to the Scottish Branch of the Town and Country Planning Association, which had been founded in 1937 largely with the aim of persuading Glasgow Corporation to adopt an overspill and new town policy. As would be expected, therefore, at a public inquiry held in 1953 the Association challenged what it thought to be a major omission from the Development Plan (Glasgow Herald 23/5/1953).

In reply, however, Glasgow - now with the Jury Report absorbed into its thinking - argued that by inference an overspill policy had been accepted in the Development Plan. Parts of the City had been zoned effectively as green belt, and a careful study of the housing figures in the Plan revealed that there would be room in the city for only 40,000 of the 100,000 dwellings that would be needed by the 1970's. The public inquiry, if it achieved nothing else, forced Glasgow to admit publically and unequivocally that an overspill mechanism had to be devised.

The first move on the part of the Scottish Office was to reconvene the Clyde Valley Planning Advisory Committee. The Committee had been disbanded after Glasgow had made known its objections to the Plan. Now those objections were no longer valid there was no impediment to a re-formation. By 1953 the Committee, drawing on the Jury report, had concluded that by 1960 no more housing sites would be available within the Glasgow boundaries, and that as a consequence between 100,000 and 120,000 houses to accommodate 300,000 Glaswegians would have to be built beyond the municipal boundaries. This dispersal, it was recommended, should be undertaken through the new towns strategy laid down in the Plan. A new town at Cumbernauld was therefore recommended.

Glasgow Corporation and the Scottish Office agreed with the Cumbernauld proposal, and despite the unwillingness of the Ministry of Housing and Local Government to designate more new towns in England and Wales, the Cabinet made no objection to Stuart's proposal to designate a further new town to take 20,000 Glasgow families. This is a clear indication of the influence of the man in Cabinet. Stuart did, however, insist that Glasgow had a responsibility to bear a proportion of the cost of the new town. At first Glasgow refused, and an acrimonious dispute between the Scottish Office and Glasgow Corporation ensued. This delayed the designation of Cumbernauld by some two years. The shortage of land for housing within Glasgow was becoming acute at a time when an ambitious slum clearance programme was being prepared. It was realised that without a formal overspill programme the slum clearance proposals would be unworkable. This forced both sides into a compromise (Smith 1977). The Secretary of State, therefore, agreed to designate a new town under the 1946 Act at Cumbernauld, whilst Glasgow Corporation intimated a willingness to pay the Development Corporation £14 per annum, extending over ten years, for each family from the City accommodated. The designation order was confirmed in 1956.

Glasgow Overspill Policy 1956-1960

By the mid 1950's, Glasgow Corporation was beginning to turn its attention from housing those on the general waiting list to rehousing those in unfit properties, and by 1957 plans were being drafted to undertake an extensive urban renewal programme (Corporation of Glasgow 1957). 106,000 dwellings located in 29 Comprehensive Development Areas were classed as warranting clearance in the period 1960-80. A further 21,500 dwellings were proposed for clearance post-1980, when only 7,400 would remain of the original dwellings in the CDA's. As only 275

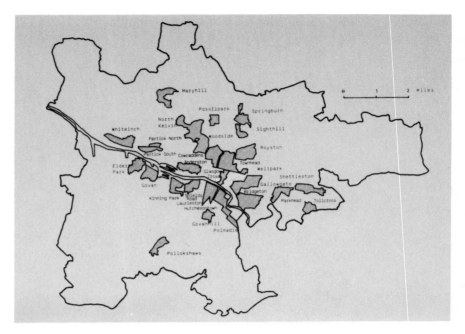

Figure 3.5 Glasgow's Comprehensive Development Area proposals
1957

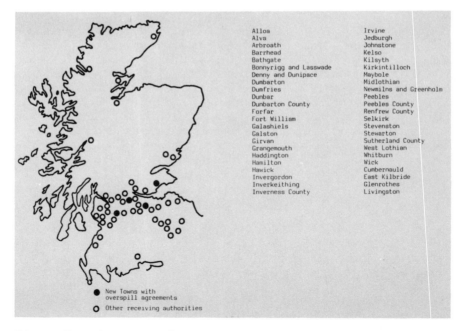

Alloa	Irvine
Alva	Jedburgh
Arbroath	Johnstone
Barrhead	Kelso
Bathgate	Kilsyth
Bonnyrigg and Lasswade	Kirkintilloch
Denny and Dunipace	Maybole
Dumbarton	Midlothian
Dumfries	Newmilns and Greenholm
Dunbar	Peebles
Dunbarton County	Peebles County
Forfar	Renfrew County
Fort William	Selkirk
Galashiels	Stevenston
Galston	Stewarton
Girvan	Sutherland County
Grangemouth	West Lothian
Haddington	Whitburn
Hamilton	Wick
Hawick	Cumbernauld
Invergordon	East Kilbride
Inverkeithing	Glenrothes
Inverness County	Livingston

● New Towns with
   overspill agreements

○ Other receiving authorities

Figure 3.6 Glasgow's Overspill Agreements with Scottish
Counties, Burghs and new town Development Corporations

acres of land could be made available on the periphery of the built up area of the City at Darnley and Summerston, and as it would be possible to replace only one third of the number of houses demolished in the CDA's, some 60,000 new houses were anticipated to be required in the period 1960-80 in overspill reception areas outside Glasgow. These proposals were incorporated in the Quinquennial Review of the Development Plan which was published in 1960.

When the urban renewal programme was first announced in 1957 it was obvious that East Kilbride and Cumbernauld alone would be insufficient to provide the requisite number of overspill outlets. The target population for East Kilbride which had originally been set at 40,000 was increased to 50,000, partly to offset this deficiency. However, according to the Clyde Valley Advisory Committee more new towns were required. Stuart was not, however, prepared to adopt such a recommendation. Seemingly he did not wish to disturb the landed society, for which he had much personal regard, farming near to Houston and Bishopton. Rather, Stuart preferred to handle the matter through the expansion of existing communities, via a Town Development Act.

England and Wales had had a Town Development Act since 1952, whereby population from congested areas could be dispersed with the aid of Treasury grants to publicly owned housing in local authorities which had land surplus to their own requirements. The Act as it stood was unsuitable for Scotland, largely because of the higher level of subsidised municipal rents there. As the receiving authorities could not be expected to subsidise rents for the newcomers, and as there was no Treasury subsidy available for that purpose, it was argued that the higher rents that would have to be charged by the receiving authorities would dissuade Glaswegians from moving into them. By 1957, however, a Housing and Town Development Act was passed for Scotland, but with a more generous system of grants than had been available in the English Act. In this way, the detrimental effects that the low rent issue in Scotland would have had in undermining an overspill policy was to a degree offset. As a result of the 1957 Act, therefore, an extra dimension had been added to the overspill recommendation set out in the Clyde Valley Regional Plan. Other local authorities were now to be brought in on a major scale to help handle the decentralisation.

Glasgow Overspill in the Early 1960's: the Return to New Towns

With the passing of the 1957 Act, Glasgow began to formalise its overspill position with the new towns. With Cumbernauld, an overspill agreement with Glasgow simply gave de jure recognition to a de facto situation. The same, to a degree, applied to East Kilbride, although in that case the Scottish Office stepped in and raised the target population of the town yet again - this time to 62,000 persons - in order that more Glaswegians could be absorbed. A third new town overspill agreement was signed with Glenrothes New Town in Fife. This was a more curious arrangement. Glenrothes had been designated in 1948 to accommodate miners in the new coal mines that were to be opened up. But by the mid 1950's, geological problems and flooding of the new shafts caused the Coal Board to abandon their plans. There was, as a consequence, no flow of population anxious to take up residence in the town. Towards the end of the decade, therefore, the town's Development Corporation was looking for new reasons to justify its existence. One was found by offering its services as an overspill reception area for Glasgow.

Local authorities throughout Scotland were equally eager during the early 1960's to sign overspill agreements with Glasgow, and by 1964, 57 (including those with Development Corporations) had been signed. This creditable number reflected the anxiety of Glasgow to secure as many agreements as possible, as well as the desire on the part of the local authorities themselves to become involved in such arrangements. Many of these authorities were experiencing falling population and declining industry, and they saw their salvation in overspill schemes bringing in not only people but jobs, some of which might provide work for their own unemployed and school leavers. Grounds for this belief were strengthened through the 1960 Local Employment Act, which gave overspill reception areas advantages of development district status, including grants, even if they would ordinarily not have qualified.

Yet even whilst these overspill agreements with local authorities were being signed, the Scottish Office was showing some concern that the scheme might not live up to expectation. Certainly, the experiences of overspill agreements made by the congested cities of England under the 1952 Act was not encouraging. Within the Scottish context, early doubts suggested that despite the large number of overspill agreements concluded, the rate at which houses could be provided would fall short of 1,000 dwellings per annum (Department of Health for Scotland 1962, para. 9). Small local authorities, it was increasingly being recognised, were not geared up to large scale building programmes. The new town development corporations, on the other hand, were. By the early 1960's, therefore, it was recognised within the Scottish Office that Stuart had been misguided in 1957, when he decided to handle overspill predominantly via local authorities and the expansion of existing communities.

In one sense, therefore, the restating of arguments for more new towns as the major vehicles through which Glasgow overspill was to be handled, represented a return to the old Clyde Valley Regional Plan orthodoxy. The decision where to site the next new town, however, represented a radical departure. The next new town was not to be in the Clyde Valley, but outside. The novel point was made that

> 'it was clearly desirable that any location in the
> already congested Clyde Valley should be avoided'
> (Department of Health for Scotland 1962, para. 9).

The site outside the Clyde Valley which suggested itself was Livingston, lying on the boundaries of Mid and West Lothian. The area offered enough suitable land to hold a town to accommodate a population of up to 70,000 persons. It was also anticipated that the site would be attractive to new industry and that rapid communications could be readily established with Glasgow. Furthermore, agricultural displacement would be less severe than would have been the case on any other site examined. The draft designation order of Livingston was issued in 1962.

The designation of Livingston can also be seen as a major departure from the new town concept as it had become recognised in the Clyde Valley during the 1950's in another sense. One of the functions suggested for East Kilbride during the mid and late 1940's, was that it should be used to attract growth industries into North Lanarkshire and thereby counteract possible high unemployment in the area. The anticipated post-war depression in that part of Scotland did not, however, materialise until the end of the 1950's. Consequently, there no longer seemed any urgency to attract new firms into the region during much of that decade. East Kilbride was no longer thought of as an industrial magnet, and the industrial role of Cumbernauld Development Corporation was in part to attract firms displaced by the Glasgow clearance schemes and so provide jobs for the new town immigrants. Unemployment rates, however, began to rise towards the end of the 1950's, when central Government shifted its policy from encouraging firms to come into the Clyde Valley simply to mop up unemployment caused by the contraction of the heavy industries to one of reconstructing the whole of the economy of the Scottish central belt. Thus in 1963, SDD issued the White Paper on Central Scotland in which the case for the industrial regeneration of that part of Scotland was argued in terms of growth areas, five of which were the already designated new towns of East Kilbride, Glenrothes, Cumbernauld and Livingston and another area later to become so designated, Irvine.

The essential thinking behind the growth area philosophy was that within a generally depressed region, it would be possible

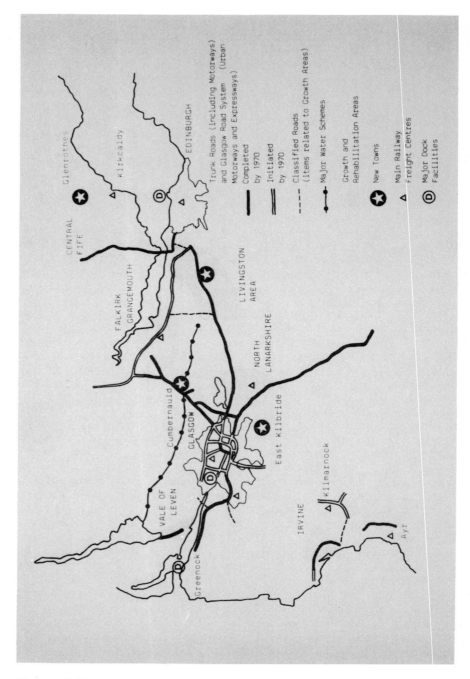

Figure 3.7   1963 Strategy for Central Scotland.   White Paper on
Central Scotland: A Programme for Development and Growth

to delineate a number of tightly defined areas where, if
government resources in the forms of infrastructure and grants
were concentrated, economic growth would stand the greatest
chance of success. This growth, it was argued, would then spin
off through linkages with firms attracted into the hinterlands
of those areas, until a time would be reached when economic
expansion would become self-generating and government
assistance would no longer be required.

That the growth area strategy should have been grafted onto
the new towns owed much to the Inquiry into the Scottish
Economy (The Toothill Report) published in 1961. In this
report, issued by the Scottish Council (Development and
Industry), the argument was put that overspill and growth areas
were different faces on the same coin. Overspill population
would provide the new industries with the workers, whilst the
workers would be attracted to the reception areas by the offer
of jobs provided by the incoming industries. But whereas with
East Kilbride, Glenrothes, Cumbernauld and Livingston, this
growth area strategy was grafted onto towns which were seen by
1962 as essentially overspill reception areas, Scotland's fifth
new town, Irvine, was designated in 1966 specifically as a
growth point.

Irvine was an old established settlement which had
demonstrated in the postwar period a remarkable rate of
economic growth. Thus, Irvine had already become in effect a
growth area and the Scottish Office was anxious to stimulate
more intensive industrial expansion. This was to be done by
providing the town with industrial estates, a wide variety of
factory premises for sale or to rent, and a readily available
supply of good housing for incoming workers, set within a high
quality urban environment. The Scottish Office concluded that
the best way of realising these ambitions was to designate
Irvine as a new town and thereby ensure that most of the
infrastructure would be established by a development
corporation. The implication was that such a body could handle
this task more effectively than a local authority, even with
support from the Scottish Special Housing Association and
Scottish Industrial Estates Corporation.

Thus, the major justification of designating a new town at
Irvine was an economic one and any role in the decentralisation
of Glasgow population was merely ancillary. The very essence
of the growth area was that it should draw in population.
Although Irvine Burgh had already signed an overspill agreement
with the City, housing Glasgow people was not the objective of
the Development Corporation, which chose to avoid any
association with Glasgow through an overspill agreement,
although the agreement with Irvine Burgh continued to run.

Meanwhile, the Scottish Office's attitude to green belt policy was simultaneously strengthened. Up to 1960, Glasgow was the only local authority which had had pressure put on it to conform to the rather nebulous green belt strategy operated by the Scottish Office. The three county authorities which adjoined Glasgow, however, had had little pressure placed on them during the 1950's, largely because none were preparing extensive developments likely to link up with the city. Even so, the Part Development Plan of Lanarkshire which included that portion of the county which adjoined the Glasgow boundary noted that,

> 'land use shall be based on the principles advocated for the Clyde Valley Green Belt in the Clyde Valley Regional Plan' (County of Lanark 1953 para. 5).

The same adherence to those principles was also noted in two other parts of the Development Plan which were published in 1962. There was a similar adherence to the green belt principles in the Renfrewshire Development Plan, although the matter was completely ignored in Dunbartonshire's Plan published in 1952 (County of Dunbarton 1952).

The 1960's, however, witnessed a more stringent attitude to green belt on the part of the Scottish Office. In 1960 the Secretary of State requested the Clyde Valley Advisory Committee to undertake a special review of the Clyde Valley green belt (Department of Health for Scotland 1960; Clyde Valley Advisory Committee 1963). Three years later a map was produced defining the green belt more generously than had been the case in the Clyde Valley Regional Plan. This gave the Secretary of State more muscle in his attempts to protect the green belt through the powers he had over development control. The Counties were certainly co-operative, at least as far as holding the peripheral growth of the Glasgow conurbation was concerned. Lanarkshire and Renfrewshire made their agreement in principle plain in Reviews of their Development Plans. Dunbartonshire's green belt proposals were incorporated in its Countryside Map which was produced in accordance with the Countryside (Scotland) Act of 1967 (County of Lanark 1962, 15; County of Renfrew 1963; County of Dunbarton 1968).

The Decentralisation of Glasgow Population
and the Reduction of Residential Densities

During the 1960's, the peripheral growth of Glasgow was generally contained by the green belt and the population of the City fell to 897,000 by 1971. Residential densities within the central areas were drastically reduced and slum clearance was prosecuted vigorously. Yet, contrary to the expectations of those involved in the Quinquennial Review of Glasgow's Plan in

1960, formal overspill policies played only a minor role in this.

The slum clearance record in Glasgow during the 1960's was impressive. The 1957 Report on the Clearance of Slum Houses, Redevelopment and Overspill had predicted that by 1969 some 47,000 of the worst 97,000 dwellings in the CDA's would have been demolished. In fact, by that date the figure for closures or demolitions in the City was 63,000. Between 1970 and 1972, a further 19,205 dwellings were closed or demolished throughout Glasgow, giving an annual average rate of 6,400 per annum which exceeded the maximum envisaged in the 1957 Report or in the Quinquennial Review of 1960.

There was, however, no close correlation between the working out of the formal overspill policy and the clearance of slums. The official Glasgow overspill scheme fell sadly behind the 3,000 families or 10,000 persons annual exodus that the Quinquennial Review had anticipated. This poses two questions. Why were the official targets not achieved, and how was it that under such circumstances Glasgow managed to undertake so successfully its clearance programme?

There are a number of reasons for the failure of the official overspill policy to live up to expectations, although a willingness on the part of a substantial number of Glaswegians to leave their City was certainly not one of them. In 1972, for example, there were 24,000 applicants on the overspill waiting lists. These potential overspill tenants, however, tended to want to remain within a twenty mile radius of the City. The failure to attract sufficient jobs in reception areas outside commuting distance from Glasgow was one of the reasons for this.

During the 1960's, Government mounted an impressive campaign to attract industry into Central Scotland. The expansion of firms in the prosperous parts of Britain was discouraged, and a formidable battery of financial incentives was assembled to tempt industrialists into Development Areas like Glasgow and its overspill hinterland. But these jobs did not come on a sufficient scale, and there was even a contraction of jobs throughout Scotland from 2,216,000 in 1961 to 2,170,000 in 1971. And what jobs did come tended to cluster within the Glasgow area. Furthermore, the outward movement of jobs from Glasgow expected to result from the demolition of older factories and workshops in the clearance areas, did not yield anything like the needs of all the reception areas. Like industry new to Scotland, what firms did move outside the city tended to remain in close proximity to it (Henderson 1974). Under such circumstances, it is hardly surprising that few

Glaswegians were attracted into the overspill reception areas. To go would have meant unemployment in many cases.

But that is not the whole story. The new towns, whether sited within a travel-to-work radius from Glasgow or not, did attract a disproportionately large volume of industry. Yet, by 1972 Glenrothes had taken only 509 Glasgow families under formal schemes and Livingston 1,086. This contrasts with Cumbernauld's 12,288 and East Kilbride's 7,173. Obviously there were social as well as economic factors to take into account in explaining why the formal overspill policies were not more successful.

This point is reinforced by the experience of East Kilbride and Cumbernauld. In 1966, there were 96 jobs for every 100 employed residents in both towns. In other words, both might have been expected to have a high degree of their employed residents working near to where they lived. In fact, 54.2 per cent of the employed residents in Cumbernauld and 40.5 per cent of the employed residents of East Kilbride worked elsewhere - in both cases predominantly in Glasgow. Thus, many who were prepared to move out to overspill areas did not necessarily wish to work in them, hence their choice to move only a relatively short distance.

Having thus, to a degree, explained why official overspill schemes did not meet expectations, the second question can be turned to. How was it that the peripheral growth of Glasgow was contained, its population fell and residential densities reduced despite the failure to meet targets for the formal overspill areas? The primary explanations are the substantial movement of population away from Glasgow without official encouragement - 'voluntary overspill' in the contemporary terminology - and Glasgow Corporation's newly devised policy of building multi-storey blocks of flats at residential densities which, whilst lower than those prevailing in the slums, nonetheless were higher than had hitherto been thought acceptable.

Official and Voluntary Out-migration

Before moving on to examine the scale of decentralisation from Glasgow, a few contextual comments should be made about the broader demographic changes that were underway within the Clyde Valley during the post-war period. The first point to make is that in terms of the aggregate population of the Clyde Valley, the regional planners in 1946 had assumed a total population of substantially the same gross numbers as still existing for the next 40 or 50 years. The background to this assumption was the declining birth rate of the prewar period, which many considered an adverse trend. In fact, there was a considerable overall natural increase in the region of about 400,000 between 1951 and 1971. This was unexpected, as was the net migration outflow of about 336,000. Because of this, the effect on decentralisation within the region created problems which were unforeseen in 1946.

Despite the stress that had been placed in the 1950's and 1960's on formal overspill policies to reduce the population of Glasgow, they played only a minor role in the overall exodus. Although between 1961 and 1971 some 65,000 persons left Glasgow under formal overspill schemes, this amounted to a little under 30 per cent of all the net exodus. It is difficult to determine where these voluntary emigrants went to, but the 1966 sample Census suggests that of the 116,600 (gross) persons who left Glasgow during the previous five years for destinations within Great Britain, 56.7 per cent remained within the neighbouring counties of Ayr, Dunbarton, Lanark and Renfrew, whilst 25.9 per cent left Scotland altogether. Clearly, many of those who left Glasgow but remained within commuting distance of the City were those moving to middle class owner occupier suburbs. Many of those who were moving much further afield were clearly encouraged to leave because of the less than healthy state of the region's economy.

Before the mechanics of population dispersal can be examined, attention should be redirected to the contributions made by the official schemes. Surprisingly, only a minority of the official overspill families came from the central clearance areas or were living under the most overcrowded conditions, so that the link between slum clearance, decongestion and overspill was by no means as direct as had been anticipated. This was because heads of those households with the greatest housing needs tended to belong to the semi- or unskilled strata of society, for whom jobs were especially difficult to come by in the overspill reception areas. Where such firms did have vacancies for semi- and unskilled labour, they tended to mop up local unemployment and only drew from Glasgow if they required persons with specific skills. Furthermore, many of the semi- and unskilled from Glasgow were dissuaded from leaving because of the higher rents that they would have to pay, notwithstanding subsidisation through Treasury grants available for housebuilding under the 1957 Act, whilst others were deterred from settling in the overspill areas near to the City because of high commuting costs.

But even if the direct benefits of official overspill schemes were limited, the indirect contribution was more impressive. Many who occupied municipal houses in Glasgow (23 per cent of movers) left under formal schemes, and so vacated dwellings which could be offered to those who were in more direct need. Other non-urgent cases who left under formal schemes released houses which, although the Corporation had no control over them, started a filtering process in the City's housing market which ultimately benefited the overcrowded and the slum dwellers.

It was through the mechanism of filtering within the Glasgow housing market that the voluntary exodus may have made its major contribution to easing the City's housing problems. Those who vacated expensive properties in some of the upper class districts of Glasgow were not, of course, directly helping the overcrowded and those living in unfit dwellings. On the other hand, because the inward movement of population into Glasgow was limited, it would seem that houses must have been released for those from the less prestigious owner occupied sector. This in turn tempted those in the poorer rented sectors to upgrade their housing status. This then left rented private property available to those living in the very worst housing conditions. It was in this way that the voluntary exodus must be supposed to have made its greatest contribution to improving the Glasgow housing environment.

High Density Housing in Post-War Glasgow

By the early 1950's, it was becoming apparent that because no extensive official overspill programme had been put into effect, densities in the new housing schemes being undertaken by Glasgow Corporation would have to be considerably higher than the regional planners would have approved in 1946. Because of the potential land shortage, the Corporation adopted a revised version of the tenement on its peripheral municipal estates such as Easterhouse and Drumchapel, where net residential densities were frequently as high as 100 persons net per acre, i.e. 40 per acre higher than those recommended in the 1940's. Then, as the 1950's drew to a close and land shortage remained acute and despite the overspill mechanism that was being developed, Glasgow, following the fashion of the period, began its extensive multi-storey flats programme. Originally these flats were intended only for the central areas, but soon they were being provided on the outskirts of the City. This resulted in many of the newly developed areas of Glasgow experiencing net residential densities only a little under 200 persons per acre.

Paradoxically, this swing towards the building of multi-storey flats was encouraged by the 1957 Housing and Town Development (Scotland) Act. Whilst encouraging Glasgow population to leave the City, Government also allowed a new subsidy to be paid to compensate for increased costs of

Figure 3.8 Multi-storey flats, Red Road, Glasgow, asserted to have been the tallest in Europe

building multi-storey blocks. Clearly, despite the efforts that were being made to move people out of Glasgow, the consequence of the Corporation building at higher densities was to retain population who might otherwise have been rehoused in overspill areas.

This was not, at the time, seen to be a contradiction of policy objectives. Because official overspill schemes were seen not to be living up to expectations, there were fears in Glasgow that the slum clearance and urban renewal programme would be drastically impeded. A way round this was to build high. In addition, despite all protestations to the countrary, especially during the early 1960's, the Corporation was not anxious to lose population on such a large scale, nor was it anxious to cut back on its house building rates. Since the 1930's, the housing committee had been one of the most prestigious on the Council, having far greater influence than any spokesmen for planning and the lower densities and higher environmental standards for which they argued. The reasons for this were that the Corporation (for very understandable reasons) believed that its first priority was to rehouse a considerable section of the City's population as rapidly as possible and, following on from that, its belief that impressive house building achievements were an important factor in securing votes at municipal elections. Building land may have been in short supply, but multi-storey blocks and prefabricated construction methods meant that annual house completion figures could be kept high. Thus, between the beginning of the overspill scheme and 1972, 48,000 dwellings were provided within the City compared with 25,000 overspill dwellings. This, it will be remembered, contrasts with an original expectation of 60,000 dwellings outside and 40,000 inside the City by 1980.

Changes in Overspill Policy in the Later 1960's

During the second half of the 1960's, and despite the designation of four 'overspill' new towns as well as an impressive array of overspill agreements signed with many local authorities, there was concern within the Scottish Development Department that not only was the pace of overspill too slow, but that overall there were insufficient outlets to meet the needs of Glasgow.

Despite the fact that the Secretary of State had approved Glasgow's Quinquennial Review in 1962, SDD began to have reservations about the City's renewal programme. The scale and progress of the City's multi-storey flat programme was disquieting, and it was thought that there was need to lower net and gross residential densities if greater space was to be

66

devoted to recreational areas. When these concerns were compounded with the realisation that it was difficult to persuade Glaswegians to move beyond the travel-to-work area of the City, even to the new towns of Livingston and Glenrothes, and that the contribution made by most of the local authorities which had signed formal overspill agreements fell sadly behind expectation, it is hardly surprising that SDD came to anticipate that the existing overspill machinery was inadequate to shoulder the burdens imposed on it.

The first corrective move that SDD undertook was to encourage some of the local authorities within the Clyde Valley to set up Land Use working parties, to assess within the context of their own development plans and the reviews which were to accompany them, how much land could be spared to accommodate the Registrar General's expectations of population growth and to take Glasgow overspill. From these consultations it became clear that there was sufficient land available at Erskine to create a new community to take some 30,000 persons. The Secretary of State gave his approval for the project in February 1967, and the Scottish Special Housing Association agreed to undertake the house building under the terms of the 1957 Town Development Act (Scottish Development Department 1969, 22).

A further report recommended that an additional new community, modelled on Erskine, should be provided at Stonehouse. But whilst this was being considered, representatives from SDD and Glasgow Corporation examined the population projections of the Registrar General. They indicated that despite the redevelopment and building that had already been undertaken, 100,000 more new or rehabilitated houses were still needed - 65,000 beyond the municipal boundaries (Corporation of the City of Glasgow and the Scottish Development Department 1970, para. 4.6). They concluded that there was insufficient output of construction in prospect to meet those needs in an acceptable timespan.

The Scottish Development Department took the findings of this Glasgow Housing Needs study with seriousness and concluded that 'from past negotiations with local authorities ... it had become clear that the only way of carrying out a larger development by 1981 would be by establishing a New Town' (Scottish Development Department 1972, para. 15). As a consequence, the Stonehouse project was upgraded to new town status and the Designation Order was confirmed in 1973.

It was against this background that the West Central Scotland Plan was initiated. However, the West Central planners had to face two eventualities that were absent even four years earlier when the Glasgow and SDD working party report was written. Firstly, between 1970 and 1973 the City's population fell from 908,000 to 850,000 – an unusually rapid rate even for postwar Glasgow. This trend was accompanied by the exceptionally poor economic performance of the region in these years, which accentuated the trend of persons seeking work elsewhere. 32,000 persons (net) were now expected to leave the City each year. The early 1970's also experienced a decline in the birth rate both nationally and locally, which meant that the Scottish Registrar General lowered his population predictions for Glasgow considerably. On this basis, the scale of official overspill expected to be necessary in 1970 would no longer be required.

Furthermore, a growing trend of owner occupation became apparent in West Central Scotland despite the region's poor economic performance. This, coupled with a move on the part of Glasgow Corporation from slum clearance to the rehabilitation of older houses, meant that the demand for official overspill outlets was reduced even more. By the early 1970's Glasgow, like many other cities, was turning away from its multi-storey flat building programme, and from its grandiose comprehensive redevelopment schemes. Finance was partly a reason for this. Multi-storey flat building and comprehensive redevelopment schemes were becoming relatively more expensive, at a time when the historic shortage of houses in Glasgow was turning into surfeit. The early signs of dereliction and vacancy were appearing. But there was also a growing awareness on the part of many of the elected representatives, as well as officials, that there were many undesirable social consequences that could arise from such schemes. Living in high rise blocks was not universally popular. There were also problems involved in breaking up communities through slum clearance schemes. The resultant shift to rehabilitation, of course, meant that the demand for official overspill outlets was reduced. The fact was now generally recognised that the overspill, whether official or voluntary, tended to draw out younger persons of higher status groups from Glasgow, leaving the City with an increasingly ageing and less skilled population. This encouraged many, including the West Central regional planners, to query the wisdom of sustained large scale programmes of decentralisation (West Central Scotland Plan 1974, esp. chaps. 2, 3 and 10).

The Move Away from Decentralisation

Despite the arguments against decentralisation the Scottish Office, at least initially, continued with the Stonehouse project. The development was to be undertaken by the renamed East Kilbride and Stonehouse Development Corporation, which was

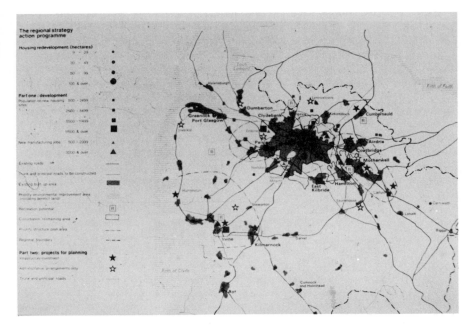

Figure 3.9   The Regional Strategy Action Programme,
West Central Scotland Plan 1974

Figure 3.10   Stonehouse, Regional Growth Point.   Erected 1975,
demolished 1976

coming to the end of its original work. The Strathclyde Regional Report (Strathclyde Regional Council 1976), however, drawing on the West Central Scotland Plan, argued for abandonment of the Stonehouse project. The case against Stonehouse had been strengthened in 1976 by the fact that out migration from the City was continuing to accelerate, whilst the birth rate continued to fall markedly. As a result of the forecasts based on these figures, the view became established that by 1981 Glasgow was likely to find that it had a large surplus of municipal houses. The priority now, therefore, was to improve the quality of the existing housing stock and the overall housing environment of the City and to encourage Glaswegians to stay, rather than to encourage them to leave. If the Stonehouse project were allowed to continue, Strathclyde Regional Council, would, of course, have been statutorily responsible for providing a number of important services, the most expensive being schools, sewerage and water facilities. Such investment, as far as the regional authority was concerned, would be better spent in areas of greatest need - especially as the recently published results of the 1971 Census had demonstrated that in terms of multiple deprivation, Glasgow remained the worst case in Britain. Indeed, further overspill could result in the under utilisation of facilities, currently provided or about to be provided within the old areas at a considerable cost.

The Secretary of State for Scotland, now Rt. Hon. Bruce Millan (replacing Rt. Hon. William Ross - a staunch supporter of new towns), was sympathetic to Strathclyde's case for dispensing with Stonehouse, and announced his decision to stop the town before considering and replying to the other issues raised in the Council's Regional Report. By that time, the first 96 houses had been completed and the first families had moved in. But why had the town been allowed to develop this far? Stonehouse had been initiated largely because the Scottish Office could have greater control over housing in the region through using the new town mechanism. The Scottish Office certainly had a profound mistrust of the old Glasgow Corporation. The City was associated with one of the worst postwar housing environments in any British city, and the history of the 1960's demonstrates that the Scottish Office had only limited real powers to prevent this. The Scottish Office believed that it could, however, play a more active role in Glasgow's affairs through the control it had over new towns. Hence its strong commitment to them. But in addition, the new towns of the region - and especially the East Kilbride Development Corporation - had proven records of success. Very good housing environments were made available for Glaswegians which would not otherwise have been provided. And the new towns probably did attract jobs into the region which otherwise

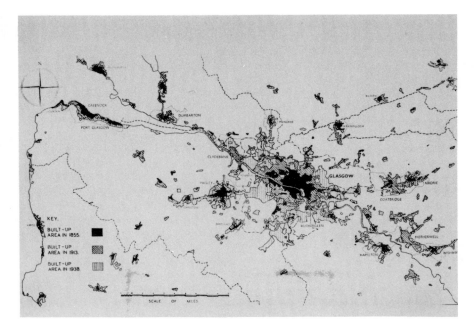

Figure 3.11   The Plan's illustration of the growth of Clydeside

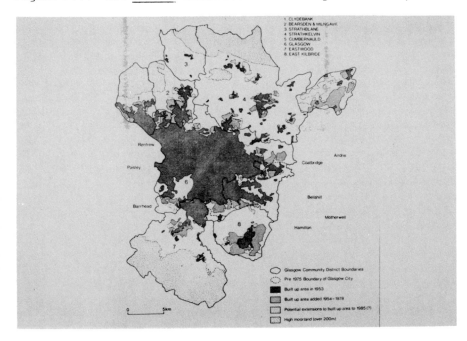

Figure 3.12   The subsequent growth of Clydeside 1953-78
(Lea 1980)

would not have come. By encouraging the East Kilbride Development Corporation to build Stonehouse, the Scottish Office had expected that it would at least give a 'winning team' the opportunity to continue with its successes.

Yet, the Scottish Office was not immune to the wider changes in planning thought which manifested themselves during the 1970's. The Scottish Office began to accept that more resources ought to be focused directly in the inner areas of urban settlements like Glasgow. The GEAR project was established in 1976 very soon after the Secretary of state's decision to terminate Stonehouse. The transfer of emphasis in urban and regional development, which this first British government direct intervention in urban renewal reflected, was represented in the transfer of senior professional staff from Stonehouse to the GEAR enterprise.

Meanwhile, as far as decentralisation was concerned, all overspill agreements made by Glasgow were terminated in 1978 after consultations with SDD, interested local authorities, the new town development corporations and the Scottish Special Housing Association. In future, any Glasgow citizen wishing to live in a new town had to make a direct application to the development corporation concerned. In this way, the formal policies for decentralising Glasgow's population came to an end.

By the end of the 1970's and the beginning of the 1980's, major planning concerns were with attempts to draw the young and enterprising back into Glasgow. To do this it would be necessary to broaden the base of owner occupation. But perhaps the final irony was that one of the main areas of planning concern was now with the outer peripheral estates, with their social problems, lack of facilities and high incidence of unemployment. This legacy was partly the result of not fully integrating dispersal policies with comprehensive planning for the whole City.

4 Community Planning and Regional Architecture

SHIELA T. McDONALD

THE PLAN AND ITS BACKGROUND

Scottish Design and Planning Between the Wars

The Clyde Valley Regional Plan was commissioned in 1943 in readiness for the time when building would again be possible for other than wartime purposes. As outlined in Chapter 3, the Clyde Valley, in common with other parts of the country, had a legacy of housing need from the inter-war and early war years: the deficiencies revealed by a survey of overcrowding in 1935 had not been remedied by 1939, further losses had occurred due to war damage and poor maintenance, and increases in household formation meant that there was a pressing need for more dwellings. The form that development might take was explored in the Plan from different points of view in two chapters, 'Community Planning and Standards', and 'Regional Architecture and Recovery of Amenities'. Paradoxically in a plan so dominated by the issue of bad housing, there is no single chapter under the heading of 'Housing'. Arising from the literary shortcomings of the member of the team who would have been responsible, the omission was compensated by extensive discussion in other chapters including those with which we are concerned here.

In the inter-war period, the region's estates of local authority houses and of private bungalows were not for the most part considered to be of satisfactory layout or design.

73

Widespread concern at the quality of development throughout
Scotland was reflected in 1935 in the reports of visits to the
Continent by the Secretary of the Department of Health
(Department of Health for Scotland 1935a) and the Scottish
Architectural Advisory Committee (Department of Health for
Scotland 1935b) when Scotland was said to lag behind in matters
of external appearance and layout. The largest of Glasgow's
estates, Knightswood, was developed from 1923 onwards with
predominantly cottage type houses at ordinary rents, and was
unusual in that it was more generously supplied than most with
parades of shops, schools, open space and a library (Checkland
1976).

Professional planners were few in number and certainly too
few in Scotland to have a direct impact on much of the
development in the inter-war years. Raymond Unwin's influence
was apparent in some layouts with culs-de-sac, short terraces,
tunnel closes and linking screen walls which had featured in
his 1915 low density township at Gretna. Patrick Abercrombie
advised on plans for a large estate at Pollok before the war:
his textbook Town and Country Planning, first published in
1933, was well known. In it he stressed the need for regional
plans. He also commented 'between Ebenezer Howard's and Le
Corbusier's conceptions there is room for considerable variety
of ideas, though perhaps the gap between the two is not so wide
as one might suppose'. This left the Scots, who are pragmatic
rather than purist in such matters, to draw on elements of the
work of both theorists. Scandinavia and Holland were much
praised at this time for sound new housing developments with
well laid out blocks of flats. One writer (Hurd 1938)
suggested in 1938 that a visitor might be forgiven for thinking
that, notwithstanding the earlier contributions of Charles
Rennie Mackintosh or the work of Tait for the 1938 Empire
Exhibition in Glasgow, modern architecture had not yet reached
Scotland.

Planning in the Early War Years:
The Plan's Immediate Influences

After 1939 the professional journals continued to draw heavily
on examples from the Continent and from the US, directing
attention to developments considered worthy of close scrutiny
when travel was again feasible. The loss of fine buildings
throughout Europe was chronicled month by month, members of the
forces were canvassed for their views on aspects of rebuilding,
and the Wartime Social Survey vigorously pursued enquiries
amongst a wider population on a host of topics under the
direction of Dennis Chapman who was to advise on the social
surveys conducted in connection with the Plan.

In 1943, the year when work began on the Clyde Valley Regional Plan, the County of London Plan was before the public (Abercrombie and Forshaw 1943). It was much debated, not only in Britain. By the spring of 1944 a copy sent to Stalag Luft III had been so well used in lectures illustrated by epidiascope that a replacement was needed. The County of London Plan contained proposals for reduced densities, decentralisation and reconstruction and placed a great deal of emphasis on the recognition and development of communities. This was the tenor of material in many detailed reports and studies called for in preparation for the surge of activity that was expected to follow the end of the war. Some of these reports were referred to by on the Plan team.

The best known, the Central Housing Advisory committee's Design of Dwellings (the Dudley Report) (Central Housing Advisory Committee 1944) talked of the need for complete communities rather than residential estates for a single social class. 'The creation of such communities depends for its success upon the collaboration of all types of enterprise, both public and private, working towards a common goal.' The report included a statement by a study group of the Ministry of Town and Country Planning on 'Site Layout in Relation to Housing.' Principles enunciated were that surrounding development should be taken into account, that density should be considered over wide areas, and that redevelopment should be over as large an area as possible at the same time, or at least to a comprehensive plan. Promotion of all types of housing was advocated but short term housing programmes which might give rise to continuous growth without a proper plan were not to be encouraged.

A great deal of attention was given to neighbourhood planning. It was this report that said:
   'For the proper social well-being of the large town,
   then, it is necessary to work out some organization
   of its physical form which will aid in every way the
   full development of community life and enable a
   proper measure of social amenities to be provided and
   arranged to advantage in each residential
   neighbourhood. The idea of the "neighbourhood unit"
   arises out of an acknowledgement of the necessity of
   doing this and offers the means of doing it'.
The population of the neighbourhood was not to be more than 10,000 and every house was to be within ten minutes' walk of the neighbourhood centre. Densities could vary according to location, higher densities being accepted near the centre, but 'never ... so high that it is impossible to include houses for families with young children, open spaces, and a range of community facilities'. The highest average net density

suggested was 120 persons per acre in the centre of concentrated urban areas only. At this figure houses and flats would be needed but 70-75 per cent of the population could, it was said, be accommodated in houses at a density of 20 houses per acre or a little over. However, arriving at reasonable density figures for housing was described as one of the most difficult problems in planning.

The Scottish Housing Advisory Committee Report Distribution of New Houses (Department of Health for Scotland 1944), also published in 1944, covered many of the same topics, but was by no means identical to the English study. The terms of reference were 'To consider and advise on the measures required to secure the most appropriate distribution of the houses to be erected in Scotland in the immediate post-war years'. A historical account of the development of public housing in Scotland was followed by discussion of the distribution of houses in relation to population, and of the shortage of staff qualified to plan for more effective distribution in the future. A great deal of importance was attached to the relationship between industry and housing, and journey to work was explored in some detail. The extent of Scotland's housing need was accepted as being very great. On this account, it was suggested that 'the responsibility for building them (houses) should be shared by housing authorities, private enterprise and housing associations'. The committee was clear that the creation of a healthy community depended on many things besides housing. Conditions of full employment and of freedom from want were necessary, as well as an adequate educational and recreational provision but it was concerned principally with the translation of the community concept into built development and concentrated on physical measures.

In discussing community facilities much reference was made to Planning our New Homes, another SHAC document (Scottish Housing Advisory Committee 1944) which had noted the limited use made of powers available under the Housing Acts to provide community buildings in local authority housing schemes. It contained examples of different approaches to layout, including Greenbelt, Maryland, in the United States, with its Radburn layout incorporating pedestrian and vehicle access and provision of local community facilities.

Planning our New Homes also gave some encouragement to modernisation of existing property where the condition of the dwellings justified it. A further sub-committee of SHAC was set up to investigate but did not report until 1947 (Scottish Housing Advisory Committee 1947), by which time the Plan had been prepared.

The Content of the Clyde Valley Regional Plan

The Interim Report.   The interim housing report issued by the
Clyde Valley Regional planning team recognised that local
authorities would be faced with an immediate demand for houses
and that this demand would be met 'to the greatest extent
possible, plan or no plan.'

Under the terms of Department of Health for Scotland Circular
No. 21/1944 local authorities were able to acquire the land
needed for house building programmes extending over the first
few years after the war. Many authorities were prepared to act
quickly.   Overall housing need in the region was calculated at
this time at over 200,000 dwellings. As this was equivalent to
rehousing approximately 35 per cent of the population, a
programme which could start smoothly and quickly was an
absolute necessity.   Only this extremity of need could have
persuaded the regional planners to report on sites for short
term use at such an early stage. They expressed misgivings
about the standard of architectural design, layout and
landscaping, and the lamentable lack of community planning in
housing developments and wrote hard words of the Scottish
Special Housing Association (a body appointed and financed by
Government) for failing to offer appropriate leadership in
these aspects of development.

The regional planners offered their own brief explanation of
what was meant by community planning, with three plans for
hypothetical greenfield sites and descriptive notes.   These
were subsequently included in the full Report with the addition
of detailed proposals for the Vale of Leven, and were
comparable to the plan for Ongar in the Greater London Plan
(Abercrombie 1945).

Development on many of the sites discussed in the Interim
Report, whether acceptable or not to the Plan team on community
planning grounds, was already under way by the time the Plan
became available to the local authorities in 1946.   It is hard
to see how the regional planners could have stemmed the flow of
development on to these sites: outlining the principles of
community planning was hardly sufficient in the absence of
immediate means of implementation.   At the very least
alternative suggestions as to substantial sites for development
would have been necessary since many of the sites under
discussion were already in local authority ownership, and
available for use without delay.

Such an outcome was also to be expected from the reactions of
Glasgow Corporation in 1945 to the First Planning Report of the
City Engineer, Robert Bruce, with its broad planning proposals

Figure 4.1   Looking north from Colston Road, Glasgow, 1975. The Plan's Interim Report on Housing Sites of 1944 had advised that Glasgow's development should be limited to the south side of Colston Road

78

for a fifty year period (Bruce 1945) and comments on the
Interim Report. The Lord Provost in a foreword said 'Glasgow's
citizens have a right to demand that their children should have
a city no less healthy and no less beautiful than that which
Mr. Bruce envisages'. And Bruce's vision was of tall buildings
on generous sites, of flats rather than houses.

The City Engineer's proposals were based on the belief that
planning for contiguous areas was necessary and by making
proposals for the conurbation, in which he included built-up
areas such as Rutherglen, Paisley and Barrhead, he aimed to
avoid a tightly drawn green belt and satellite towns. He
claimed 'some small originality' in his approach. His
proposals for transport were more fully worked out than those
for other aspects. He talked of a number of neighbourhood
units forming a community area, thought poor people should not
live on dear land near the city centre and proposed the
improvement of existing housing schemes. He extolled the
merits of the modern tenement and cited as evidence of the
desirability of the tenement privately owned and rented flats
in Glasgow built in 'excellent sandstone and very pleasing
architecturally', with net densities of 100 to 196 persons per
acre.

Energy saving was one reason given for developing flats
rather than houses. Another was the focus of the contemporary
discussion of flats versus houses on the possibility of
reducing costs through serial production. Bruce's positive
assurance that flats would be cheaper than houses must have
convinced the Housing Committee: by 1946 the first experimental
scheme of ten storey flats was being designed for a site at
Paisley Road West (Worsdall 1979) and much public housing was
to take the form of 'modern tenements'.

Community Planning. The Plan itself continued to be phrased in
ambitious terms:
> 'One of the chief objects of this Report is to
> present a wider view, to propose the provision of
> houses on so vast a scale that completely new
> communities are created, industry moved wholesale
> from its present unsuitable siting, threatened
> agricultural land reserved for vital growing of food,
> and recreation, fresh air and sunshine brought to
> everyone's doorstep.
>
> The Regional Plan, therefore, envisages an organic
> pattern of inter-related communities, economically
> and socially balanced, evolving from the City of
> Glasgow, linked by a regional system of
> communications and parks, and based upon sound

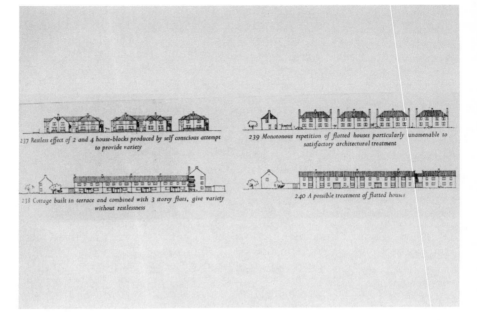

237 *Restless effect of 2 and 4 house-blocks produced by self conscious attempt to provide variety*

239 *Monotonous repetition of flatted houses particularly unamenable to satisfactory architectural treatment*

238 *Cottage built in terrace and combined with 3 storey flats, give variety without restlessness*

240 *A possible treatment of flatted houses*

Figure 4.2 Design Guidance in the <u>Plan</u>, 1946

Figure 4.3
Abandonment at Ferguslie Park,
Paisley, 1974

Figure 4.4
Demolition at Blackhill,
Glasgow, 1980

industrial proposals.

   The   application   of   this   method   of   orderly
development to the City of Glasgow and to the large
and small towns and villages alike, will ultimately
result in a more compact type of development, but at
the same time with a marked reduction in density and
with   an   increased open space provision in all the
main urban centres and villages of the region'.

In the team's view the redistribution of population with
associated uses was at the heart of the proposals. Without a
thinning down of the exceptionally high densities in the
centres no substantial improvement in living conditions was
feasible. When illustrating the principles of development in a
New Town context the Plan suggested sub-division of the
neighbourhood into groups of at least 300 houses which could be
'either tall blocks of flats, detached houses on large or small
plots, or any of the intermediate types of dwelling, such as
terrace houses'. A hierarchy of roads, with footpath routes to
the schools was advocated. Much of the discussion of standards
dealt with children's playspace, school playing fields, other
space for organised games, and parks. Where land could be
bought at agricultural value 'generous treatment of open space
will always succeed provided care is taken not to lose
compactness of communication' - no worries there about the cost
of maintaining open space, but joint use of land for public and
school playing fields was recommended as was the development of
nursery schools on the ground floors of blocks of flats. The
acreage proposed for open space fell in the areas of highest
density to 4.5 acres per 1000 population.

Although the Plan drew broadly on the contents of the major
reports of the period it did not spell out the extent of its
agreement with one or another where differences in content and
emphasis might have justified comment. For example, on the
question of balance 'the organic pattern of inter-related
communities, economically and socially balanced' lacks the
qualification (and greater realism) of the Dudley Report's 'at
least not so unbalanced as to be restricted to one type
or income level only'. This is one place where, regrettably,
connections between parts of the Plan were not made; the Plan
mentioned outward movement of the 'well-to-do' (para. 745) but
failed to discuss the possible consequences for community
planning of continuation of this movement. There were none of
the specific reminders of the SHAC report of the need to draw
upon many and varied resources and the different approaches of
the local authorities, private enterprise and housing
associations in each locality. It could be argued that some of
the detail in the reports lay outside the field of a Regional

Figure 4.5 Weaver's Cottage, Kilbarchan, Renfrew

Plan, but this might seem too fine a distinction for a plan at such an early stage in the evolution of either regional or statutory planning. Thus while no mention was made of the suitability of different levels in blocks of flats for different types of family, nor was there discussion of modernisation of existing dwellings, yet both topics had been raised in SHAC reports, and linked community planning with aspects of the regional architecture to which the Plan gave much attention.

Regional Architecture and Recovery of Amenities. The chapter on 'Regional Architecture and Recovery of Amenities' stressed particularly the importance of the application of the best architectural skills and the use of landscaping and tree planting in the 'great replacement of obsolescence' which it foresaw. It was a chapter in which the special interests of one of the Senior Technical Officers were apparent. Alan Reiach, as Secretary of the Sub-Committee on Housing Design had contributed to the SHAC report on Planning our New Homes. He had also prepared with an architect, Robert Hurd, a cautionary guide entitled Building Scotland which was published by the Saltire Society (Reiach & Hurd 1944). A reviewer wrote of this second, enlarged edition:

'Building Scotland is a challenge to all patriotic Scotsmen to put an end to the follies and mistakes in building that menace their heritage. It must reach every town and county councillor, every library and every bookstall in Scotland.

Its message is presented with such admirable directness that it is hard to believe that anyone reading it could fail to be goaded into action or at least preventive action where that is necessary' (Hill 1945, 84).

The Clyde Valley Regional Plan offered Alan Reiach an opportunity to press its message home in a specific context, and its message did not favour Victorian architecture. At the time a great deal of attention was focused on historic buildings because of the destruction of so much of Europe's heritage. A re-evaluation of Britain's vernacular architecture was taking place with the realisation that many old buildings falling into severe disrepair might be lost altogether. Much of the material in Building Scotland and in the Plan dealt with the vernacular and drew lessons from its form, scale and colour for the building of housing especially. This was delightfully presented in the Plan with a variety of illustrations, calling attention to the pleasing qualities of domestic buildings in villages such as Eaglesham, Kilbarchan and Ochiltree. The architecture of the nineteenth century received rather less

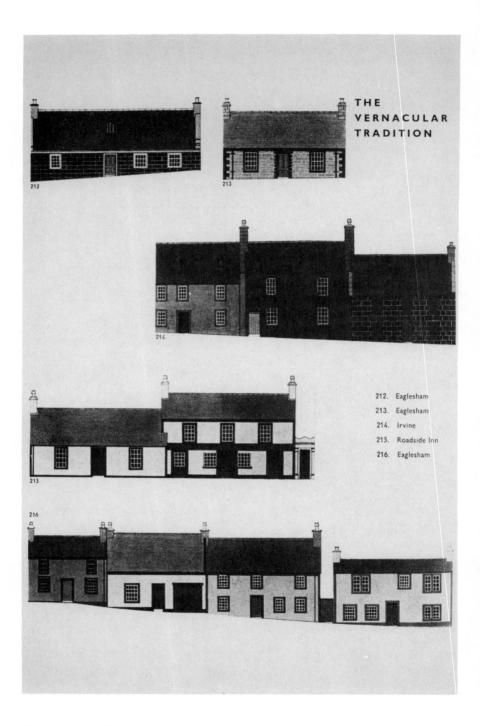

THE
VERNACULAR
TRADITION

212. Eaglesham
213. Eaglesham
214. Irvine
215. Roadside Inn
216. Eaglesham

Figure 4.6 The Vernacular Tradition illustrated in the Plan

attention. 'Greek' Thomson was singled out for praise, and
Hamilton, Wilson and Mackintosh were mentioned. The sentence
'It must be emphasized that such architects were the exception
- in fact they stand out all the more in contrast with the
mediocrity of the great bulk of the work of the period'
demonstrates the thinking in the chapter which was written
before the upsurge of interest in of Victorian architecture.

The attitudes of the time to older tenements were often
highly critical. Planning our New Homes talked of the 'old-
fashioned tenement, with its cramped dwellings on congested
sites'. Jacob Crane, Director of Urban Development in the US
National Housing Agency said in 1945 'In Edinburgh and Glasgow
a large proportion of the population live in caves - families
of five and more in one room, stone caves without private
sanitary facilities. That, it seems to me now, is the worst
housing I was shown in Britain' (Crane 1945).

Crane also commented that stone was not in his view a good
material for small houses - it was expensive, cold and damp.
It had already proved too costly for most housing. Planning
our New Homes had echoed the views of the Architectural
Advisory Committee of 1935 in suggesting that substantial
improvement in the external appearance of Scottish housing
would stem from production of a satisfactory facing brick.
This would be preferable to the drabness of the harled surfaces
of much local authority building, and the point was reiterated
in the Plan.

While there was an interest in the Plan in conserving the
village architecture the overall emphasis was on new building.
This outlook was not affected by the findings of the SHAC sub-
committee on modernisation (Scottish Housing Advisory Committee
1947). There were many question-marks over the feasibility of
modernisation. It was said that from the landlord's point of
view modernisation was not as a rule an economic proposition,
but might be from the point of view of the local authority and
the state since it would postpone the need for replacement of
older houses, and maintain for a substantial period the value
of the capital investment in public buildings, streets and
services in an older neighbourhood. The report recognised that
financial assistance from public funds would be necessary if
modernisation of houses was to be carried out on a large scale
within a reasonable space of time. It also said
'Notwithstanding the wide field for modernisation, it is not a
substitute for new building' and this view was widely shared,
especially by the politicians.

THE PLAN'S PLACE IN THE SUBSEQUENT HISTORY OF DESIGN AND PLANNING

The 1950's: The Prelude to Comprehensive Redevelopment

Conditions of economic stringency prevailed when the Plan was published in 1949 in final form with the full complement of illustrations. Some of the suggested community groupings had already been ignored in developments on the outskirts of Glasgow, and some doubts had been expressed about 'this ridiculous community concept' by sociologists and architects who suspected that only considerations of 'neighbourliness' were relevant in a changing society in which people were less dependent on the local area (ASB Study Group No. 1 1946). The Plan had been commended for noting that:

> 'It is not too much to say that, if a reasonable standard of decency of living is to be aimed at, the major proportion of the communities of the region require complete replacement during the next twenty-five years',

and the City of Glasgow through its response to the reports prepared by the City Engineer (Bruce 1945; 1946) had insisted on its ability to tackle its share of the problems within the municipal boundary rather than risk any loss of power and prestige through adoption of greenbelt and overspill concepts (Grieve 1960).

By 1949, too, the participants in the preparation of the Plan had scattered, some to work outside the Region, some to carry the thinking of the Plan into local authorities in the Region, some to spread the Plan's philosophy in a teaching role, and yet others to return to central government.

In the short term some of the fullest realisation of the thinking in the Plan on community planning and domestic architecture took place in the New Town of East Kilbride, the development of which has been described elsewhere (Smith 1979). The form of the development contrasted strongly with that of Glasgow's outlying estates at Pollok, Drumchapel, Castlemilk, and Easterhouse. In these estates every warning given in the Plan seemed to be forgotten in the rush to provide houses. Substantial numbers of three and four-storey walk-up blocks of flats were put up without the attention to detail in siting and landscaping that had been called for in the Plan. Some sites (not enough) were left for later provision of a variety of other uses but development of these uses was slow and haphazard, distances of dwellings from recreation and employment were often considerable, and the importance of sensitive housing management was rarely recognised.

Figure 4.7   Development Corporation housing, East Kilbride, 1974

Figure 4.8   Housing for the elderly, Kildrum, Cumbernauld

The responsibility for community centres, village halls and playing fields lay mainly with the Scottish Education Department. A document produced in 1947 (Scottish Education Department 1947) made it clear that while the Education Authority could take an interest in these facilities it did not follow that an Education Authority must or should provide them wholly at its own expense. The expression 'there is some debatable territory which will require to be approached with some care' introduced discussion of the importance of co-operative planning for social, educational and recreational facilities. Education has not proved to be the most co-operatively inclined of departments at either central or local level, and it is possible to speculate that the saga of failure of provision to keep pace with development might have been less gloomy had initial responsibility been allocated differently.

By the late 1950's the day on which no further land would be available in Glasgow was fast approaching, and a new stage in amelioration of Glasgow's problems was imminent in which the City Corporation would take the initiative in negotiating overspill agreements with towns often far from the City. The worst of the overcrowding seemed to have been handled by rehousing but the redevelopment of many of the worst of the buildings could not proceed without more elbow room as was clear from consideration of the proposals for the first Comprehensive Development Area in 1956. These proposals were for Hutchesontown/part Gorbals and only 10,000 or so of about 27,000 inhabitants were expected to be rehoused in the area (Corporation of the City of Glasgow 1956). Shops, factories and offices (often, like the dwellings, in a structurally unsound state) were affected by the proposals. Dispersal was seen as a necessary complement to redevelopment, and Cumbernauld New Town was designated in 1956 to aid the process in a locality identified in the Plan. It was to prove innovative in its approach to town design with a departure from the neighbourhood principle, densities higher than those given in the Plan, an emphasis on a strong central core, and a pedestrian system (Wilson 1960). Osborn and Whittick (1977) in their description of Cumbernauld's development drew a distinction between the siting and the design of the town. The choice of site for the designated area led to development on a windy ridge with a high rainfall. This was widely criticized but did limit the take of agricultural land.

In March 1960 a fire disaster in a bonded whisky store made the hazards of Glasgow's congestion horrifyingly apparent and gave added emphasis to sentences from the Survey Report of the Quinquennial Review of the Development Plan such as this:
    'An estimated 100,000 new dwellings should be built
    between 1960 and 1980 and these must have better

facilities and more space around the buildings than
the dull, internally crowded and extremely congested
tenements they will augment and replace'.
By 1961 the 'overspill' programme had become fully
operational and was receiving substantial publicity.

The 1960's: Comprehensive Development Areas and the Plan in
Hindsight

The proposals for Hutchesontown/part Gorbals had received a
mixed reception when they were first announced and further
comment was stimulated around the time of the opening of the
first 96 houses in the area by an article by a sociologist at
the University of Glasgow, Tom Brennan, in The Scotsman in
April 1958 and by his book Re-shaping a City (1959).   Brennan
argued that overspill did not derive from poor condition of
property but from overcrowding. He noted that occupancy rates
were falling but that the outer areas had occupancy rates above
those proposed in CDAs, and he suggested:
    'The city might maintain its overspill programme on
    the assumption that large numbers of people will be
    moving to the reception areas and new towns, not from
    the   centre   but   from   the   housing   estates.
    Alternatively it can be more generous than has
    hitherto seemed possible with the space which will be
    set free by demolitions, and so achieve a greater
    thinning out of buildings with a corresponding saving
    in expenditure.   It might, on the other hand, shift
    the whole emphasis of its plans and decide that the
    maintenance and renewal of the fabric of the city
    rather than a general ability to accommodate its
    citizens is the more urgent problem'.

A follow-up leader in The Scotsman expressed support for some
reconsideration of policies, and argued that physical solutions
gave   insufficient   attention   to people.   Several   other
commentators called for reappraisal of policies, not all for
the same reasons.   Professor Alec Cairncross of the Chair of
Applied Economics in the University of Glasgow questioned the
whole cost of the overspill operation, as did the minority
Progressive group on the Glasgow Council.   Ian Nairn, an
architectural journalist, discussing Glasgow in 1960, said of
the Gorbals:
    'I would plead with them (the planners) really to go
    and have a look at the Gorbals. It was laid out on a
    grid, with immensely dignified, four-storey, stone-
    built terraces. To the shame of its creators, it was
    designed as a working-class rabbit warren and hence,
    naturally, it slid into slums.   There are far too
    many people living there, and the state of the

89

backyards and the communal stairways with their
lavatories on the half-landings are intolerable and
must be altered. However, the actual outside
appearance, in other circumstances would be applauded
as a splendid piece of urban design' (Nairn 1960).

Crane's comments on tenements (Crane 1945) had given no hint
of a fresh and discerning eye recognising the sombre dignity of
Glasgow's buildings. He had seen the appalling living
conditions inside the buildings, as had the Clyde Valley
planners, and his vision and that of many subsequently involved
in the planning process was coloured by those conditions and
knowledge of the serious structural and sanitary deficiencies
of many of the properties. By 1960 when the Survey Report of
the Quinquennial Review of the Development Plan was completed
in the Corporation of Glasgow there was still a greater
sympathy for Grassic Gibbon's 'vomit of a cataleptic
commercialism' (Gibbon 1934) than for Ian Nairn's 'splendid
piece of urban design'. It could hardly have been otherwise
for the planners, who were hard pressed by City councillors
intent on expanding house production, and who had, as well as a
formidable acquaintance with the living and working conditions
of the inner areas, a greater understanding of the complexities
of the density question than the majority of the commentators
who persistently failed to grasp the lesson of Table 33 set out
in the Plan some ten years previously. The effect of doubling
the net density in an area of fixed extent was shown not to
result in a doubling of the population if due consideration was
given to needs other than housing. Many people attracted by
Bruce's contention, that a higher proportion of open space was
available if flats were built instead of houses, did not
appreciate that this was an argument for building high and not
one for high density. So it was possible for Brennan in his
book to write of the Gorbals that 'with well planned buildings
of several storeys such a density of occupation (164 persons
per acre) becomes not only tolerable but quite pleasant. The
plan for the new Gorbals itself shows what can be done. One
may ask whether it is quite impossible to create the conditions
in which even the present density of 450 or something like it
would be tolerable'.

When considering proposals for development, the planners had
also to bear in mind the content of the latest section of the
Scottish Housing Handbook on Housing Layout, (Department of
Health for Scotland 1958). The further limitations imposed by
sunlight and daylight recommendations were more stringent than
those discussed in the Reports commended in the Plan. This
made it well nigh impossible to conceive of an acceptable form
of development which would accommodate 450 persons to the acre.
The proposals for clearance, redevelopment and dispersal thus

90

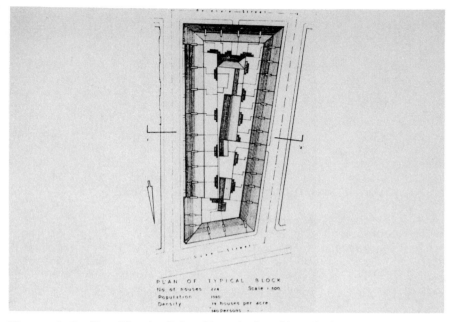

Figure 4.9   The Plan's Duke Street density study

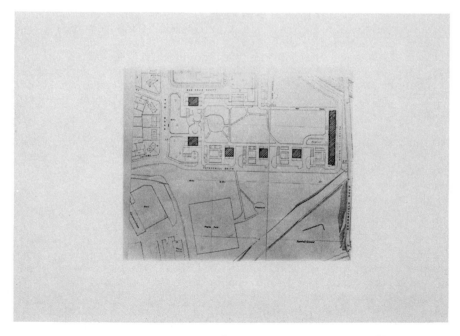

Figure 4.10   Site plan of the Red Road multi-storey flats, Glasgow

remained in 1960, partly because modernising existing tenements meant accepting densities even higher and standards even lower than those for which planners were already castigated by other members of the planning profession, who thought that the comprehensive development proposals were outrageous because they perpetuated the difference in standards between Glasgow and elsewhere in the country. Perhaps this dilemma was in Robert Grieve's mind when he spoke of the danger of developing to lower standards than were considered acceptable elsewhere (Grieve 1960). The late J.R. James, then Deputy Chief Planner of the Ministry of Housing and Local Government, put the point forcefully when he suggested that the day would come when anyone associated with development in Glasgow at a density of 150 rooms per acre would be branded as a criminal.

And all the time people were clamouring to be rehoused, thereby putting the local politicians under constant and unrelenting pressure to maintain a public housing programme which at its peak in the 1960's reached 5,000 dwellings per year. People did not like their living conditions and the politicians had to be seen to be taking action.

There was nothing in the Plan to encourage stepping up of the efforts to modernise dwellings which were tentatively proceeding mainly in the owner occupied private sector under the Housing Acts of 1949 and 1950. But the shortage of professional staff to initiate a programme, and the building industry's increased emphasis on prefabrication and greater mechanisation encouraged by central government turned attention away from short-term modernisation as an acceptable alternative, or indeed as a necessary complement, to demolition and redevelopment. Neither was there anything in the Plan to discourage the building of high flats.

Alongside the potential of planned redevelopment, where some emphasis could be put on provision of facilities, there were many isolated multi-storey housing developments on restricted sites where difficulties were often inherent in the basic design of the block, with lack of variation in house size, and in the site, and with lack of access to shops and other uses. While the Plan had made little mention of the detailed aspects of high flat blocks some problems had been foreseen in the discussion in Planning our New Homes. Committee members had expressed reservations about development of blocks of more than six storeys, and the use of upper floors for families with children (Scottish Housing Advisory Committee 1944). Physical planners in Glasgow made their initial studies on the basis of no families with children living more than four floors off the ground: their hopes were largely frustrated by a housing allocation system which involved prospective tenants of a block in drawing lots. But this is not the place to expand on the problems generated in this period: it is sufficient to show that the Plan's influence in this period was sometimes negative in that a re-reading of the Plan at this time would not raise questions about several significant strands of public policy.

The 1970's: The New Policies of Rehabilitation

It was not until the 1970's when many more misgivings had been expressed over the disruption of social networks on redevelopment, that rehabilitation became a major part of Corporation policy. By then not only had the worst housing been demolished but the valuation of nineteenth century architecture had also changed. J.M. Reid had written perceptively (Reid 1960) of the quality of Glasgow's Victorian centre and praised the Corporation for its decision to preserve Greek Thomson's St. Vincent Street Church. The publication of The Architecture of Glasgow by Gomme and Walker in 1968 further directed attention to the scale and quality of the architecture and townscape as did the amenity societies and the Scottish Civic Trust. The advantages of the compact urban form of the 'finest surviving example of a great Victorian city' (Esher 1971) were now acclaimed. It is not unreasonable to suppose that much stronger support for retention and modernisation at an earlier stage especially in the Plan might have resulted in the transfer of resources to a programme of tenement improvement for, despite all the difficulties, there is little doubt that greater pressure on central government from the giant Glasgow could have led more quickly to the introduction of favourable legislation. Other places in the region such as Greenock and Paisley would have benefited from such moves. As it was, an emergency programme of repairs following the damage brought about by the great gale of 1968 gave added stimulus to changing attitudes.

The politicians of the 1940's and 1950's thought of reconditioned tenements as 'second best'; clearly some of those moving from tenements many years later would have thought likewise (Buttimer & McDonald 1974). More recently, community initiatives encouraged by the availability of financial support from the Housing Corporation have helped to revitalize some areas of tenements (Robinson 1980). In the 1970's environmental improvements also proceeded rapidly in areas with dwellings above the tolerable standard, partly through EEC backed District initiatives and partly through the efforts of the Scottish Development Agency's land renewal division. This division took over the financing of land rehabilitation by and for the local authorities in 1975, and with an expanded budget has made an impact of the kind envisaged in the Plan. The greening of the East End as part of the Glasgow Eastern Area

Figure 4.11 Gable painting by James Torrance, Govanhill,
Glasgow. Sponsored by the Scottish Arts Council

Figure 4.12 Custom House Quay, Glasgow. The simplicity of
good design recognised by the Civic Trust Award 1975

Renewal scheme has a psychological importance which would have been appreciated by Abercrombie and his team: it owes much to the Plan's influence on the West Central Scotland planning team, which resulted in that team's proposal for an Environmental Improvement Task Force.

The importance of such schemes in retention and revitalisation of existing communities is now appreciated, and, despite all the criticisms levelled at the content of the CHAC Report and the enthusiasm of its time for 'social balance' and 'community', there is widening support for the view that some variation in house type and tenure could make a contribution to improvement of amenity and social character in many areas, even where demolition of some existing houses may be a necessary preliminary to action. The scale of action required in the core of the region with its peripheral estates may be relatively and absolutely greater than elsewhere, but the potential benefit to the Strathclyde Region was obvious and the Structure Plan of 1979 laid emphasis on environmental improvements and the need to increase the range of choices open to the people of the region in terms of tenure and house size. These were stated to be essential elements of the strategy for tackling deprivation which was identified as a priority for action in the Regional Report of 1976.

The fact that in European Architectural Heritage Year, 1975, conservation schemes went ahead in a number of the very places identified in the Plan was at least partly due to the holding operations prompted by the Plan over the years.   It is a pointer to the tenacity of ideas as well as of individuals that colour wash on municipal roughcast, gable paintings, stone cleaning, and a substantial use of facing brick for new housing have all occurred to help to transform the appearance of inner areas of Glasgow in the late 1970's. The work of the Plan in this field may be seen as the precursor of both Conservation Areas and design guides.

What Responsibility had the Plan for the Course of Clydeside Renewal?

Although Tom Johnston, Secretary of State for Scotland at the time, has said (Johnston 1952) that a major factor in the decision to go ahead with regional studies for the east and the west of Scotland in 1943 was a desire to retain independence from Whitehall as planning legislation mushroomed, there is relatively little that is specifically Scottish in the Plan. In this the Plan contrasted sharply with the contemporary Regional Survey and Plan for South-East Scotland (Mears 1948). Perhaps Abercrombie brought more from the south than has been realised.   Certainly in the spheres of community planning and architecture, the most obviously Scottish content lies in the recognition of the qualities of the region's vernacular architecture and this section, as has been shown, was strongly influenced by Robert Hurd who was unashamedly a nationalist although not himself a member of the team.

Many of the Plan's proposals for community planning were not implemented, but here it is worth remembering that the Clyde Valley was not the only part of Britain in which provision of community facilities lagged behind completion of houses. The extent of the failure in the Clyde Valley may be more strongly related to the political pressures imposed by the scale of the housing problem in the core of the region, and the weakness of the planners' influence on detailed implementation, than to an over-emphasis on the physical components of residential development. Nevertheless, despite the humanity of the Plan the people of the region were not assertively present on all its pages. The Appendix on Paisley said 'But a little thought suggests that simply to transfer a family from the only living conditions it has ever known, to set it down in an entirely new and strange environment, and to expect it immediately and unaided to alter its whole way of living, is to reveal a belief in miracles which is as naive as it is unfounded in actual experience'. And yet that is in effect what happened. It was only in the New Towns in the early years that staff resources and a range of facilities were more readily available to ease the transition. The fact that there are now a great many combinations of voluntary and social services at work in Scottish public housing estates, does not mean that the potential of some of the residents could not have been more fully realised had more of the services been available at a much earlier date in the spirit, if not the letter, of the Plan's recommendations. But could the Plan have done more to ensure that the spirit did not wholly evaporate as the ink dried on its paper? Perhaps it could not, in that it simply reflected what proved to be the idealistic rather than radical socialism which permeated the introduction of the many social welfare measures of the late 1940's.

Professor Dix has commented on Abercrombie's optimism (Dix 1981), and it may in retrospect seem that he was overly optimistic. The programme he was working to was a long-term one, and the expectation was that new legislation would take care of difficult questions of finance, land ownership and compensation. Abercrombie saw no need for the team to become involved in such issues. On local authority boundaries he had written in Town and Country Planning (Abercrombie 1943)
   'There can be no doubt that a logical scheme of
   planning upon a theoretic background can only be
   attempted on a Regional scale, when for the purpose

of arriving at the best results the boundaries of authorities are banished from the mind'.

The recommendations in the Plan for a regional authority tried to make the banishment of boundaries a practical possibility but was not acted upon until local government reorganisation in 1975. What Abercrombie did not stress was the necessity of keeping in mind the nature of the functions and responsibilities being planned, for since there are serious dangers in lack of realism over powers and resources for implementation, especially in advisory planning schemes, as well as advantages in unfettered vision. It is doubtful if planners have fully understood the uses and limitations of visionary and optimistic proposals. Indeed, the planners of the new Strathclyde Region had cause to ponder this very point on being faced with an adverse response to their proposal to aid the inner city through de-zoning of housing land elsewhere in the region in the Consultative Draft Structure Plan of 1977. This was a proposal which could only succeed where no planning permission existed, a situation which did not universally apply.

The Plan itself said 'Both in the local and regional scale, much further study is required as to the essential social character of the rural and urban communities. The value to the planner of such information can hardly be over-estimated'. Thirty-five years later it is humbling to recognise that this is still a field of which little is known. Faced with the challenge of high job losses in Strathclyde as a whole, no-one knows whether the personal rigours of unemployment will be any less in the planned communities of the New Towns than in the peripheral urban housing estates. One point not in dispute is that each of these forms of development involves its residents in high energy costs. There can be little doubt that in the renewed interest in the 1980's in tenement-living which resulted in keen competition for ownership of flats in East End blocks modernized by SSHA, the cost of energy is as much a factor as is their Victorian detailing or their social character. Perhaps more consideration of the phasing of development and of resources for implementation could have led the team to less blanket condemnation of existing development and a more Geddesian approach to gradual renewal. It is unlikely that it could have provided the force wholly to resist the onslaught of system building in the 60's which has given the region a new legacy of problems in the 80's, for reasons which could not have been foreseen by the planners of the Clyde Valley team when they expressed the hope that the replacement of the slums of yesterday would not 'become a problem, even greater still, for the future to solve'.

Figure 4.13 Wyndford, Glasgow. Saltire Award for Good Design, 1968, to the Scottish Special Housing Assoc.

Figure 4.14 Tenement block awaiting clearance, Maryhill, Glasgow, 1976

Figure 4.15 Private housebuilding, North Woodside, Glasgow, 1982

The absence of a chapter on housing in the <u>Plan</u> may have been a factor underlying the lack of discussion of modernisation. In many respects, what was said in the <u>Plan</u> was not unlike what was being said elsewhere.   The attitudes in the 1940's to much of the existing housing were highly critical, which had a reinforcing effect on the clearance policies of the local authorities in the 1950's and 60's, when opportunities for policy reappraisal were not taken up.   Had there been a separate chapter on housing, it seems likely that modernisation would have received a mention and that very mention might have meant stronger pressures for action.   Who can say?   Human frailty cannot be discounted as a factor in planning activity any more than in other spheres, and it seems to have entered into the <u>Plan</u> giving individuals more scope to develop their separate interests while superficially handling a topic in an integrative way.

5 Industry

JOHN R. FIRN

THE APPRAISAL OF INDUSTRY OF THE CLYDE VALLEY

The Plan's Place in Clydeside's Industrial History

Amidst the decline and recession of the 1980's, it is worth remembering that a century earlier the growing industrial complex of the Clyde Valley had the same aura of technological excellence and leadership that is presently displayed by Silicon Valley in California. Since 1945 the Clyde Valley has seen its strengths gradually and continually eroded, and the general atmosphere has been one of decline and dependence, where corporate and governmental horizons have sharply contracted to the extent that longer term forces of industrial and economic change are unconsciously ignored.

In 1943, at the start of this period of comparatively slow growth on Clydeside, a small group of people took a step back from short-term concerns and, in the Clyde Valley Regional Plan, produced a longer term view of the region's strengths and weaknesses which for pure inductive reasoning has not yet been improved upon. In this chapter, their evaluation of the region's industrial potential will be examined; their recommendations assessed; and the long-term impact upon subsequent industrial development appraised. As will be seen, the Plan is still an influential and stimulating view of a European region which remains a challenge to its people, planners, and government.

The Analytical Background. There are always problems in retrospective evaluations of the impact of complex and substantial documents such as the Clyde Valley Regional Plan. The inherent difficulties caused by inter-temporal differences in knowledge and perception are magnified when the principal analytical issue concerns the Plan's approach to the problems and potential of industry in the West of Scotland: any evaluation of this requires not only a detailed understanding of the structure and performance of local industries, but also of the relationship between them and other industries elsewhere in the United Kingdom and overseas, and the ever-changing and little understood long-term dynamic forces that shape industrial change. In all of these areas the extent and sophistication of the economist's ignorance overshadows any knowledge and manipulative ability that he possesses: this remains as true today as in 1946, despite the theoretical, technical and empirical advances claimed for applied economics in the last forty years. In reviewing and appraising the impact of the team upon the subsequent industrial development of the most important economic area in Scotland, we must be constantly aware of the context within which they worked, deliberated, and reached their conclusions.

The first issue is whether the analysis made by the team of the industrial problems of the Clyde Valley was the best that could be achieved with the evidence and experience at their disposal. While there are grounds for some reservations on this central question, it cannot be doubted that the industrial policy proposals that emerged from the analysis have had a profound, although perhaps not always entirely beneficial, effect upon the post-war economic development of the region and of Scotland. What then were the factors that shaped and determined the Plan's industrial review?

The pre-eminent influence, in both a conscious and subconscious sense, affecting the team was certainly the Second World War. In 1945-1946, when the Plan crystallised, the war had just ended, and consequently the national and international economic future was uncertain. The danger of a severe post-war slump and recession (as in the early 1920's) loomed large, and the role of government in such a situation was unclear, for Kenesian economics had not by then become an accepted part of the national scene (Winch 1969, Chap. 12). The return of a Labour Government in 1945 had brought a new commitment to positive state intervention to improve economic prospects, both by implementing the 1944 White Paper on full employment (Employment Policy 1944) and by taking into public ownership major industrial sectors such as iron and steel, a development that had important implications for the Clyde Valley. But overall, there was an air of economic uncertainty, only partly countered by a feeling of being able to make a new start.

Regional planning on the scale attempted by the Plan was very much in its infancy, and there were few precedents for the regeneration of a highly industrialised region like the Clyde Valley, although the Tennessee Valley Scheme in the United States and Abercrombie's earlier plan for Greater London were two important influences, as was the 1940 report of the Royal Commission on the Distribution of the Industrial Population, which effectively shaped most of Britain's regional development policies until well into the 1970's. In retrospect, the economic analysis in Barlow is strangely descriptive and superficial, and its belief that the control of the location of new industries should be the basis for regional development had serious long-term repercussions that still haunt British regional policy.

The Plan team, like Barlow, worked in an area where economists had singularly failed to be involved. Industrial economic theory and regional analysis in the 1940's were heavily biased towards description, and few of the seminal works shaping these fields had appeared. (Richardson 1969, 429-442). The explanations of regional decline advanced by Barlow, and which subsequently became accepted wisdom for a whole generation of civil servants and town planners, had a geographical and administrative base rather than an economic, industrial or corporate one.

In Scotland, little applied research into the Scottish economy and its constituent industries had been undertaken by either government or university departments. Regional planning in Scotland in 1946 was the responsibility of the Health Department, and consequently it could not be expected to have expertise on industrial economics. In the Scottish offices of the Board of Trade (which then had responsibility for industrial affairs) the primary function of officials was to administer United Kingdom policy, although after 1949 they became more of a pressure group for Scotland. There was a lack of statistical material on the Scottish economy let alone on industrial conditions in West Central Scotland, and few of the sectors had been covered by statistical surveys during the inter-war period. Usually the planners had only one set of observations of a highly aggregated nature at their disposal, and this often influenced their analysis, and indeed, policy (Oakley 1947, 81). For example, the 1935 Census of Production, which should have yielded valuable information about the structure of the region's industries, had by 1939 been only partly analysed and the War effectively prevented detailed regional tabulations from ever appearing.

The lack of interest in applied economic analysis was a 1940's feature of Scottish universities, and this situation was to remain until the early 1960's, with one or two notable exceptions (Cairncross 1954; Cairncross 1958, 219-241). A total unconcern with industrial problems in the Clyde Valley is evident in the academic publications appearing in the early post-war period, a stark contrast to the interesting and comprehensive analyses of the earlier industrial growth of Glasgow in the seventeenth and eighteenth centuries (Macfie 1955, 81-103) which seems to have dominated research in Political Economy departments. There was one exception. The Plan team had access to a perceptive document on economic change in the region, namely the Industrial Survey of the South West of Scotland, undertaken for the Board of Trade by economists at the University of Glasgow in 1932 (Board of Trade 1932). This identified as a prime cause of industrial decline the apparent slow response of industries in the Clyde Valley to technical change, and a growing dependence upon foreign technology. In 1946, and indeed now, this remains one of the single most important economic weaknesses within the industries of the Clyde Valley. It was not identified in the 1946 Plan.

It is unfair to judge the industry chapter of the Plan by modern standards of regional economic analysis but in retrospect it is clear there was no rigorous or well-defined research strategy specifically designed to identify the economic problems and potential of the area's industry. This partly reflects the prevailing state of regional planning but also demonstrates the relatively small role played by economists in the Plan. There was only one part-time economist formally attached to the team compared with the 11 economists behind the plan for the Lothians in the mid-1960's (Grieve and Robertson 1964, 29).

The industry analysis in the Plan relies very heavily upon description, yet it is hard to see how it could have been otherwise: few clear precedents in terms of regional industrial analysis; a relative scarcity of reliable and timely economic information and data; poorly developed statistical techniques; and extremely slow and cumbersome methods of data collection and analysis. The team fully recognised its inability to adequately tackle an analysis of the region's industry, and called for "... an enquiry into the set-up (sic) and location of each of the Region's industrial groups." This suggestion was ignored, and an important opportunity was missed, very probably because the economic expertise that existed in the Scottish Office at that time simply failed to appreciate industrial policy at a regional level. Had it been taken up the results might have had a major impact upon postwar Scottish economic and industrial policy.

The industrial studies in the Plan, whilst fairly comprehensive and coherent descriptions of the situation existing at the
end of the War, also suffered through aggregation, and as a
result, the team failed to appreciate the degree of industrial
diversification that had already taken place, both amongst the
smaller firms in Glasgow and, more importantly, in some of the
leading local companies that dominated the local economy.
Indeed, a principal weakness of the Plan was the gap between
statistics and individual companies, a problem that remains to
this day.

The team spent a considerable amount of time talking with
local businessmen about industrial prospects and the possible
changes they would face in the uncertain post-war world. Such
unstructured interviews and discussions probably contributed
little to any analytical understanding of the real difficulties
facing the region's enterprises, especially when the absence of
empirical data meant that conclusions of the discussions were
unrelated to a statistical analysis of industrial trends at a
sectoral level, which is a precondition for validating and
scaling interview results.

The Plan team wisely refrained from using the results of
these discussions as a basis for policy, and indeed, recognised
that there was still much to learn about industrial
development, and they outlined topics which should be covered
by any subsequent enquiry:
> '... are the Region's industries well organised; are
> their buildings and machinery up-to-date; is their
> management progressive; are there too many small
> units and what schemes of rationalisation are
> necessary to increase their competitive efficiency;
> how far are Glasgow's industries handicapped by
> location on congested sites where the planning of an
> up-to-date production flow is impossible?'
> (380).

Those familiar with current research into regional economic and
industrial development will be impressed by the sophistication
of these questions, but depressed by the fact that most remain
unanswered.

Despite the difficulties facing the team's attempts to
analyse the region's industry, the Plan indicated a range of
structural and performance problems which in combination gave a
compelling picture of regional industrial decline, with an
urgent need for sustained and imaginative economic policies and
programmes to reverse the situation, especially at the
corporate level. Although the Plan does not formally set out

the individual industrial problems it does, within the Industry chapter, indicate ten separate but obviously inter-related causes of the poor performance of the region's industry. It is worth briefly examining each of these.

The Clyde Valley's Industrial Problems

A dependence on declining industrial sectors. The region was heavily dependent upon the declining, essentially nineteenth century industries of coal, iron and steel, shipbuilding and mechanical engineering, and failing to diversify into the newer light industries that the team believed characterised the Midlands and the South-East of England. The Plan looked enviously at those regions with '... a wide range of industrial skills, like Birmingham, (which) have been able to see many of their old industries die away during the past half century without losing the general prosperity' [342]. Thirty years later, the post-1979 recession showed very clearly that possession of these newer industries was no guarantee of economic prosperity and Birmingham's relative industrial decline after 1974 surpassed that of the Clyde Valley. Concern was indirectly expressed about the proportion of employment concentrated in the service sector of the region's economy and the question was put (in relation to the UK) as to whether "... in terms of the manpower shortage (sic) ... it is sound economy for Britain to maintain such a great proportion of its manpower in the 'non-producing' industries" [263]. This attitude that the service sector is 'non-productive' reflected a lack of understanding about the contribution of the tertiary sector that persisted until relatively recently.

Poor industrial management. Although the team avoided the key question as to why the enterprises in the old and declining sectors failed to diversity into the new products and technologies of the light industries, it nevertheless hinted at one reason when it described the heavy industry complex that dominated the thinking of the region's influential businessmen:
'... business sentiment seems rather uninterested in
light industry and is inclined to look down on it;
the Area has so long thought in terms of tons ...
that mental reorientation is not easy' [358].
This perceptive and quite subtle appraisal of the Clyde Valley's orientation to heavy industry was fully justified, and until the 1970's industrial planning and policy remained committed to supporting and preserving local industrial dinosaurs whose day had long passed.

A low level of new firm formation. The region's economy, especially after the wartime armaments boost, continued to be driven by big, heavy industrial plants which predominantly employed unskilled and semi-skilled labour. There were few higher-grade and technological staff: namely "...just the men who so often break away and start up for themselves" [345]. This poor indigenous response to the opportunities presented by new technologies, products, and markets, should have been given priority in any industrial policy devised for the region, but very little understanding then existed of the entrepreneurial element in economic growth, despite the Clyde Valley's own performance in the preceding century when the sudden flowering of local entrepreneurs laid the foundation for the region's industrial greatness. Entrepreneurship, even after four decades, remains an area of socio-economic behaviour that is little understood, and consequently one difficult to affect by policy (Storey 1982, Chaps. 9 and 10).

The impact of the War. There was a recognition, based on the post World War I experience, that the regional economy had been artificially boosted above its long-term trend rate of growth by the armaments and ammunitions factories opened in the region after 1938, and by the extra business generated for existing enterprises, especially in the shipbuilding and mechanical engineering sectors, by government expenditure on wartime needs. The end of the war was therefore seen as leading to a certain degree of unemployment in the region, especially in Glasgow. Recent research however suggests that the distortions caused by the heavy armament programme of the First World War probably had a relatively greater impact by effectively and permanently distorting the structure of many leading local enterprises (Hume and Moss 1979).

The rationalisation of local enterprise. Rationalisation of production facilities through take-overs and mergers had already been taking place, most visibly amongst the cotton textile plants in the region [249]. This was seen almost as inevitable in the iron and steel sector [316] and amongst shipbuilding firms [333], and pointed to yet further unemployment in the future, principally amongst male employees. But while rationalisation had begun to gather momentum in the inter-war years, the Plan team noted a more ominous development which was to become a central concern of the Scottish economy from the 1970's, namely that "... rationalisation of concerns controlled from England has resulted in the closing of several Scottish factories" [351]. In the area survey of the Vale of Leven, the Plan pointed out that the main financial interest in the United Turkey Red Company (now a subsidiary of English Calico Ltd) was "... now the Prudential Assurance Company and therefore controlled from England". Concern over this gradual loss of local control of the region's enterprise would increase in later years (Scott and Hughes 1980), and if the true significance of this structural shift had been seen in 1946,

106

measures might have been devised to preserve and encourage important local enterprises to restructure themselves through managerial improvement rather than through mergers.

Labour market problems. Weaknesses in the regional industrial structure were seen as having a serious effect upon local labour supply, both in qualitative and quantitative terms, but this part of the Plan's analysis is somewhat vague, confused, and contradictory. Whilst a lack of local job opportunities since the inter-war depression had led to a heavy net migration from the Clyde Valley of "... the better type of young semi-skilled men whose loss further drained the area's resources" [347], the Plan commented favourably on the outstanding labour adaptability of the region noting that the wartime achievements in training local labour to new skills should "... dispose of that often expressed view (held in some quarters of the South) that Clydeside labour is unsuitable for light industry" [370]. A further contradiction lies concealed in the Plan, namely a fear that the skills of the region's miners might be dissipated in light industries [284], whilst at the same time concern is shown over a potential lack of male employment in the mining areas. The large run-down of the mining industry predicted was a genuine concern for the Plan team, who forecast that as the local coalfields became worked out, some 19,500 jobs would be lost by 1975.

The Red Clydeside image. The team, unlike many subsequent regional planning teams elsewhere examined, with little data to help them, the important question of industrial relations. The image of the area as militant "Red Clydeside", dominated by strikes and stoppages, was already well established in 1946, but the team dismissed this view with a brief judgement that there was no justification for labelling the Clydeside worker as unco-operative, for "...judging from recent labour disturbances it is mainly in the Midlands and in London that labour unrest is most marked" [359]. Later research would confirm the broad disagreement that most modern industrial relations observers would have of the Plan's view, although by the late 1970's, the region seemed to be moving towards a period of labour relations harmony with many of the newer plants being totally non-unionised - something almost inconceivable in 1945.

A growing spatial imbalance of residence and workplace. Apart from direct economic problems, the Plan isolated a number of locational constraints which were thought to affect the efficiency of the region's industry. Haphazard expansion of major urban centres, especially Glasgow, had produced a lack of co-ordination between residences and workplaces, average journey-to-work distances had risen, and consequently "... the cost in time and money, though not easily assessable in hard cash, must be exceedingly high" [477]. Nearly twenty years were to pass before urban economists began to measure these costs with any rigour, and planners attempted to bring housing and industrial location back into balance.

A shortage of industrial sites. Concern was expressed about a distinct shortage of industrial sites throughout the region and the absence of new factory buildings. The team believed that enterprises operating in the centre of Glasgow, especially in manufacturing, were severely restricted through an inability to expand in-situ. The strange view emerged that "... if the hoped-for expansion of industry takes place in Glasgow many light industry concerns [was there not meant to be a shortage of light industry in the region?] will, in any case, have to vacate their premises, where incapable of expansion, or reconstruct them and expand by starting up another factory elsewhere, thus adding to their overhead expenses by running two establishments" [482]. This statement beautifully encompasses the almost total lack of knowledge that existed in 1946 about the structure, distribution and operation of industry within urban areas: it was an area that was to remain shrouded in darkness until the 1970's. The team's argument implies that urban entrepreneurs act irrationally, and indeed, that intra-urban industrial mobility was a form of non-economic behaviour. In fact, manufacturing and service enterprises within Glasgow, as in other urban areas, had been mobile for decades, and expansion by moving to a larger site or factory was until recently the rule rather than the exception. The team forecast gradual but fairly substantial industrial decentralisation from Glasgow to other parts of the region, such as the industrial estates on the City's periphery and at sites that were later to be designated New Towns, but misunderstood the mechanism of decentralisation which, when it subsequently occurred, was achieved principally through the combination of firm closures in the city and the immigration of new manufacturing plants to peripheral locations from elsewhere in the UK and overseas.

An absence of modern factories. Most manufacturing enterprises in the City of Glasgow were, through the impact of urban economic dendrochronology, operating in buildings and works that dated from the last quarter of the nineteenth century. Small firms in important industries were often operating out of the cheap and easily available production facilities offered by lofts, railway arches, and (especially in Glasgow), out of the back court factories that provided employment for many of the people living in the teeming tenements that encompassed them. To the planners of 1946 conditions like these in inner urban areas meant that local industry was "handicapped from the start

108

in its efforts to compete with more fortunate (sic) Southern rivals, housed in modern factories in good surroundings" [483]. In reality many of the Clyde Valley's economic and industrial competitors at that time (especially in sectors such as clothing and light engineering) were also operating in similar cramped conditions in the old, decaying inner areas of Birmingham, Liverpool, and London. Glasgow had no monopoly of industrial squalor, and the team failed to foresee the industrial consequences of a housing oriented drive for urban renewal.

The predominance of environmental dereliction. Finally, the team pinpointed a problem that has continued to haunt the region, namely that to both inhabitants and outsiders its image was that of the grime, decay and dereliction associated with industrial decline. The team painted a depressing scene of a region characterised and dominated by "...horrible slums and shapeless towns, abounding smoke pollution, abandoned collieries and old works falling to pieces (and) ... no-one can fail to notice the conditions of industrial squalor and congestion that exist in large parts of Glasgow" [492, 482].

Of course similar conditions existed (and still do exist) in other industrial areas of Britain, and Glasgow in 1946 was probably no more depressing than Birmingham, Liverpool, Manchester or indeed London. But this image of the Clyde Valley, and of Glasgow in particular, as being the worst urban environment in Britain (and perhaps in Europe) was strong and widespread, and it has persisted to the present day offering a major challenge to those charged with attracting industry and capital to the region.

When all the above problems and difficulties are considered, one cannot escape the conclusion that in 1946 the long-term economic viability of the Valley's industries was even worse than the planners feared. But had the Plan team correctly identified the major issues of concern with respect to the industries of the Clyde Valley; had they identified the principal problems, and more importantly their basic causes?

The benefit of hindsight and subsequent research into the region's industrial performance and structure enables us to be fairly certain that the team's analysis picked up the more important weaknesses in the performance, location, and structure of local industry in the West of Scotland, although more by intuitive deduction than by analytical management. The basic causes of this economic underperformance were never really researched let alone identified, and consequently what appears in the Plan is more a collection of symptoms than a confirmed diagnosis of the types of economic and industrial

109

illnesses underlying the industrial economy of the Clyde Valley. But if we remember the context in which the planning team worked, then we can see that such analytical sophistication was well beyond the theoretical and practical capabilities of the current regional analysis and plan-making. Even with the advances made in understanding the dynamics of regional economic growth and change that have taken place during the past 25 years, it is still difficult to isolate and identify the basic cause of economic and industrial development at the regional level, especially where socio-cultural factors such as entrepreneurship are involved (Firn 1974, 47-72; Swales 1979, 225-241).

The Strengths of the Clyde Valley

Whilst the Clyde Valley Regional Plan team were fairly successful in their general identification of industrial problems, it had virtually nothing to say about the positive aspects of the region's economy. It did not formally outline the economic strength and comparative advantages of industries and enterprises in the valley, apart from a mention of new companies that had moved into the area from elsewhere. Yet effective policies for regional industrial regeneration require that local comparative advantages together with growing and dynamic companies and sectors be sought out, identified, encouraged and built on.

It is therefore curious that few positive aspects of the region's industries can be found in the Plan. There are references to the obvious quality of the labour force and its adaptability, and a vague belief is expressed that "... in theory the industries which can be expected to start up in the Region are almost limitless ... (many have arrived) ... and others no doubt will come" [417]. There are also some heartening words about the general engineering sector:
> '... which has an outstanding reputation for skill, inventiveness and enterprise ... (and) ... whilst the prospects for it are likely to be bright for some years to come, it is essential that the huge pent-up demand for its traditional products should not be allowed to interfere with the industry applying its experience and ingenuity to the development of other lines of manufacture' [246].

The implications of this accurate comment on the need to encourage market and technological change in the region's major sectors totally escaped the attention of those involved in industrial and regional policy right through until the 1960's, by which time it was too late for many of the firms involved. Textiles, and iron and steel, were singled out as sectors with good prospects, but there is little evidence for such optimism in the surveys of industries made in the Plan. It must be assumed that these views were based on unpublished work and on judgements reached after discussions with local business, and were intuitive and subjective assessments of future prospects. The postwar history of textiles and iron and steel has confirmed that the optimism expressed was largely misplaced for both have contracted severely.

The team noted that certain towns and areas within the region were showing signs of economic prosperity. Kilmarnock, for instance, had "... an air of great prosperity and drive ... (with) ... a very varied and prosperous industrial structure" [1588-9]. But most of the other large towns in the region, such as Airdrie, Coatbridge, and Hamilton, were actual or potential economic problem areas, where the loss of male jobs in traditional industries had exceeded employment created in new industries.

THE PLAN'S INDUSTRIAL STRATEGY

The Three Levels of the Plan's Strategy

Whilst never labelled as such, the Clyde Valley Regional Plan contained within it a clearly defined industrial strategy for the region, which still has relevance for those involved in industrial development, both in Clydeside and in the other conurbations that are now experiencing the decline and despair first encountered on the Clyde.

The team's industrial strategy for the Valley had two broad objectives: the attraction of a greater supply of new industries from more prosperous parts of the United Kingdom; and an improved intra-regional distribution of employment and housing. Few of the specific 34 recommendations in the Plan for industry are economic and industrial policy as we would understand it today. Many were incapable of implementation by any planning authority, either at national or regional level, as they required economic powers substantially greater than then available, or indeed, than those existing today. The objectives were stated with conviction and sincerity, though in the cold light of retrospection they appear more as planners' rhetoric. In 1946, however, the proposals appeared to form a coherent strategy, especially when viewed in conjunction with the proposals made in the Plan for regional government.

There are three levels at which the Plan suggested action be taken to improve the industrial future of the Clyde Valley: by central government at the national (United Kingdom) level; by the Scottish Office; and by local authorities and regional administrations within the Clyde Valley itself. These three policy levels were thought to form an inter-related programme of action, although the Plan was vague on the administrative links between the levels necessary to achieve the Plan's objectives. The subsequent experience with the West Central Scotland Plan revealed the importance of the politics of regional planning to the implementation of proposals.

The National Dimension

At the United Kingdom level, the Plan called for greater guidance to town planners on the criteria for efficient industrial location. For instance, the relative priorities of the need for areas to solve unemployment problems versus the requirements of industries to remain clustered for technical efficiency: a question still unresolved mainly because such questions can never be answered in economic terms alone. The team also recommended that the Barlow Report be fully implemented, and that the Distribution of Industry Act of 1945 be strengthened to give greater positive powers of control over industrial location. Central government was urged to use the purchasing powers of industries that were (or were to be) nationalised to stimulate the demand for goods of industries in the Clyde Valley and thus encourage them to expand (Lever 1974, 111-122). The Plan also called for the decentralisation of Government offices to towns in the region, and quoted the example of Newcastle-upon-Tyne's selection as the headquarters of the new Ministry of National Insurance.

Variants of these recommendations have appeared in many of the subsequent policy proposals advanced by political parties in Scotland and the UK. Few of those drafting such policy documents will have read the Clyde Valley Regional Plan or realised that their new ideas have a long and respectable ancestry. However, in 1946 the industrial restructuring of the Clyde Valley was principally to be achieved through the direction of manufacturing industry at the UK level, and here the Plan has important lessons for contemporary planners.

The proposals for industrial development in the Clyde Valley relied on the UK government fully implementing the policies contained in the 1944 White Paper on Employment Policy, especially the measures which would be used to tackle regional imbalances in employment. The 1945 Distribution of Industry Act, while a useful first step, needed strengthening if the region was to receive its fair share of new industries. The Plan's industrial policy therefore rested on an acceptance that new light industries would be steered to the region from other parts of Britain, and thus a strategy was required that would mobilise the resulting employment in support of other Plan objectives such as the establishment of New Towns and the provisions of new jobs for the declining towns of North Lanarkshire. Improving the efficiency of indigenous enterprises was important, but an area where the planners rightly felt they had no competence, and specific proposals for local companies would have to wait until after the more comprehensive and specialised industrial enquiry.

The team accepted that the industry likely to be steered to the region by the 1945 Act would be mainly female employing branch factories of Southern firms, "... to an appreciable extent developing here to supply the local industrial market" [406]. The Plan sought for a better ratio of male to female employment as:
'... the prime necessity is the introduction of several substantial new industries employing thousands of men rather than the setting up of concerns merely to supplement the basic industrial structure ... we say quite frankly that the present developments cannot possibly meet the Area's fundamental requirements and the problem has yet to be faced" [409-410].
This problem remains at the core of the region's performance, and since 1970 it has become acute throughout the Clyde Valley.

Many of the fears about regional reliance on branch plants which surfaced with some force during the late 1960's and 1970's, were thus first outlined in the Plan:
'Reliance on English initiative means that industrial policy is controlled from the South. The future of these (firms) is a matter of speculation; will they stay when the consumer-goods boom is over, or again concentrate production in their headquarter factories? In a period of slump a branch factory would undoubtedly be the first to be closed; ...(and) ... Rolls Royce are abandoning much of their aero engine factory and reconcentrating production at Derby' [412].
But the Plan felt it was possible to over-emphasise the dangers of this type of development, for:
'... these Southern firms are, in many instances, of established reputation, ... which ... is a guarantee of reliable employment with diminished risk of commercial failures. (Therefore) ... these branch factories are to be welcomed for the local employment which they give, for the likely resultant expansion of linked or subsidiary industries, for the new ideas which they bring to Scotland and for the skill which labour acquires in industrial work with which it was not previously acquainted" [412].

113

The possibility that such new branches would supply only the Scottish and Northern Ireland markets was also of concern, and the team argued that attracting concerns with nationwide (UK) sales and a strong export position was essential:

'Without this wider market ... once depression overtakes the basic industries, the purchasing power of the local population falls and with it their purchases of consumer-goods, resulting in unemployment in these light industries ..." [413].

In reality attracting export-orientated light industries would not improve the region's economic situation, for they would equally be affected by recessions in other national economies. While a spread of export markets can help ameliorate the effects of international depressions, it cannot remove them altogether and consumer goods enterprises in the West of Scotland, many foreign-owned, were to feel the effects of such overseas recessions in the post-1970 period.

The Plan recognised that implementation of the industrial recommendations would be difficult in the absence of a national plan for industrial location, and virtually impossible unless the 1945 Act was given both positive and restrictive powers. The difficulty of guiding market forces to support industrial development was accepted, for:

'... the planner has no guarantee, without industrial conscription, that individual concerns will act in such an accommodating manner and come at his behest. We cannot normally ... compel industrialists to start up branch factories, ... nor compel (them) to start up a factory at all if he is not interested in a particular venture ...' [384-388].

Thus success depended upon the effectiveness of the inducements offered to industries to settle in the area, unless:

'... the State is willing to enter production by running factories where they are most needed for full employment'.

The Plan also foresaw that West Central Scotland would be competing with other Development Areas for the mobile new industries, and that it would face a strong challenge from the reconstructed industries of the South of England as they replaced their war-damaged factories and plant with modern equipment.

The Plan team were fully conscious of their limited power to tackle the industrial problems of the Clyde Valley, but nevertheless considered that these national proposals would enable a start to be made. Yet, with the advantages of hindsight it is starkly apparent that not one of the industrial recommendations was directed at the basic problem in the region: the declining competitiveness of indigenous manufacturing enterprises, especially in export sectors, upon which the region's economic prosperity depended, and which still dominated the Clyde Valley's manufacturing in 1946. To neglect them in favour of winning a share of the UK's mobile industry (especially when the Team recognised the problems inherent in such a policy) was not an optimum long-term economic strategy for the region. Had a greater economic input gone into the Plan, as with the 1932 Board of Trade Survey, it is possible that this seduction by the clean, modern, diversified light industries of the South would have been avoided, or at least placed in context.

Action at the Scottish Level

The most important and immediate action to be taken at the Scottish level was the preparation of a National Economic Plan for Scotland, of which the Plan would be a major component, together with similar plans for the other main Scottish regions. A co-ordinated set of regional economic plans remains an unfulfilled objective in Scotland, principally because of the difficulty of grasping the political thistle of establishing priority sectors and areas when all the nation claims to have some special reason for prior treatment, but partly because co-ordination has tended to imply constraints rather than competition.

The Plan called for the 1945 Act to be applied to all Scotland, with the central objection of steering new industries to areas of major need, and specifically to the Clyde Valley which the team considered had the first claim to mobile firms. In retrospect Dundee and parts of the Forth Valley also had severe economic problems, but on scale grounds the Clyde Valley rightly was given priority to be the principal target destination for light industry. The team recognised that this component of the strategy had its problems, and noted that:
> 'Light industry is, in itself, no panacea for a region's industrial troubles but, if present in sufficient volume, it can be a valuable stabiliser and an absorber of an area's labour surplus' [403].

The stark truth was that if such steering failed, there would be no real alternative to an emigration of industry and population from the Clyde Valley, especially from the declining mining communities, whose miners would then be encouraged to migrate to the expanding coalfields in Ayrshire and the East. An intensive publicity campaign at home and abroad was suggested to inform people (exactly who was not clear) of the region's labour skills and its industrial variety, although elsewhere the Plan had faulted the area's lack of diversification! Finally, there was a call for greater use of Scottish enterprise in the development of new industry in Scotland and "... not leave the field so much to Southern firms" [514]. The apparent policy contradiction between encouraging Scottish enterprise and seeking out mobile firms from the South, continued throughout Scotland's postwar economic policy, although when the indigenous sector performs as badly as it has done since 1946, the contribution of employment from all sources must be pursued.

Perhaps the most important regret on looking back to the Plan's proposals for Scottish industry in 1946, is that the critical importance of encouraging, supporting and defending Scottish enterprise and entrepreneurs was not given greater priority and advanced to a position of high visibility. The message was clearly there in the analysis and deliberations of the team, but inexplicably got lost in their concern for more ephemeral objectives.

The Proposals for the Clyde Valley

The, recommendations for the Clyde Valley itself depended upon success at the national and Scottish levels. Plans for industrial diversification at a sub-regional level were suggested, each based upon a number of adjacent towns and communities forming a coherent economic unit. New industry attracted to the region was to be steered to areas of high unemployment, with priority given to locating enterprises providing male employment to areas, especially North Lanarkshire, with the greatest decline in mining and heavy industries such as iron and steel. New Towns were to be established as balanced industrial communities, based both on immigrant enterprises and firms decentralised from Glasgow and other congested central urban areas in the region. It was proposed that the entry of new industry to Glasgow be carefully regulated, and restrictions placed on further expansion of the Hillington Industrial Estate on the Western edge of the City which was proving an attractive location for firms from elsewhere in Britain, and for enterprises leaving central Glasgow. A series of new industrial estates throughout the region was recommended, as was a programme of environmental improvement to remove the worst of the scars left by industrial decline.

Amidst the Plan's industrial recommendations for the Clyde Valley were two which were prophetic and important. Firstly, there was the call for the creation of a strong Regional Authority, which would have a major role in the planning of industrial development in the Clyde Valley. It would control the New Towns; co-ordinate the plans of local authorities; and advise on the distribution and location of industry for the Conurbation and central part of the Clyde area which it considered formed the largest coherent economic unit. Such a regional authority, had it then been established, would have had a marked effect upon the distribution of industry, though unlikely to have contributed much to the solution of the economic problems facing local industrial enterprises. But, it was one of the early steps in the thinking that eventually produced Strathclyde Regional Council in 1974.

The second interesting proposal was the possibility of rationalising and relocating the region's steel industry to a new waterside site on the Clyde. This was not a new idea for in 1929 H.A. Brassert and Company, a firm of American consultants specialising in the steel industry, had recommended the relocation of the Scotish steel industry to an estuarial site in the West of Scotland (Campbell 1980, 126). The Plan foresaw the move being made in stages to a true integrated complex in North-East Renfrewshire where:

'... iron ore could be unloaded direct to a great integrated unit consisting of ore-crushing and sintering plant, a battery of coke ovens, blast furnaces, steel furnaces and rolling mills where the maximum fuel and transport economies could be obtained by the use of coke-oven gas and the transfer of hot metal direct from blast furnaces to steel works. Steel from it could be floated by barge to the adjoining Clyde shipyards... Such a project ... would seem to be the logical final stage in the series of amalgamations that have taken place in the inter-war period' [316].

The Plan admitted that the old steel-making areas of North Lanarkshire would be heavily affected by the accompanying closures of out-dated plant and acknowledged that the economic effect would be painful. But similar developments were happening elsewhere, and industrial logic pointed to such reorganisation in the region, and:

'In retrospect it may be found that such upheaval marked one of the great turning points for the better in the West of Scotland's industrial history' [319].

Thirty years later, the great steel location debate still aroused passion: the technology had changed; the ideal location had moved further west to Hunterston; the steel industry had been nationalised (twice); plants in North Lanarkshire were either closed or under perpetual threat of closure; and an attempt to develop a modern coastal integrated steel facility at Hunterston collapsed in its early stages. An internationally competitive integrated steel plant was by 1980 an objective for the Clyde Valley that was unlikely to be achieved.

It is difficult to identify other proposals in the Plan designed to assist industrial regeneration of the Clyde Valley, and thus the ideas outlined above represent the team's industrial strategy for the region. How are we to appraise them? The ideas and concepts might now seem naive and were often directed at solving the wrong problems, but these are merely superficial criticisms, for the Plan's industrial proposals were undermined by a central, more pervasive failing, namely that the recommendations were simply ideas which could not be translated into action because they were unrelated to specific programmes of action for designated people and institutions to implement; were oblivious to the scale, source or type of money and resources required for implementation; and were politically and institutionally inept. Quite simply, the Clyde Valley Regional Plan was not an economic or industrial plan, but a planner's manifesto for industry, prepared at a time when such interventionist positivism was seen as offering the only hope of breaking with the Clyde Valley's industrial past. But in an area that had been one of the birth-places of democratic socialism, such an approach was understandable, and in many ways has perhaps had a greater influence on the subsequent economic and industrial evolution of the Clyde Valley and Scotland than a more operational plan, costed down to the final pound. To see this, it is necessary to firstly review the post-1946 industrial development of the region and then look at the influence of the Clyde Valley Regional Plan on this.

CLYDE VALLEY INDUSTRY: 1946-1982

The National Perspective

Since the Plan, far-reaching and substantial changes, quantitative and qualitative, have occurred in the industries of the Clyde Valley, leaving the area very different from that known to the planners in the early 1940s. Some developments have been unexpected, but many of the broad trends were foreseen in the Plan. The detailed changes, their causes and consequences have been well documented elsewhere (West Central Scotland Plan Team 1974d; Slaven 1975; Randall 1980) and will not be recounted here except where they have relevance to the broad strategic themes of the Plan or where they are a necessary backdrop to subsequent planning developments.

The postwar industrial history of the Clyde Valley, like all British regions, has been principally determined by developments in the UK economy, and during the 1946-1982 period three important economic shifts have taken place which have had an impact upon the Clyde Valley. First, the postwar years have seen a slower real rate of growth in the British economy and its constituent industries compared to other major industrial nations, resulting in an increasingly harsh and less competitive international trade environment than might have been expected even in 1946. Second, partly as a response to this initial factor, there has been (until 1979-80) a slow but continuous expansion of public sector intervention in the economy through a wide range of mechanisms not yet fully documented or understood. Third, and perhaps most important, there has been a continuing integration of the constituent regional economies of Britain, partly through regional policy, but mainly through policy and market developments in such as industrial organisation; employee compensation, industrial relations and trade unions; and transportation and communications. The result has been an overall narrowing of inter-regional differentials in virtually all the economic and social indicators used to delineate relative regional prosperity. The overall effect has been to simultaneously integrate the Clyde Valley into the UK economy, and also make it increasingly dependent upon economic and industrial developments that have their origin elsewhere. In this sense, present and future regional planners will face harder tasks than their 1946 predecessors if they wish to make a significant impact.

Structural Changes

The Clyde Valley's industrial structure in the 1980's is far different from that of the 1940's as is revealed by examining the broad shifts in employment structure over the past four decades. What stands out most clearly is that the industrial structure of the region in 1959 was not too dissimilar from that found in 1939. Some decline in agriculture and other primary industries was matched by growth in the services sector (concealing an obvious spatial mismatch); and most of the traditional and heavy manufacturing industries had actually grown in employment although their share of manufacturing employment had been reduced by the rapid growth of the newer sectors, such as electrical and electronic engineering which had begun to arrive in the Valley in the 1950's. The region had survived the war, and the demand for its engineering products remained strong in Commonwealth and European markets, creating the national economic growth rates of the 1950's which now appear as a vanishing golden age.

Then in the 1960's, a rapid and comprehensive collapse of the Clyde Valley's traditional industries began, and by the late 1970's over 100,000 manufacturing jobs had been lost in the

Table 5.1

Structural Changes in Employment in the Clyde Valley: 1939, 1959 and 1979

Industrial Sector	Clyde Valley 1939		West Central Scotland 1959		Strathclyde Region 1978	
	Number '000	%	Number '000	%	Number '000	%
Primary Industries	50.5	6.7	46.2	4.6	17.7	1.8
Agriculture,Forestry,Fishing	14.5	1.9	10.5	1.1	8.6	0.9
Mining, Quarrying	36.0	4.8	35.7	3.5	9.1	1.0
Manufacturing Industries	333.0	44.3	441.8	44.3	331.3	33.8
Food, Drink, Tobacco	36.0	4.8	42.7	4.3	42.8	4.4
Metal Manufacturing	40.0	5.3	38.2	3.8	25.7	2.6
Engineering	90.0	11.9	90.0	9.0	62.7	6.4
Shipbuilding, Marine Eng.	47.5	6.3	52.4	5.3	27.0	2.8
Textiles and Clothing	72.5	9.6	73.2	7.3	46.7	4.8
Other Manufacturing	47.0	6.4	145.3	14.6	126.4	12.8
Construction	63.5	8.4	65.5	6.6	72.1	7.3
Service Sector Industries	306.0	40.6	443.4	44.5	560.0	57.1
TOTAL	753.0	100.0	996.9	100.0	981.1	100.0

Notes:

(1) Figures on a strictly comparable basis are not available, but the areas and sectors shown above for the three dates are sufficiently comparable to be a guide to broad structural change.

(2) The sectoral groupings are as follows: Food, Drink and Tobacco (1968 SIC III); Metal Manufacture (VI); Engineering (VII + VIII); Shipbuilding and Marine Engineering (X); Textiles and Clothing (XIII + XIV + XV); Others are the remaining orders.

Sources:

1939: Clyde Valley Regional Plan, 1946, p.69, table 4; West Central Scotland Plan, Supplementary Report 1, The Regional Economy, p. 130; 1978: Census of Employment, June 1978 (latest available).

area, together with another 30,000 in the primary sector, principally in coal mining. The growth in service sector employment was fortunately large, and thus employment in the region was maintained at a high level. But jobs created by growth in office and white collar occupations are not filled by redundant miners, or steel and shipyard workers, and consequently levels of net emigration from the Clyde Valley remained high as these victims of industrial decline sought employment elsewhere. By the 1980's, the Clyde Valley was no longer a regional economy driven, dominated and determined by the large-scale heavy manufacturing enterprises upon which the area rose to international pre-eminence and prosperity. It is now clear that the contraction of the region, especially that of the Clydeside Conurbation at its core, was not unique, as the subsequent history of the other British conurbations reveals (McCallum 1980, 14-53), merely earlier.

This rapid decline in the international competitiveness of local industry is not well understood, but it seems likely that it has its roots back in poor corporate decision-making in the early decades of this century, and in the distortion of the regional economy through the high demands made on its heavy industries by armaments and defence in the First World War. The comprehensive analysis of the decline in the manufacturing base of the Clyde Valley undertaken by the West Central Scotland Plan (WCSP) in the early 1970's pointed to a whole range of explanatory factors (poor industrial structure; low labour-productivity; low levels of indigenous enterprise and entrepreneurial activity; poor management; a depressing environment; and a shortage of business finance), but never quite identified the prime causes nor resolved the apparent contradictions (West Central Plan Team 1974d, Part 2). It is not possible here to review changes that have taken place in individual industries, but a few brief comments may prove helpful in setting the background for the planning developments that took place in the Clyde Valley after 1946.

As noted above, the primary sector, has declined sharply in the region, both in absolute and proportional terms. In agriculture, the family-owned 'farm-towns' of the 1940's have largely been replaced by capital intensive units that are the new dominant rural industry. Coal mining, under attack by oil, gas, and nuclear power, has virtually disappeared from the area, with Scottish production being increasingly concentrated at large pits outside the old Lanarkshire coal fields, and with output increasingly being devoted to electricity generation. The period since the Plan has also seen the once-proud iron and steel industry rise to a peak of important in 1958, when a new integrated steel strip mill hinted at in the 1946 Plan [318] was steered by Government to Ravenscraig in

121

Lanarkshire. It then slowly collapsed as its traditional markets disappeared under the pressure of foreign (especially Japanese) competition. The region's mechanical engineering industries remained fairly buoyant until the 1970's, when like their counterparts elsewhere in Britain, they entered the long recession which followed the oil-price rises of 1973, pushed downwards by persistent low investment in new designs and facilities.

The region has also seen new industries develop since 1946, the most notable of which have been electrical and electronic engineering, and the motor vehicle industry, neither of which had been foreseen by the Plan team. The growth in automotive manufacturing, which many hoped would see the region re-enter a sector where it had once been a world leader (Orr and Orr 1958a, 209 pp), never took firm root and the major car factory that the UK government brought to Clydeside in 1962 finally closed in 1981 after an unhappy existence under a number of owners (Hood and Young 1982, 61-80). The experience of electronics has been much brighter, and the Clyde Valley has steadily evolved into one of Europe's largest concentrations of advanced electronics manufacture, and by 1981 was already at the forefront internationally of the semi-conductor and optronics technologies that would essentially shape much of the industrial development of the 1980's and 1990's: the Clyde Valley had become the heart of Silicon Glen. Although the manufacturing sector as a whole has declined, new industries, enterprises and products have become established, including aerospace engineering, oil and gas production equipment, cameras, computers, integrated circuits, fine chemicals, medical electronics, pharmaceuticals, and a wide range of other high technology products. Some traditional sectors have also flourished, including the production, blending, bottling and shipping of Scotch Whisky, which by 1980 had grown to be Scotland's largest export earner; and also specialised areas of the heavy engineering sector such as mining equipment. Thus, even within the decline, it was possible to find Clyde Valley enterprises that remained competitive world leaders in their products.

Major changes also were seen in the region's tertiary sector. Perhaps the most visible to residents returning to Glasgow after a thirty year absence were those affecting the transport systems where trams, trains, and river traffic had given way to road, and latterly, air transportation of both people and goods. Most service sector industries continued their growth throughout the post-war period and ameliorated to an extent, the unemployment stemming from manufacturing decline. The main engines of tertiary sector expansion were central and local government bodies, both of which had a far wider economic and social remit than in 1939, although the 1980's appears to be a decade where such continued extension cannot any longer be taken for granted. The region also managed to partly fulfil one of the Plan's wishes by attracting some central government offices (National Savings Bank; British National Oil Corporation; parts of the Overseas Development Administration and the Ministry of Defence) and the headquarters of public bodies such as the Scottish Development Agency. Against this some losses took place when local industrial companies were nationalised, and head office functions disappeared. The private sector tertiary industry all showed continued resilience throughout the post-war period, and Glasgow remained one of the UK's main commercial, financial, professional services, and trading cities. By 1980, the region was effectively driven by non-manufacturing enterprises and services - a situation with important and far-reaching policy implications.

Qualitative Change

Far more important than the bald figures of post-war structural shifts in the Clyde Valley are the qualitative changes that have been seen in local industry since 1939, and, as will be seen, the Clyde Valley Plan team anticipated many of these.

The most fundamental development has been in the corporate structure of the local economy. In 1946, the manufacturing base of the Clyde Valley was still in essence that of the pre-First World War period, with large, locally-owned (often by descendants of founders) heavy engineering companies (typically in old urban factories) exporting capital goods to the Empire and the developing world. Thirty years later, the position was radically different, with a more apt characterisation being a manufacturing base dominated by smaller, non-local branch plants and subsidiaries exporting light industrial goods to Europe and North America. The scale of change over a brief period was dramatic, and the reasons and impacts of it have not yet been fully examined or understood. The principal result was that the Clyde Valley had developed a degree of dependency that even the Plan's team would have despaired over (Firn 1975, 393-414). By 1980 it was widely recognised that high levels of external ownership present long-term development problems at the regional level, and a renewed emphasis on policies aimed at encouraging indigenous growth emerged.

Much of the product diversification in the region came about through the arrival of plants from other parts of the UK and overseas rather than by internal invention and by local industry, and consequently the older indigenous sector declined rapidly over the post-war period, especially after 1960. This

123

decline, unrecognised by government, together with the low rate of formation of new enterprises by local entrepreneurs, combined to produce a situation where the region was increasingly unable, via the use of its indigenous resources, to counteract the forces which were driving it into a downward spiral. The process was hastened by a continuing series of takeovers of local enterprises by larger UK and international groups, by which many famous Clyde Valley companies ended up as mere manufacturing units in multi-plant companies, and thus less able to determine their own products, marketing or future.

The Plan team had not foreseen this, but they had predicted the branch-plant phenomenon, and many of the region's industrial crises in the 1960's and 1970's were visibly played out in some of the larger branch plants, principally at Linwood. Sadly, the team's belief in the enhanced long-term stability of branch plant employment was not justified by events, for initial research has indicated that their closure rates have been above those of similar-sized local plants in the same industries (Henderson 1980, 152-174; Hood and Young 1982, 29-30).

Another qualitative change of some postwar importance has been the steady expansion, especially in manufacturing, of public sector ownership and influence in the local economy. Since 1946, many industrial sectors have found themselves entering the public sector through a variety of mechanisms (nationalisation; rescue; take-overs; or new corporations), and the Clyde Valley industrial structure ensured that it was the location of many of the major operating units in such industries. Coal, shipbuilding, aerospace, vehicles, and transportation systems all became publicly-owned, and consequently, both in employment and output terms, the West of Scotland developed an exceptionally high level of dependence upon government for industrial decision-making. Further, many private sector enterprises relied upon the public sector for orders, and yet others (especially in the 1970's) were only kept in operation through financial assistance from government.

The nature and structure of the labour force in the Clyde Valley also underwent noticeable changes over the postwar period, and showed the same trends as those experienced nationally. The participation of women in all sectors of the regional economy expanded compared to the pre-1939 position, and between 1961 and 1978, the female share of total employment rose from 36 to 42 per cent, and to as high as 55 per cent in the tertiary sector. The skill composition of the local labour force also changed, with pressure evolving on the labouring and unskilled jobs that had always lain at the base of the heavy industrial economy of the West of Scotland. In line with the

Plan's views of 1946, the newer industries entering the Clyde Valley had found no difficulty in training labour up to the standards they required, even in the complex, high-technology semi-conductor plants that developed in the late 1970's.

The areas's 'Red Clydeside' industrial relations image was unfortunately reinforced in the 1966-1974 period by a series of major industrial disputes and work-ins, with the Linwood car plant and the Upper Clyde shipyards dominant. Subsequent research confirmed that the poor comparative industrial relations of the area was mainly attributable to these two industries and a very small number of other specific firms, and closer inspection revealed that much of the trouble could be attributed as much to deplorable management systems and attitudes as to employee militancy. The media concentration on industrial disputes rather than the more usual accord between management and unions, failed to identify a more fundamentally important long-term trend, namely the contracting role of trade unionism in the local economy. Many new manufacturing plants, especially those from overseas, were non-union (IBM had operated one of its most competitive plants in Greenock from 1954 without a union or a single stoppage); other plants which had been standard bearers of union power declined under market forces; and, especially after the onset of the severe recession in 1979, workers increasingly accepted a harsher wage and salary regime as they faced the prospect of redundancy and unemployment. These particular changes struck deep into the socio-economic fabric of the West of Scotland, and whilst the visible results in terms of unemployment were horrendous when compared to the levels experienced in the 1950's and 1960's, there was a feeling that when the ever-expected up-turn arrived in the international economy, the more flexible and individualistic workforce in the West of Scotland would once again show its productive power.

Whilst Clydeside labour had changed fundamentally since 1946, so also had the premises in which their days and nights were spent. Much of the older, dilapidated industrial property in the urban areas was demolished in the 1960's and 1970's, under the impact of urban renewal, road development, and local planning strategies, most of which however, were hopelessly ill-adjusted to the needs of industry and commerce. Glasgow's small, old-established manufacturing and service traders were especially badly affected, and contraction, relocation, or closure was often the inevitable response. The large incoming firms were well treated with modern, well-serviced factories being provided by the New Towns and the Scottish Industrial Estates Corporation (the latter having existed under a series of designations since the mid-1930's), usually on industrial estates around the periphery of Glasgow and the larger urban

Figure 5.1 Work-in at Upper Clyde Shipbuilder's, 1971. Yard
meeting

centres. The smaller firms, which often required a central urban location for efficient production, were less visible; thought to be less important; and consequently, usually left to fend for themselves, with often fatal results.

The late 1960's saw the first change in this pattern, with the Ronald Lyon Group successfully providing industrial sites and buildings on cleared industrial land in Glasgow, and their success, together with a much improved understanding of the locational requirements and dynamics of urban industry and commerce, resulted in a steadily increasing provision of attractive, well-designed, small-scale industrial premises in inner city areas, initially in Glasgow, but later in all the main towns in the region. By the 1980's, the success of these units, especially in the East End of Glasgow, on the Clyde Ironworks site in Cambuslang, in Clydebank, and in the North Lanarkshire towns, indicated that entrepreneurship in the West of Scotland could emerge if provided with appropriate facilities. Indeed, the new environment for business in the Clyde Valley which emerged from 1977 onwards, principally under the aegis of the Scottish Development Agency's (SDA) property and environmental development programmes, meant that, unlike 1946, it was now the turn of the urban industrial areas of the South East and the Midlands to envy the fortunate enterprise of the Clyde Valley, "... housed in modern factories in good surroundings" [483]. Qualitatively, the region had been slowly transformed into one of the more attractive industrial areas of Western Europe, and the City of Glasgow at its centre had begun to regain some of its Edwardian grandure and self-confidence.

PLANNING AND CLYDE VALLEY INDUSTRY: 1946-1982

The Adoption of Growth Area Strategy

Immediately after the War, comparatively few dramatic or visible events happened to the Clyde Valley economy, and thanks to a comparatively strong infusion of new industrial companies to Scotland, the relative position of major economic variables did not weaken compared to the rest of the United Kingdom. But at the end of the 1950's Scotland's economic and political position began to slip and attempts were made to improve its relative economic situation. The initial response, namely the ill-conceived Local Employment Act of 1960, achieved very little and perhaps even worked against the long-term interests of Scotland and the other regions by the fact that it concentrated assistance in the most distressed industrial areas where the unemployment rate remained above 4.5 per cent. This approach not only discriminated against successful areas like the New Towns, but because of its essentially negative orientation also prevented the formulation of any positive and coherent development strategy. In Scotland, bye-election results began to turn against the Conservative government, and in 1959 it became clear that a more fundamental reappraisal of regional policy was required.

About this time some prominent British planners and economists became aware of the concept of growth poles, first advanced by the French economist Francois Perroux in 1955. The concepts Perroux discussed related to industrial sectors rather than spatial areas - a vital distinction ignored in the sudden and largely inexplicable conversion of British administrators and regional planners to the virtues of French-style indicative planning. In Scotland, the first move in the re-appraisal of regional policy was the establishment of a Committee of Enquiry into the Scottish Economy by the Scottish Council (Development and Industry), chaired by Sir John Toothill of Ferranti. The Committee, which had the active support of the Scottish Office as well as Scottish industrialists, economists, and planners, produced a report which was (in retrospect) revolutionary in its approach to regional policy. It recommended that the use of local high unemployment as a criteria for regional assistance be replaced by a policy that concentrated government policy and public-sector investment on areas that offered the best prospects for achieving long-term economic growth. This advocation of growth areas was influenced not only by the ideas of Perroux, but also by the self-evident economic and industrial success of the Scottish New Towns, especially East Kilbride which had prospered since its designation in 1947. Closer examination of the Toothill Report reveals that, as in the Plan many of its conclusions were not based on detailed research, but what cannot be doubted is the impact which it had in Scotland. It offered a decisive break with the past, which was taken, and in 1963 the legendary White Paper on Central Scotland was published, which adopted the approach of the Toothill Report and built around it a detailed physical planning strategy for the Central Belt of Scotland. Eight 'Growth Areas' were designated, including all the existing New Towns, where concentrated government investment in economic and social infrastructure, such as housing, roads, schools, power and communications, would encourage both the expansion of existing industry, and more importantly, attract new enterprises in growth sectors from other more prosperous regions or countries. Integrated physical and economic planning would ensure that industry was supplied with skilled labour; would develop into fast-growing industrial complexes taking full advantages of potential technical inter-plant linkages; and would benefit from the general external economies supposed to exist around such growth poles. Consequently, the whole area would take-off on a future path of self-sufficient economic growth at which point further regional aid would no longer be required. Five of these Growth Areas were in the Clyde Valley - East Kilbride, Cumbernauld, North Lanarkshire, Vale of Leven and Irvine, and thus for a while, the West of Scotland appeared to be set fair for a period of co-ordinated industrial expansion. It was perhaps a high point in regional industrial planning, never since reattained.

Growth Areas as official policy had a very short existence. The Scottish Labour Party, which effectively dominated political events in Scotland, had never shown enthusiasm towards a policy that by definition selectively discriminated against some areas, usually Labour Party strongholds! The advent of a national Labour Government in 1964 meant that the brief life of Growth Areas began to ebb away, and although a muted and heavily disguised version appeared in the 1966 Plan for the Scottish Economy, the Growth Areas concept made its final appearance in the 1969 plan for the North East of Scotland. Unfortunately, nothing has emerged to take the place of Growth Areas, and thus the 1970's saw Scotland and the Clyde Valley facing the prospects of major economic and social change, especially the advent of North Sea Oil and gas, with no coherent economic or industrial development strategy or even guidelines to capitalise on new opportunities: a tragedy for the Clyde Valley's industrial skills and tradition which appeared tailormade to meet the new demands of ocean engineering.

One lasting innovation of the changes in the aftermath of the Toothill Report was the creation within the Scottish Office of the Scottish Development Department in June 1962. This development, which strengthened the administrative machinery required to back up comprehensive regional planning, also produced the 1963 White Paper. The Chief Planning Officer in SDD, Robert Grieve, had been a member of the Plan team, and thus the ideas of the 1946 Plan were kept alive and to the fore in the work of the Department. The New Towns; population overspill from Glasgow; the need to help the older areas of North Lanarkshire; the importance of modern industrial estates: all found their place in the 1963 White Paper, and all can be found in the Clyde Valley Regional Plan. Thus in 1963, as Grieve himself stressed, "... the basic tenets of the Clyde Valley Plan even yet hold good; the important factors and their likely changes still exist in much the same form and they are changing in the expected ways."

Yet there was one fundamental difference between the 1946 and 1963 strategy. In the former, regional policy (with the exception of the proposed New Towns) concentrated on providing employment opportunities in the areas of greatest economic distress and need; with the 1963 Growth Areas developmental efforts were to be focussed on the centres with the greatest economic potential, although the inclusion of the Vale of Leven and North Lanarkshire in the 1963 list of designated areas reduces the distinction, whilst demonstrating the importance of politics in the regional planning process.

The strategy that evolved in 1963 showed little advance in the appreciation of the more fundamental industrial needs of the Central Belt or the West of Scotland and, in dealing with the region's potential for growth, the 1963 White Paper is less sophisticated than its 1946 predecessor. The simple message is: designate an area, direct public investment into its infrastructure, and industrial growth will emerge. The important questions raised in paragraph 380 of the 1946 Plan were unresearched and unanswered. In both 1946 and 1963 industrial policy was not a Scottish Office concern and detailed consideration of major industrial economic problems was seen as being best left to the Board of Trade. From 1966 until 1974, there was no comprehensive industrial strategy for the Clyde Valley, nor indeed for Scotland as a whole. The result was that a number of organisations and groups were able to fly rather flimsy kites offering instant salvation to the West of Scotland, such as the Scottish Council's Oceanspan concept and the Hunterston Development Corporation's ideas for a deep-water industrial complex; neither of these were taken very seriously for very long and both dropped from view. It is however interesting to note that in both the Oceanspan and Hunterston plans could be detected the influence of Francois Perroux, and of concentrated investment.

Throughout most of the early 1960's Scotland's outwardly prosperous appearance masked serious and worsening industrial trends that required urgent remedial policies, especially in the Clyde Valley. Attention was diverted away from the very real industrial problems of the City of Glasgow by the relatively greater success of the surrounding New Towns, and the growing imbalance between the location of housing and employment within the region was largely ignored. The apparent ease by which immigrant companies could be captured, a policy goal that played a key role in both the 1946 and 1963 Plans, led to a comparative neglect of existing and potential indigenous industry. These problems remain with us still, but they have at least been firmly delineated in the West Central Scotland Plan, and it is to this that we should now turn our attention for it marks the next important step in the post-war development of the Clyde Valley.

The West Central Scotland Plan

By 1970 disillusionment with Growth Areas had set in, and the continuing visibly poor economic performance of the industries of the West of Scotland, reinforced by the political pressure stemming from factors such as the collapse of shipbuilding in the Upper Clyde in the early 1970's, led to a demand that the Scottish Office re-examine the economic problems of the area. The intention was to produce a new policy for the future, that would enable the region to get nearer to its economic potential and reverse the almost continuous industrial decline that had been an unvarying feature of the post-war scene. In 1971 the authorities in the region, advised by the various departments of the Scottish Office, agreed to undertake a new regional planning exercise. The committee's objectives aimed at preparing and maintaining an advisory, economic and physical plan for West Central Scotland, an area approximately equivalent to that covered by the Clyde Valley Plan a quarter of a century earlier. The study team of the Committee began work early in 1971, and after a period of exhaustive study released their Consultative Draft Report in May 1974, followed by other volumes which dealt with various aspects of the study in more detail. One of the most important of these was the supplementary report on the regional economy.

The tasks facing the (three) economists on the West Central Plan team was daunting, but the results of their work is certainly impressive, although reservations have been expressed about their basic research methodology. The symptoms of economic decline in the region were described in detail, but the team encountered difficulties in identifying the causes of decline. In the end they opted for an unranked mix of factors to explain the region's economic performance. Poor labour-productivity and high unit labour costs (although here the statistical problems were formidable); bad industrial management compared to the rest of the United Kingdom; poor industrial relations; a poor record of new company formation; possible problems in the supply of business finance; a high level of external ownership and control in the local manufacturing sector; higher transport costs; and the poor quality of the local environment and infrastructure: overall, an evaluation not too far from that reached in 1946. Like the Clyde Valley Regional Plan twenty-eight years earlier, identification of symptoms had proved easier than diagnosis of the basic causes of decline, especially that of the indigenous manufacturing sector, and its failure to switch production to new products, markets and technologies. As in 1946, it was generally appreciated that such a complex question required greater research effort than the team had available.

The policies in the West Central Scotland Plan for dealing
with the region's problems are very different from those in the
Clyde Valley Regional Plan, in that greater attention is laid
on the economic and industrial aspects, and on the need to make
the region's enterprises and industries internationally
competitive. They recognised that the existing industries
within the region hold the key to future development, and urged
the Government to set up a Strathclyde Economic Development
Corporation (SEDCOR) to help local firms achieve greater
efficiency. This aspect of the proposals marks perhaps the
greatest advance over the recommendations in the Clyde Valley
Regional Plan.

But, as with the Clyde Valley Regional Plan, the West Central
Scotland Plan team called for increased central government aid
in attracting firms from outside the region to settle in West
Central Scotland, including higher capital grants, thus
increasing the regional development differential between the
Special Development Area status of the West of Scotland
(granted in 1971), and the other Development Areas. The
political pressure of the New Towns was then demonstrated very
clearly by the fact that they were also able to wring Special
Development Area status out of the Government in order to
protect their attractiveness against Glasgow, despite, firstly,
the relatively greater need to encourage industrial development
in Glasgow, and, secondly, the apparent success of the New
Towns in attracting new enterprises in the post-war period
without high levels of grant. The 1974 plan also stressed the
importance of offering attractive industrial sites and advance
factories to incoming and expanding firms.

Both the West Central and Clyde Valley plans made cases for
the decentralisation of central government offices to the
region as a means of improving local long-term employment
stability. Government accepted the arguments of the West
Central Scotland Plan team and agreed to decentralise at least
10,000 civil service jobs from London and the South-East to the
West of Scotland, although it rightly accepted that there was
likely to be powerful opposition to such proposals from the
civil servants involved and their unions. The West Central
Scotland Plan called for larger financial inducements to be
introduced to attract private sector office employment to the
region, and like its 1946 predecessor, stressed the importance
of improving the region's physical environment, estimating that
this would cost at least £675m by 1981. On the question of how
the proposals were to be financed, the Clyde Valley Regional
Plan was less convincing, but by 1975 it was being argued that
a substantial proportion of the funds would be channelled
through the proposed Scottish Development Agency, thus fuelling
allegations that the new body would in practice be a

Strathclyde Development Agency.

There are certainly many points of similarity between the two plans in their handling of the problems and potential of the region's industry, but the 1974 plan represented a definite advance in that it recognised that the basic economic problems are industrial rather than specifically regional, and that they should be tackled by policies and programmes that would enable a specific company focus. The 1946 Plan, while stating perceptive and relevant things about constraints facing enterprises in the Clyde Valley, still considered the solutions lay in the implementation of appropriate national macro-economic policies, which in restricted policy areas might be allowed to have a Scottish focus. Whilst such a view was acceptable in the then regional policy framework, this approach is now regarded as insufficiently direct to encounter and overcome the competitive market problems facing individual enterprises in a region. Postwar experience has clearly shown that broad policies are not likely to solve specific corporate-level problems, unless it is believed that the problems are identical in each sector, area or company - a patent nonsense. The West Central Scotland Plan, by taking policy down to the enterprise level, and more importantly to the problems and opportunities of local indigenous enterprises, marked a major step forward in regional policy, and by doing so, set a precedent that would eventually be followed by a succession of develpment agencies and enterprise boards throughout Britain.

Industrial Planning in the Clyde Valley in the 1980's

Much of the initial commitment to the industrial strategy of the West Central Scotland Plan fell away sharply in the late 1970's, although its central policy recommendation, SEDCOR, was brought into life in late 1975 as the Scottish Development Agency, and given a broad remit to tackle industrial and environmental problems in a co-ordinated and determined way that echoed the approach set out in the West Central Scotland Plan. The region did, however, receive its first comprehensive development plan covering the future evolution of its industry in the Strathclyde Structure Plan of 1978, which had elements of the 1946 and 1974 plans in it, but which was comparatively mechanistic and sterile compared to the vision of the earlier plans. The Structure Plan also had little to say about industrial development as it is generally understood, but it did at least set down a framework in which potential spatial conflicts of industrial location could be resolved.

It is still too early to evaluate the industrial impact of the recent planning innovations introduced after the West Central Scotland Plan, but it is clear that a number of important new policy trends have appeared, which individually and in combination have the potential to significantly improve the long-term industrial competitiveness and self-sufficiency of the West of Scotland economy. It is thus worth closing our post-war review with a brief discussion of these, as in many ways they represent a totally different approach to the Clyde Valley Regional Plan.

The first development is that policy and programmes have become firmly refocused on the City of Glasgow and the larger urban centres in the Clyde Valley. The first step towards this came with the Springburn Study of 1967, which questioned the Clyde Valley Plan's decentralisation thesis and urged that greater attention be paid to the employment needs of Glasgow. The West Central Scotland Plan was the principal cause of the refocus on the City of Glasgow, and was responsible for both the cancellation of Stonehouse New Town and the combined environmental - economic - social development approach that was initiated in the Glasgow Eastern Area Renewal (GEAR) project which was headed by the SDA. The renewed emphasis on urban areas has continued since then, and under such initiatives as the GEAR programme, a wide range of assistance and support has been offered to existing and potential enterprises in the inner city areas of the Clyde Valley. By the early 1980's the results of this were already visible, and, for example, the new small industrial premises provided by public and private-sector developers were being rapidly taken up - often by new local enterprises. Further, this new orientation towards urban economic development was additional to, rather than instead of, industrial programmes in the rural areas of the Valley and in the urban periphery where much of the new industrial investment between 1946 and 1975 had taken place. The support for urban manufacturing was also paralleled by a renewed emphasis on commercial and service sector projects in inner city areas, and Glasgow City in the early 1980's was the scene of a number of significant new developments, including a new national Exhibition Centre for Scotland.

The second significant trend was the swing back of industrial development priorities towards the indigenous enterprises of the Clyde Valley, and from 1975 onwards public sector bodies, led by the SDA, began a long-term programme which aimed at building up and strengthening the international competitiveness and efficiency of the local industrial base. The downturn in mobile industrial projects within Britain that followed the 1973-4 oil-based recession was only one of the factors that argued for a more self-reliant approach to economic and industrial growth for the region, but it was also increasingly realised that many of the older industrial companies in the Clyde Valley had a future provided their management could be assisted to adopt contemporary planning, production and marketing methods while resisting the temptation to sell control of their companies for either short-term profits or on the naive belief that a larger parent company universally brought sales and salvation. By the 1980's few people involved in industrial development in the Clyde Valley still believed that the area's economic problems could be solved by mobile industry, and the results of a long series of subsidiary and branch plant closures, led to a greater emphasis being placed on providing financial and management assistance and support to local enterprises especially in the small firm sector. The range of support schemes and development projects were many, and included new ideas such as enterprise zones and freeports; science parks and innovation funds; enterprise awards and venture capital schemes - all aimed at enhancing the development of local entrepreneurs and enterprise in the Clyde Valley.

The broad movement generally visible in the 1980's was the relatively rapid flowering of a large number of local economic development initiatives, whose variety and originality defied co-ordination by any regional plan. These local schemes really stemmed from a joint Scottish Office - SDA desire to soften the impact of the closure of the BSC steelworks at Glengarnock in Ayrshire, and the formation in 1978 of a special Task Force to provide an integrated package of industrial and environmental help for the area to ease its transition towards new sources of employment. A second Task Force was provided soon after for Clydebank to tackle the problems caused by the closure of the once-giant Singer sewing-machine works, and from these the SDA evolved (via projects in Leith and Dundee, both of which were outside the Clyde Valley) the integrated project approach to local area development. Each of these essentially involved the Agency, Regional and District Councils jointly agreeing to commit funds to implement fully-specified programmes for developing local industry and improving the environment. Each was based on a detailed analysis and evaluation of local needs and opportunities, and, more importantly, each was in some way unique. (Scottish Development Agency 1982, 55-63). All were time-limited and were to be completed by a fixed date, agreed before funds and resources were committed. By 1983, local initiatives were in existence in Glengarnock, Clydebank, Motherwell, Port Dundas, Coatbridge, Paisley, Kilmarnock and a number of other areas in the Valley, and others were in course of preparation. Such variety allowed experimentation, and ensured active local participation, especially from the private sector enterprises in each community. This movement towards self-help which identified local areas throughout the region was at odds with the Clyde Valley Regional Plan view of the world, but perhaps represented a first step back along the road towards local enterprises contributing much of the future growth for the region and its population, instead of the previously widely-held belief that such growth was the responsibility of central government.

THE INDUSTRIAL IMPACT OF THE CLYDE VALLEY PLAN

The principal conclusion that emerges from any consideration of the Clyde Valley Regional Plan and its impact of industrial development in the Clyde Valley is that the evolution on local enterprises and individuals has been largely unplanned, except perhaps in marginal ways of location. The major forces shaping both sectoral and spatial change had origins that have lain either outside the Clyde Valley, or in decisions and policies directed at other economic and industrial objectives. It cannot therefore be maintained that the Clyde Valley Regional Plan ushered in an era of co-ordinated planning for industry at the regional level, where resources were deployed in coherent programmes towards agreed policy objectives. Yet, the influence of the 1946 Plan has been there throughout the post-war period, and in its absence, it is unlikely that we would have seen either the Growth Areas experiment, the West Central Scotland Plan, or indeed the Scottish Development Agency, as the individuals and institutions responsible for these initiatives were all heavily influenced by the Clyde Valley Plan.

The increased, though far from satisfactory, understanding that now exists about the West of Scotland economy permits us to be fairly certain that the Plan has not greatly influenced the direction or rate of structural change in local industrial sectors, and has had no real impact upon the more important factors that determine the competitiveness of a region, such as industrial efficiency and technological innovation; yet to be fair to the members of the Clyde Valley Planning team, these were areas in which they and their successors openly admitted ignorance and earnestly requested advice (McCrone 1965, 135). It is also important to remember that industrial policy was never seen as forming the core of the Plan's strategy in the manner of the West Central Scotland Plan; the Plan was essentially designed to tackle the urgent need to rehouse 700,000 people in the Clydeside Conurbation, who were then living in overcrowded and depressingly substandard housing conditions. The industrial recommendations made by the team in 1946 were therefore seen as being complementary to the programme for rehousing the population and for decentralising them from the high densities of the central urban area. It is against this central fact that the achievements of the Plan must be judged.

The priority given to the need to improve the conditions of life for the residents of the Clyde Valley was perhaps responsible for the comparatively small input made by economists and industrial experts. Consequently the Industry chapter, while full of perceptive, intuitive insights into the problems and opportunities facing industry and commerce in the Valley in 1946, certainly has its problems. The view taken in 1946 of the region's industry is largely an inward-looking one, a definite weakness in a region heavily export-orientated in its basic industries. The condition, needs, and potential of industrial enterprises in the urban areas, above all in Glasgow, were never really understood, and thus the Plan advanced large-scale urban clearance and redevelopment schemes without appreciating their impact upon local urban economies, and especially on the myriad of small firms which in fact comprised the bulk of the Clyde Valley's enterprises as well as a substantial proportion of its employees. The orientation in the Plan towards large enterprises also created problems: the belief in the big technological fix that first appeared in the Plan persisted throughout the post-war period, and manifested itself in demands for steel plants (Ravenscraig and Hunterston); for car factories (Linwood); and for oil refineries and petrochemical complexes (Hunterston and Bishopton). Such campaigns have created jobs (in retrospect often depressingly temporary) for Clydeside, but they did so largely through political pressure at a national level and thus were often bought at a high social cost and also at the price of long-term economic efficiency. Finally, as we have seen, the failure of the Clyde Valley Plan to investigate the basic causes of industrial decline in the indigenous enterprises in the region (although this was admittedly difficult in the immediate post-war period) meant that the industrial policy priorities that emerged, namely a combination of strengthened national economic policy and an attempt to capture immigrant light industry, was one that in retrospect was not in the best long-term interests of the West of Scotland. The Plan team clearly recognised the dangers in adopting such a strategy, yet it nevertheless set a trend in regional policy that lasted until the 1970's. This is, perhaps, the most important single industrial legacy of the Plan (Firn 1981, 5-19).

Despite its faults and shortcomings, the Plan remains an influential document, even though the industrial chapter's recommendations remain largely unimplemented and indeed, unimplementable. The impact it had upon a whole generation of planners in Scotland and elsewhere will ensure that its particular approach to industrial development is never forgotten. The continued comparative failure to arrest the industrial decline of the West of Scotland, raises fundamental questions about the most effective means for positively influencing long-term industrial change at a regional level in an advanced industrial economy, and of the potential and relevance of an indicative regional plan such as The Clyde Valley Regional Plan. In a world dominated by multi-national companies and supra-national political groupings, and where national economic and political conditions are becoming increasingly subservient to international events the pursuit of effective regional economic and industrial development will remain a major challenge. The uncertainty facing the 1946 Plan team as they set out on their task, which seems daunting even in hindsight, will certainly be the main link with their successors in the future.

6 Transport Planning

MILLER ALLAN

Transport Planning in the 1930's

Nineteen hundred and forty-six was a particularly difficult year in which to plan transport facilities on a long term basis. Before examining the Clyde Valley Regional Plan's proposals it is important to recognise the context within which they were made. Prediction must involve uncertainty but existing trends can often be used with advantage. Unfortunately at that time both the type and the scale of the problem were about to change dramatically. Like many of their contemporaries the team preparing the Plan were to have difficulty in interpreting the signs, although their estimate of future traffic growth was remarkably accurate. They suggested a growth factor of 6 over the next twenty years - in contrast to the Ministry of Transport's own estimate of between 2 and 4 - but they failed to identify where the main impact would materialise. Previously, interest had centred on the problems of inter-urban transport and it was assumed that a radical approach to these same problems was now overdue. Any coincidental problems in towns and cities could readily be solved by the logical development of electrified tramways and railways. Just as in America, however, car ownership was about to increase at an unprecedented rate while the relative importance of goods vehicles would decline in numerical terms. Thus the issues which had dominated transport planning in the 1930's were soon to be overshadowed by those related to the motor car and especially where it was used for the daily journey to work.

One of the most striking features of the transport proposals in the Plan was the preoccupation with motorways. The operational benefits which would be derived from an extensive network of new roads were examined at length and the influence of contemporary ideas and events was obvious. The Special Roads Act was not to be passed until 1949 but such roads had been discussed in Britain for many years and indeed the first lengths of dual carriageway construction had already appeared. Overseas, events had moved more quickly. Italy had built her first autostrade in the 1920's and Germany had laid the foundations of her modern autobahn network in the following decade. These had impressed a British delegation in 1937:

> 'No less than 224 persons, including 57 members of
> both Houses of Parliament - a deputation "in size and
> representative character almost without parallel in
> the history of international relations" - visited
> Hitler's Reich ...' (Bagwell 1974, 275).

One of the most influential statements at that time had come from Sir Alker Tripp (1942). An Assistant Commissioner for Traffic at Scotland Yard, he was soon to advise Abercrombie in the preparation of his plans for London. In America architects and planners had already experimented with layouts which were intended to separate road traffic from people. Tripp had recognised the advantages of a hierarchic arrangement of roads and he distinguished between 'arterial', 'sub-arterial' and 'local' types with appropriate uses and standards for each. Like others he was attracted by the symmetry of idealised road networks and he favoured an arrangement of ring and radial roads for towns because it had fewest junctions. This was clearly an advantage in the days before flyover structures became commonplace. Official thinking was much influenced by Tripp's ideas and the Ministry of Transport incorporated them in the first advisory design manuals to be produced for British roads. Further development of these principles was to follow in the Buchanan Report Traffic in Towns (Ministry of Transport 1963) and in design manuals later.

In the presence of such influences it would have been surprising indeed if the Plan had not referred to the motorway concept but Abercrombie had a special incentive to include this. The Institution of Highway Engineers had proposed a plan in 1936 for almost 3,000 miles of motorways throughout Britain. Ten years later an official road programme was about to be announced but it was expected that the motorway content would be confined to England. The Clyde Valley planners considered that this was inconsistent with the status of a Development Area and were quite explicit.

'Official policy with regard to motorways in Scotland
is not clear, but it would appear that no motorways
are in contemplation north of the Border. Surely
this is a shortsighted national policy. Efforts are
being made to popularise this Development Area and
eliminate its sense of isolation. Furthermore,
Glasgow is one of Britain's main ports, the centre of
many vital and important industries and a commercial
city of the first importance. We do not understand
the official attitude' (para. 1009).

It was hoped that the balance could be redressed but this did
not happen. The Ministry announced plans in May 1946 which
confirmed the planners fears' -800 miles of motorway were
included, but only in England, and indeed this imbalance has
continued to the present time. The few inter-urban motorways
which have since been constructed in Scotland have failed to
match the rate-of-return criteria which prevail generally in
England where traffic volumes are understandably greater. Now
that the more intangible benefits of motorway investment such
as regional industrial development are regarded with some
scepticism the imbalance seems likely to be permanent.

Transport Planning in Glasgow During the Second World War

The transport recommendations in the Plan were intended to meet
the needs of the region but they were linked inevitably to
those of Glasgow itself. These had just received detailed
attention from the Master of Works and City Engineer, Robert
Bruce. His visionary First Planning Report (1945) proposed the
rebuilding of the entire city centre and the restructuring of
much of the remainder, including the development of new housing
estates at the edge of the city. This would require to be
complemented by a new transport system and in the manner of the
time he planned to build several radial motorways and two ring
roads. Glasgow is bisected by the River Clyde and in 1945 no
roads crossed the river on the western or downstream side of
the city centre. A new road bridge and a new road tunnel were
included in the plan. Bruce also realised the possibilities of
a refurbished rail system and he proposed an electrified rapid
transit network to serve the suburbs and beyond. The tracks
were to be located in the central strips of the dual
carriageway roads wherever possible, and in tunnels under the
city centre, but the detailed design was left for later, as
Abercrombie was to do also.

Bruce was critical of the impact of the old railway lines and
bridges on the appearance and functioning of the city core.
His civic design required that the four existing railway
termini be paired off and moved outwards. The line of his new

141

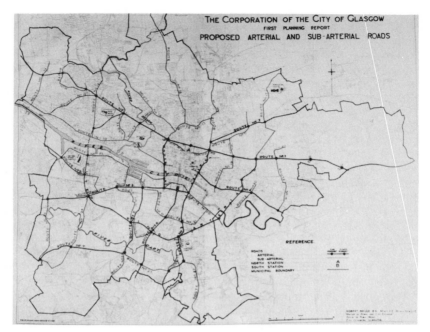

Figure 6.1 Highway Plan, City Engineer's First Planning Report, 1945

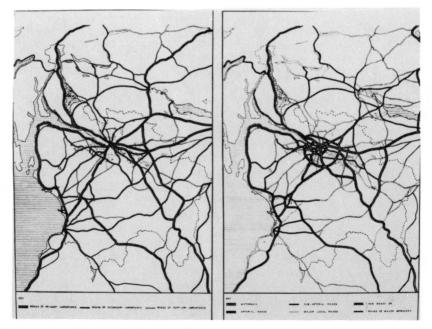

Figure 6.2 The existing regional road system of 1946 (L.) and the Plan's proposals (R.)

142

Inner Ring Road was chosen to serve these new locations, although the termini were also to be connected directly by a new underground rail link. This was to be an extension of the existing rail system on the south side of the river. Bruce was quite specific:

> '... it is clear that the railway system has never been properly related to the road system - to remedy this unsatisfactory estrangement of the two principal means of transport, the plan calls for alterations in railway lines and railway stations' (Bruce 1945, 15).

The stations were never relocated although two of them were demolished much later so it is instructive to note that transport planners did not subsequently question a continuing commitment to the original road line. The north and west flanks of the Inner Ring Road were completed in 1972, crossing the river via the Kingston Bridge, and plans for the remainder were still under active discussion in 1981. Ten years earlier the Clyde Tunnel had been opened further downstream on the alignment of Bruce's Outer Ring Road, but by 1981 it appeared that this was likely to be the only part of his original concept which would ever be built. Hindsight suggests that a single compromise located between the two ring roads could have been adopted profitably once the original justification for two had clearly been superseded.

Bruce's plans, and especially those for transport and for the inner core of the city, appear now to have been grandiose. This was a common failing of others at the time, of course. The whole of the city centre would have had to become one vast Comprehensive Development Area but that particular concept had yet to be accepted. But while land-use redevelopment would have presented many problems it is worth noting that the administrative framework necessary for the construction of the principal road system was already available although the capital expenditure would have been exceptionally high. For many years highway engineers had been planning and constructing road schemes in Britain whereas town planners had been confined to a more subservient role.

Transport Planning in the Plan

The chapter in the Plan on Transport and Communications was underpinned by one major philosophical theme, integration. Several distinct aspects of this were discussed but were not always fully or consistently develped. This was regrettable because the ideas, though not altogether novel, were certainly worth emphasising and might otherwise have been accepted sooner.

At the broadest level the integration of transport planning with other forms of planning at the regional scale was advocated. Unfortunately the relationship envisaged was somewhat one-sided and there was to be little scope for interaction. It was assumed that:

'... a comprehensive transport and communication plan will be prepared by the Ministry of Transport in association with the individual interests involved, and in the light of the Regional Plan' (para 928).

The transport system was expected to suit the requirements of the Plan and the idea of choosing a land-use strategy after an examination of its transport implications was missing. Of course this would have raised serious analytical problems at the time but when the necessary computer techniques did become available the possibilities of a cybernetic approach continued to be ignored. Transport planners were content to rely upon - and indeed they encouraged the production of - very dubious forecasts of land-use and socio-economic characteristics for their primary input. There was little or no attempt to modify the land-use predictions in the light of the transport infrastructure which appeared to be necessary.

It was also implied that regional transport requirements should be consistent with those of Glasgow itself. Here the consequences of interaction were seriously underestimated. The regional team was prepared to accept most of Bruce's transport recommendations and then graft the regional network onto them. For example, in discussing road-rail interchanges it was noted that:

'... we are not primarily concerned with the detailed replanning of the centre of the City of Glasgow' (para. 1135).

But neither plan could have been expected to predict the extent of the shift of emphasis from inter-urban to urban traffic problems which had yet to come, though Abercrombie and his team clearly had premonitions:

'... two serious disadvantages must be faced. First, a heavy increase in motor traffic in the centre of the City will create an almost insoluble parking and garaging problem, and second, a vast increase in road congestion is inevitable. It is impractical to suggest the planning of motorways from all points of the compass into Glasgow, and in the absence of complete segregation between pedestrians and motor traffic such an increase in congestion will have a corresponding effect on road accidents ... this problem in the near future will be one of the most difficult town planning problems to be dealt with in the City of Glasgow' (para. 1238).

The congestion of the regional network was to become quite insignificant compared with that which would occur within the main conurbation. In 1974 the West Central Scotland planners were to note:

'... with (a few) exceptions, only isolated sections of the inter-urban (highway) network require immediate improvement ... some schemes undertaken in the past were premature and had only an indirect effect towards solving the basic problems of the region' (West Central Scotland Plan 1974, 251).

It has been clear for many years that the regional road proposals in the Plan were unnecessarily lavish. Unfortunately the underlying philosophy in 1946 was to influence urban transport planners later as they struggled to cope with peak-hour congestion.

A third form of integration discussed in the Plan was the efficient allocation of traffic to the appropriate modes. Bruce had just stated his view unequivocally:

'The cardinal feature of the proposals is that it is regarded as sufficient if one means of speedy transport is provided for the residents of any particular area, that is, it is not part of the proposals to provide alternative means of making direct journeys' (Bruce 1945, 26).

The competition between bus and train which had occurred during the prewar years was deployed by the Plan but it rather missed the point to suggest that:

'... everything should be done to reduce the number of public service vehicles plying into the centre of the city ... (because they) are not eminently suited to meet peak traffic requirements' (para. 1239).

Glasgow corporation did cooperate by withdrawing services from areas beyond the city boundary but the bus and the tramcar were soon to contribute far less to congestion than the motor car.

Finally, arising from these considerations, an integration of the various agencies involved in planning and operating transport services was proposed. This was to be a Regional Transport Authority similar to the London Passenger Transport Board but with responsibility for freight as well. The 1947 Transport Act was imminent and the nationalisation which was anticipated was seen as a suitable stimulus for such a concept. It was a creditable suggestion and it deserved a better fate. The gulf which often exists between planning thought and political feasibility is underlined by the fact that more than twenty-five years were to pass before the introduction in 1972 of the Greater Glasgow Passenger Transport Authority with executive powers to coordinate transport services. Moreover, progress since then in reconciling competing interests has been absurdly slow.

Roads. Much the longest section of the chapter on Transport and Communications in the Plan, and the part which had the most prlonged influence, dealt with roads. These were considered from the national and regional standpoints. The physical deficiencies of the existing road system were catalogued with a level of detail which now seems wholly inappopriate in a document of this nature. There was a further flaw. Nowhere was there any discussion at all of the construction costs of the proposals nor any explicit attempt to evaluate the potential benefits of such expenditure. This would have surprised no one at the time, of course.

As we have seen, considerable emphasis was placed on a new motorway system expanding outwards from Bruce's city network to serve the new towns and the region generally. Techniques were not yet available, however, to convert the traffic volumes which had been predicted with remarkable accuracy into the corresponding road space which would be required for them. As a result, the design was too lavish. In all, three new ring roads were envisaged when two would have sufficed, repeating the mistake which Abercrombie had made in his City of London Plan a year earlier and with similar consequences. This must be seen as a significant influence on the scale of the highway plans which appeared in detail during the next twenty-five years.

A curious feature of such a comprehensive study of regional transport was the wholly negative approach to the question of road passenger transport. As has been seen, the Plan had advocated strongly that such services be reduced within the city. This is all the more surprising when it is remembered that Glasgow at that time operated one of the most extensive and commercially viable tramcar systems in Europe even if it was not the most comfortable! There was a widespread conviction, however, that buses were a primary cause of congestion in city centres and the planners were confident that electrified railways held the key to success. This had merits of course, but the limitations of such an approach were to continue to affect policy for many years and it was 1974 before it was concluded that:
> 'Within the public transport sector ... buses are of
> overwhelming importance compared with rail or
> underground... Looking at the 1960s there is little
> evidence of any coherent and dynamic policy aimed at
> stimulating patronage and the effectiveness of the
> bus network' (West Central Scotland Plan Team 1974c,
> 236, 243).

Railways. Glasgow had an extensive warren of undergound
railway lines in 1946 - 'fuming burrows' was the description
of Hamilton Ellis quoted in H.B. Morton's anthology A Hillhead
Album (1973). These had been driven with considerable
ingenuity through the sandstone and limestone beds on the north
side of the River Clyde. The two main lines passed below
Central and Queen Street Stations and there was a complementary
system on the south side of the river. This was also based on
two stations, Central and St. Enoch, but there were few
tunnels. There was also the Underground railway, a pocket-
sized version of the London system, electrified but limited to
a single circle line which linked fifteen stations in the
western half of the city. The Underground had been operated by
the Corporation Transport Department for more than half a
century with considerable financial success and it had given
excellent service to the citizens.

   The railways suffered from two main difficulties -
duplication of services and the shortcomings of steam
locomotion. In the early 1930s, a Royal Commission and other
studies had recommended extensive main-line electrification in
Britain but this had gone unheeded. The Clyde Valley Regional
Plan now recognised the advantages of such a course while
others still hesitated. It suggested significant changes such
as the interconnection of Central and St. Enoch Stations to
become in effect a single station and the closure of the other
two termini -all of this at odds with Bruce's proposals - but
it was unable to deal with the technical design which he left
to rail experts later.

Air and Water Transport. The Plan also dealt extensively with
air transport and with harbour facilities, and with the
movement of freight by rail in connection with the steel-making
industries of the region. In each case, however, technology
has advanced so dramatically that most of the reasoning has
been invalidated. Seaplane bases have no relevance today and
Prestwick Airport, though it was already flourishing in 1946,
the very year that London Heathrow became a civil airport, has
stagnated since then by international comparisons. In 1980
Heathrow handled sixty times as many passengers as Prestwick
and Glasgow's own Abbotsinch Airport handled some six times as
many. Ships have increased dramatically in size too and, as
will be seen later, this had had drastic repercussions for
harbour facilities on the River Clyde.

Impact of the Plan

The realisation of a significant proportion of the Plan's
proposals would have required finances on a scale beyond the
means of local government at the time. Even ten years later

147

the City of Glasgow was spending on new road construction an average of only £7,000 annually, a truly derisory figure in view of the mounting problems. So the Plan had little immediate impact but the stage had been set and the curtain would soon be lifted.

The first act belonged to British Railways with their new-found access to public funds. Sir Robert Inglis, an eminent railway engineer of wide international experience, was asked by the British Transport Commission for an appraisal of passenger transport provision in the Clyde Valley. Inglis duly report (British Transport Commission 1951), building on an earlier study by E.R.L. Fitzpayne (1948), the long-serving director of Glasgow Corporation's Transport Department. Extensive electrification of the suburban railway system was recommended on the grounds that such an improvement would attract passengers from the buses which were finding it difficult to maintain peak-hour schedules in the city because of traffic congestion. Inglis endorsed many of the arguments of Bruce and Abercrombie but his railway design details were quite different and he considered that three ring roads would be unlikely to be necessary. He rejected their various proposals for the four railway termini on operational grounds and he advocated the redevelopment of Central and Queen Street Stations and the abandonment of the others. These changes duly followed and his report initiated a process of regeneration of the local railway system which has continued to the present time. Indeed, even before construction began on the new highway network in the 1960's the conurbation was already served by an extensive new electric rail system on both sides of the River Clyde.

The second act was delayed because the road system required funds of a different order but again Glasgow took a lead over other cities in Britain. The scent of regional economic growth was in the air, to be led it was hoped by the provision of the appropriate infrastructure, and motorway construction was booming in Europe and America. When the city's Development Plan was reviewed (Corporation of City of Glasgow 1960) and intentions of building ring roads and radials were confirmed, a team of engineering and planning consultants, in collaboration with American advisers, was already preparing a detailed design for the Inner Ring Road. The line for this was largely that which had been suggested by Bruce and approved by Abercrombie. Twenty-nine Comprehensive Development Areas had been designated within the city by then and the new Road could be incorporated fairly easily with some of these. Central Government subsidies were now available for as much as 75% of the construction cost so it is hardly surprising that the city fathers were enthusiastic.

The Inner Ring Road Report (Scott & Wilson, Kirkpatrick & Partners 1962) was published one year before the Buchanan Report, and within ten years the north and west sections of the Road were completed, including the massive Kingston Bridge over the River Clyde. This cleared the water at a height which allowed the passage of shipping but by this time, paradoxically, the wharves upstream lay virtually unused as more and more ships sought deep-water facilities nearer the sea. In 1981 the construction of the remainder of the Ring Road was likely to be abandoned, the result of changing expectations of traffic growth and of the many other criticisms which have been made in recent years of urban motorway building. Yet this cannot detract from the enlightened terms of reference which the Corporation of Glasgow set out for their consultants as early as February 1960. The influence of Bruce and Abercrombie remained clear and it was hardly their fault that highway planners later were to suffer from what might be described as an excess of enthusiasm.

Throughout Britain, work on transportation studies gathered pace during the 1960's and Glasgow was no exception with the majority of its councillors confident of reaping future benefits. The Inner Ring Road Report was followed by the more extensive Highway Plan for Glasgow (Scott & Wilson, Kirkpatrick & Partners 1965); the first of five volumes of the Greater Glasgow Transportation Study appeared two years later (Scott, Wilson, Kirkpatrick & Partners 1967) commissioned by the Corporation on behalf of the local authorities who were represented on the Clyde Valley Planning Advisory Committee, the Public Transport operators, and the Scottish Development Department. Meanwhile, the influence of the Plan remained. The Clyde Tunnel was opened in 1963 on the alignment of Bruce's Outer Ring Road and work on the Inner Ring Road culminated in 1970 with the opening of the Kingston Bridge. An attempt was made, too, to fulfil the Plan's proposition for not merely increasing the traffic capacity of one of the city's main radial routes, Great Western Road, but for constructing a motorway there between some of Glasgow's finest architectural facades. This was one of the Plan's most bizarre recommendations when set beside its concern for the conservation of the region's inheritance of vernacular architecture. Great Western Road had been built by a Turnpike Trust set up in 1836, through the large estate of Kelvinside and it had been flanked later by terraces of mansions of exceptional architectural merit. A less suitable location for an urban motorway would be difficult to find. Fortunately, the eagerness of the highway engineers to avoid the 'disproportionate expenditure' which Bruce had claimed would be required for alternative lines, and to overcome the alternative 'constructional difficulties' foreseen by Abercrombie, was

Figure 6.3   Monkland Motorway, Port Dundas, Glasgow

Figure 6.4   Kingston Bridge,
Glasgow.   Completed After
Abandonment of Quays Upstream
By the Vessels for Which It
Allows Clearance

matched eventually by vociferous public opposition. A Public Inquiry in 1970 had only limited effect on the scale of the engineers intentions for Great Western Road but five years later the new Strathclyde Regional Council halted the scheme together with others inherited from the former local authorities.

It is hardly surprising that other changes from the intentions of the Plan took place. Land-uses which had been anticipated in 1946 simply did not materialise - there was no new steel-making plant at Erskine, for example, where a new dormitory town was built instead - and transport technology changed dramatically. Reference has already been made to air transport and to shipping. In the latter case the Plan had called for improved road and rail links in order to improve the efficiency of the extensive harbour facilities on the upper reaches of the River Clyde. Long before such improvements could take place, however, efficiency was to be achieved in a quite different way. There were three factors involved. First, the size of ships increased steadily to be followed by the containerisation concept. Dockside handling equipment was revolutionised and eventually new berths for container traffic were built at Greenock some twenty miles downstream from Glasgow. Other deep-water facilities were constructed on the Firth of Clyde far from Glasgow - for oil tankers at Finnart on Loch Long and for ore carriers at Hunterston. By 1981 only the granary trade retained a major port interest in the Upper Clyde at Meadowside although moves were afoot to introduce vegetable oil processing in connection with harbour facilities at Shieldhall.

The second factor was the change in the pattern of trade. Steady decline in coal exports was more than matched by a rise in petroleum imports though this has now declined with the development of North Sea Oil production using pipeline transport. Thirdly, the administration of the different harbours on the river was integrated, as Abercrombie and others had suggested, when the Clyde Port Authority was inaugurated in 1965. This facilitated the development of downstream harbours at the expense of Glasgow where almost all shipping activity withered with the parallel decline of the shipbuilding industry. It would be difficult to find a more apt illustration of the changing transport circumstances which are the subject of this chapter than the scene presented on the north bank of the River Clyde today. Not so long ago the docksides like those of the Queen's Dock were alive with activity and jammed with goods awaiting export, but they were hemmed in by congested cobblestone roadways which were crossed by uneven railway sidings at frequent intervals. Today, the Clydeside Expressway and two electrified railway lines curve

smoothly past miles of empty quays. Commuters, one to a car or
packed in trains, scarcely have time to notice. What would the
hauliers and warehousemen of the past have given for such
facilities?

The Changed Emphasis of Policy After 1968

The 1970's saw a considerable reversal in the earlier emphasis
on road construction. This took time, of course, and work
continued on a number of important parts of the highway
network. On the north bank of the river the Clydeside
Expressway was opened in 1973 between the Kingston Bridge and
the Clyde Tunnel. Regional roads received attention too. The
link between the conurbation and England, M74/A74, was
substantially upgraded though not to full motorway standard,
much to the frustration of its regular users. By the end of
the decade the Renfrew and Monkland Motorways (M8) were
complete so that it was at last possible to traverse the
conurbation from west to east, via the Inner Ring Road, without
leaving the motorway system.

But the days of massive road construction were numbered;
public transport was about to become a legitimate partner. The
Transport Act of 1968 was a significant watershed in the
history of transport provision in Britain. Central Government
funds became available to provide infrastructure for all public
transport services and to subsidise operating costs too. This
was a facility which had been available previously only to the
British Railways Board. Now Passenger Transport Authorities
and their Executive counterparts were to be set up in the main
conurbations, modelled on the London Transport Executive which
was soon to be responsible to the Greater London Council.
Glasgow's Passenger Transport Authority was authorised in 1972
but although it was a personification of Abercrombie's
'regional transport authority' his aim of integrated planning
was to remain elusive. In 1974, nearly thirty years after he
was writing it was still possible to note:
> 'Despite the level of competition between bus and
> rail to meet movement demands, there is little
> evidence of effective integration of the two
> networks, either operationally or in terms of service
> policy. Partly for this reason, very few trips use
> both bus and rail modes to exploit their different
> characteristics of flexibility and speed and there is
> little use of buses in providing feeder services to
> the rail network. Similarly lack of integration
> between car and rail travel means that station
> parking capacity is little developed and 'park and
> ride' trips quite few at present' (West Central
> Scotland Plan Team 1974, 247).

Perhaps too much was expected of the rail services at the outset. The unrelenting intervention of the motor car and an implacable bus industry struggling to retain its share of the market have together obscured the potential of the latter for providing flexible services with adequate commuter capacity for most circumstances.

After 1968 a simplified system of specific road construction grants remained in operation but this disappeared with local government reorganisation and the introduction of the Transport Policies and Programmes which were required thereafter from regions and counties each year. These were to form an important input to the new Structure Plan process and to justify the transport elements of the annual Rate Support Grant from the Exchequer to the local authorities. The allocation of capital and revenue funds for transport services was now to be decided locally.

These changes occurred in response to public concern at the projected cost both in financial and environmental terms of the flood of urban transport plans which began to appear before the end of the 1960's. Glasgow's experience was typical and the Public Inquiry in 1970 into the Great Western Road scheme was an early focus of these opinions. It was frequently claimed that it was unfair to spend large amounts of public funds on road construction and maintenance while city bus services deteriorated through lack of subsidy to meet the shortfall in fare revenue. There was merit in the argument particularly in Glasgow where a relatively low level of car ownership prevails, but it was overstated. Bus and goods vehicles require suitable roads as well as cars and indeed they create most of the maintenance requirements of the system. Also, if the cost of the first proposals of the Greater Glasgow Transportation Study (Scott, Wilson, Kirkpatrick & Partners 1968) appeared to be heavily biassed in favour of road construction this was considerably influenced by the fact that an extensive rail system already existed, much of it electrified. Furthermore, the Study Team were adamant that city-centre commuting by car should be discouraged by the restriction and appropriate pricing of public parking space.

But the Study's proposed road programme was excessive and subsequent refinements to the forecasts and the analyses have confirmed this, although critics who have suggested that no further road construction can be justified cannot be taken seriously. It is impossible to assess the extent of the Plan's influence in encouraging the over-ambitious road plans which appeared some twenty years later. The discussion of motorways concentrated on their use outside the city but the ideas must have carried over to the urban schemes later, though it must be

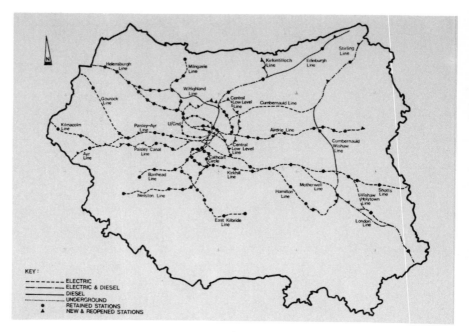

Figure 6.5 GGTS Volume V: 1978/85 Investment Programme –
Recommended Rail Network,1974

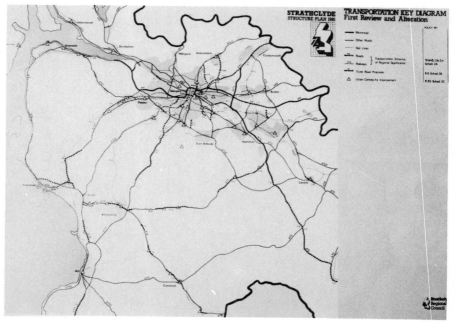

Figure 6.6 Strathclyde Structure Plan 1981, Transportation Key
Diagram

acknowledged that these were designed at a time when every conurbation was anxious to take full advantage of the Government funds which were available. It is only fair, too, to note that Abercrombie's regional transport plan was conceived with his crucial themes of population overspill and industrial regeneration in mind. His system would have served East Kilbride and Cumbernauld well whereas Glasgow's insistence on building peripheral housing estates was not anticipated. These were also poorly located in relation to the rail network, which made matters worse.

In the Clyde Valley as elsewhere in Britain capital and revenue expenditure on public transport infrastructure grew steadily during the 1970's. Though lacking the scale of Tyneside's Metro scheme two major projects were completed by the end of the decade, both in the centre of the conurbation. Utilising the former Central Low Level line (renamed the Argyle Line) the Clyderail scheme linked the British Railways networks on either side of the River Clyde. With eight new stations it provided a fast rail link into the heart of the region's busiest shopping and commercial centre. At the same time the city's Underground railway was completely refurbished with new track, new stations and new rolling stock. This was long overdue since it had scarcely changed during its eighty year life! As a result of these schemes the various public transport systems are at last quite well integrated. There are major interchanges at Govan, Partick, Central Station and Queen Street Station and many stations have park-and-ride facilities. Once more the ideas can be traced back: Abercrombie had included interchanges at Partick and at Central Station.

Meanwhile firm road plans were shrinking quickly. The Greater Glasgow Transportation Study continued until the new Regional Council assumed responsibility in 1975 for strategic planning. Thereafter, successive Transport Policies and Programmes have recorded the latest statistics of population and car ownership, the constraints of the Government's 'cash limits', changing views of the environmental and social costs of urban motorway construction and the inequity of disproportionate expenditure on new roads compared with the level of fare subsidies on public transport. These were all matters which had been pertinent for many years but which had nonetheless been disregarded hitherto. By the time that Strathclyde Region's first Structure Plan was presented for Examination in Public in 1979 few routes were considered to be sufficiently important to merit firm reservation any longer. The Secretary of State produced his Final Decision Letter in January 1981 and reflecting current attitudes he deleted some of these routes as well. The most important proposal was the completion of the Inner Ring Road with the south and east flanks but here he suggested that the Regional Council should reconsider and in particular that they should 'assess the feasibility of identifying an alternative solution with less damaging environmental effects'. By 1983, some reduction of the intended scale of the East Flank of the Ring Road had occurred, but the Regional Council had abandoned the prospect of crossing the Clyde to complete the South Flank.

The Balance of Influence of the Plan

The acid test of any plan is to assess in retrospect the extent of its influence. One of the benefits of such an examination is the insight which it should afford of the planning system which supported and developed it. In relation to its transport proposals the influence of the Plan does suggest a number of lessons. The most universal of these concerns the subsequent neglect or misinterpretation of earlier assumptions and reasoning.

For example, Abercrombie's transport proposals were consistent with his ideas for population overspill and industrial regeneration linked with new town development. This was one of the main reasons for including a wide Outer Ring Road which would pass though East Kilbride, where the main route from the south and England would reach the conurbation. When Glasgow insisted that rehousing problems could be solved within the city boundary the premise changed yet the wide ring concept remained and indeed when the detailed design appeared some twenty years later the ring was even wider. The river crossing at Erskine, for example, which was one of the few elements of the Outer Ring Road to be built, was located some five miles downstream from where Abercrombie had intended. Bruce's public transport plans were ignored too, so that when people were moved out to the new peripheral housing estates they found communications to be exceedingly difficult. Local employment, shopping and recreational facilities were all slow to appear and residents were faced with long and expensive journeys to their former haunts.

The relationship between Bruce's proposed South Station and the Inner Ring Road provides a second example. When the first was rejected the location of the second could have been reconsidered but the opportunity was overlooked with lasting repercussions. A related issue here concerns the failure of the early planners to recognise the need for adequate parking space beside railway termini within the city centre. This may have been excusable when car ownership was insignificant but later it became abundantly clear that parking provision would be necessary if trains were to compete successfully in the lucrative inter-city transport market. This should have provided a much more compelling reason for relocating or redeveloping some of the termini than the arguments used by Bruce and Abercrombie, yet it seems to have been ignored completely.

There was also some over-emphasis of rural motorways in the Plan though this was hardly damaging in itself because later costs were to inhibit premature construction anyway. Only when congestion forced the issue were schemes pushed forward. But the exaggerated scale of the rural proposals may not have been questioned rigorously enough when transport planners were faced with escalating traffic problems in the city itself. Engineers later, when discussing the effect of former road line reservations in relation to their own computerised traffic analysis, pointed out that:

> 'While it would be misleading to say that the traffic analysis did not affect the outline of the highway plan, its major influence was to determine the capacity required from the individual road lines' (Hodgen & Cullen 1968, 230).

Reference has already been made to public criticism of excessive expenditure on road construction in Britain compared with financial support for ailing public transport services. In the Clyde Valley there is little doubt that the Plan must share some of the blame for this, though it need not have been misinterpreted to the extent that it was. In any case, the criticisms have been exaggerated, which few should find surprising. Certainly, parts of Strathclyde Region are characterised by some of the lowest car ownership levels in the country while public transport fares are among the highest. A balanced assessment, however, must also recognise two things. First, the existing public transport infrastructure in the region in the 1940's was more highly developed than in most other areas of the country so that only modest expenditure was required to convert it to the effective system of today. It was inevitable, therefore, that capital expenditure on road construction should appear to be inequitably high in comparison. Secondly, it is also true that there has been nothing to prevent public transport fare subsidies from being higher. Local government has to meet competing demands from other service sectors and it is quite misleading to suggest that more road construction necessarily implies higher fares for those who must use buses and trains. The trade-offs need not be confined to each sector internally. It is perhaps also worth noting that financial appraisal within other service sectors is usually considerably less rigorous than in the transport sector.

The record of the Regional Council since its inception,

Figure 6.7   Erskine Bridge, Lower Clyde

Figure 6.8   'Blue Train' leaving Bellgrove Station, Glasgow,
Transclyde Rail

however, stands comparison with most in the country. The proportion of their capital expenditure on transport which has been allocated to road construction in recent years has been similar to the average for Britain as a whole, ranging between 60% and 70%, when the Scottish average has been consistently higher at around 75%. At the same time, direct subsidy (including Concessionary Fares support) to public transport services has risen steadily from 35% to 50% of revenue expenditure, with much of the remainder meeting road maintenance and operational costs, both of which are partly attributable to public transport operation. The corresponding proportions for Britain and Scotland during the same period have averaged only 30% and 25% respectively. Some criticism may be made, however, of the relative proportions of the public transport subsidy which have been allocated to bus and rail services in the Region. In recent years, under agreements sanctioned by Section 20 of the Transport Act of 1968, British Railways have received consistently greater subsidies than all other public transport services taken together. Since the former continue to carry considerably more passengers each year, this imbalanced policy must now be questionable.

7 Agriculture and Land Allocation

FRED HAY

Agriculture and the Plan

A continuing issue in postwar planning literature has been the need to strike and to maintain a satisfactory balance between urban and agricultural (or frequently rural) land use. Urban growth has been regarded as necessary and inevitable, but its containment was nevertheless seen as crucial. In other words there was a need to "economise" in the amount of land to be transferred from agricultural to urban use. Planning techniques were thus required to ensure that the scale of the nominally irreversible process of urbanisation was controlled. The fundamental question is whether techniques can be developed which entail rational assessment of each and every instance of potential transfer, or whether it is necessary to fall back on what are more or less arbitrary conventions or formulae. This chapter examines the Clyde Valley Regional Plan's treatment of agriculture from this perspective and with two objectives: first, to provide a clear picture of the allocative techniques in the Plan; second, to assess the extent to which there have been any significant departures from these techniques in subsequent Scottish planning.

What with the exigencies of wartime and the shortage of data on the social and economic features of the region, what was described by its authors as no more than "an outline plan for the development of the Clyde Valley Region" (para. 1) could possibly not be expected to contain detailed blueprints for

160

each individual sector of the economy of the region. Certainly there were no specific proposals for development of the region's agriculture; had there been any, this assessment of the impact of the Plan would have been rather more straightforward. But the Plan nevertheless had far-reaching implications for agriculture: it proposed residential and industrial developments entailing substantial encroachments onto agricultural land. Thus it is legitimate to focus attention on how the Plan resolved the problem of achieving the "correct" allocation of land between these competing uses, in particular without making specific development proposals for agriculture. In so doing some fundamental issues of planned resource allocation are raised.

The Plan's chapter on agriculture was specially contributed by the Chief Land Officer of the Department of Agriculture for Scotland, at the time, T.B. Manson, and was thus unique in not being written by a member of the Clyde Valley Regional Planning Staff. The larger part of it comprised a descriptive account of agriculture in the Clyde Valley, dealing with aspects such as the climate and soils which underpin the agricultural industry. The remainder examined the agricultural implications of the spatial growth of urban land uses proposed in the larger part of the Plan. Additional references were made to agriculture elsewhere in the Plan, some surprisingly radical to have attracted no comment from Manson.

There was certainly no lack of awareness in the Plan of the inevitable competition between agriculture and other uses for the limited available supplies of suitable land:
> 'It is one of the tragedies of the Clyde Valley Region that so much of the very limited area of first-class agricultural land in the region has already been taken up for building and that still further encroachments are inevitable' (para. 66).

The topography and climate of the Clyde Valley Region are rarely sufficient to prohibit agriculture. Virtually all land not built upon is in one or another agricultural use, given typical market conditions and productivities. More land for other uses inevitably means less land for agriculture. Moreover, there is an equally inevitable differential impact according to land "quality": for largely economic reasons the best agricultural land is also the best for other uses - level and well-drained - is at relatively low altitudes, and in close proximity to existing urban centres.

However, identifying this essential feature of land allocation is not the same thing as solving the problems which arise from it. From the land use perspective the main problem for the Plan to solve was the conflict of interests with respect to urban encroachment on agricultural land. If the Plan was to resolve the conflict openly then clearly-stated criteria for resource allocation were required. Manson included in his chapter a set of 'First Principles' for the guidance of the Plan team. In descending order of importance, the Principles suggested minimum interference with A and A+ land, serious consideration before a dairy farm was sacrificed, no truncation of farms, no strip development, avoidance of flat land for building, saving of topsoil and general rehabilitation of derelict land. But Manson's Principles were not transformed by the Plan into specific criteria. Instead the problem was occluded: no more land should be transferred out of agriculture than was "necessary", begging the question as to the basis of the necessity - although with careful choice of words this could seem like an argument of much greater substance:

'It should be only in respect of those developments of the highest importance from the regional and national points of view that this agricultural land should be diminished' (para. 68).

In essence this reduces to no more than the unexceptionable assertion that social as well as private considerations are relevant in determining the allocation of land among competing uses. If they were not it might be difficult to justify planning at all. But how are such considerations to be given expression?

The orthodox rational technique is cost-benefit analysis, the careful evaluation of the anticipated costs and benefits of the proposed change, initially in private terms but modified to incorporate social priorities and values. To arrive at the solution in this context entails answering a central question: how much food shall we give up to get how many more homes and jobs? Agricultural land produces food; urban land accommodates homes and jobs. More homes and jobs mean less food production - a trade-off exists, notwithstanding any subsequent subtleties of argument. The challenge confronting the regional planners was to demonstrate the social necessity of a particular boundary between these uses, with its implied particular mix of the complementary outputs from the land resource. But to answer this question meant first of all establishing how much food needed to be given up - that is, ascertaining the capabilities of the region's agricultural industry. This was not done, even although the cost-benefit approach was hinted at in the agricultural chapter. No agricultural target was set out in the Plan, and virtually no attention was paid to the possibility of a trade-off between the outputs of the competing land uses. But an urban output target was developed, in terms of homes and jobs. Consequently the Plan stands accused of adopting a one-sided approach to the problem of land

162

allocation, rather than seeking the most appropriate balance between competing uses in terms of the contribution which each use could make to the economic and social well-being of the region. On the one hand, although Manson discussed the need for agricultural output and even tried to measure the output loss consequent upon the planned urban extension, he did not go so far as to propose the necessary output target for the region's agricultural industry. On the other hand the members of the planning team discussed urban land requirements in virtual isolation from the needs of agriculture, and made no reference to Manson's calculations.

Manson wrote that:
    'It is believed that there is an unanswerable case
    for the expansion of agriculture for economic, social
    and health reasons ...' (para. 1278).
He then proceeded to consider the need for improved availability of cheap food in a national rather than a regional context. No consideration was given to the present or future food requirements of the region, nor to the proportion of these requirements which could best be contributed by the region's agriculture, as opposed to being brought from elsewhere. Of course the technical capacity to do such calculations was not immediately available; but given that this was a plan, it should have pointed towards the areas in which some technical capability was required.

Manson argued that the proposed urban expansion into farmland would have a "demonstrably serious" effect on the agricultural production of the region, and made an attempt to quantify this, in terms of a reduction in the output of the dairying industry, the most important individual agricultural enterprise of the Clyde Valley region. An accurate estimate was not possible because the region was not coterminous with the county boundaries used for statistical analysis; nevertheless, Manson suggested that the region would lose perhaps as much as two per cent of local milk production. The estimation procedure could be found wanting on several scores, particularly in respect of its neglect of the effect of possible changes in markets, costs, prices and technology. But the more serious criticism is that elsewhere in the Plan there was no discussion of the estimated loss, imperfect thought it may have been, and no explicit indication that specific locations for urban developments were selected to minimise the effect on agricultural output.

Manson described the region's agriculture in 1944 as being dominated by dairying based on pasture, with cropping for stock feed and cash entering the farm economy where the best land permitted; as altitude increased towards the moorland stock rearing increased, in particular sheep rearing. Specialist cropping of fruit and vegetables both on a field basis and under glass were sufficiently significant - particularly east of Glasow in the middle valley of the Clyde - to merit special mention. In general, however, Manson felt that the region was badly furnished with the means of producing fresh fruit and vegetables for the conurbation, and that there was therefore considerable potential for expansion of market gardening; such a sentiment had obvious implications for retention of the best land in agricultural uses.

The structure of agriculture in the Clyde Valley has, of course, changed considerably since Manson's account. The region's tilled area is less than half what it was then, both in absolute extent and as a share of the total tilled area of Scotland. Within the tilled area the greatest reductions have been precisely in respect of some of the crops for which Manson saw considerable potential: vegetables and fruit. With due regard for the problems of statistical comparison the region's contribution to the Scottish acreage of fruit and vegetables has possibly fallen to a quarter of what it was in 1944. (This will not be true of course for each individual fruit and vegetable type). Conversely, increasingly efficient utilisation of grassland, together with greater dependence on imported feedstuffs has led to a virtual 50 per cent increase in the total numbers of both cattle and sheep, sufficient indeed to increase the region's share of the national sheep flock, though not so in the case of cattle. However, the livestock position is rather more complex than this simple comparison implies, particularly in the case of cattle. The region's dairy breeding herd has in fact shrunk by 20 per cent, but its beef breeding herd has increased almost eight-fold; nevertheless, the former is still two and a half times larger than the latter. Relative to the rest of Scotland, these changes have increased the region's share of the dairy breeding herd to a third since elsewhere the decline has been greater, while its share of the beef breeding herd has increased five-fold though to no more than 10 per cent over the period, in contrast to a more than four-fold increase in Scotland as a whole. Therefore, although it is even more true today that the region's agricultural economy is livestock-based, the implication of these changes within this sector is that the shift away from dairying (which, though less marked here than elsewhere, has still reduced the region's share of milk output in the Scottish Milk Marketing Board area by three per cent compared with 1944) has not been accompanied by the marked increase in beef fattening which has occurred in the rest of Scotland.

Some of these changes appear to be consistent with the

hypothesis that the more intensive (e.g. cropping) uses of farmland have been squeezed out by the transfer of the best land out of agriculture, though the ready availability of supplies of fruit and vegetables from the south, the rising cost of energy, and the relative return from milk and beef will have exerted a significant influence in the same direction. If it is indeed the case that urban encroachment has been the main factor, then a higher social valuation placed by the Plan on the maintenance of agricultural capability either from a purely regional or a national standpoint, should necessarily have constrained the proposals for urban expansion to a significant extent.

With no forward-looking assessment of agriculture's capabilities and no advocacy of a particular contribution in terms of food production, there was no sense in which the particular extent of urban encroachment entailed by the Plan could be described as a rational compromise, in terms of a trade-off between the outputs of the competing land uses. Various reasons could be put forward for the absence of the cost-benefit approach, such as the dependence of agricultural development on national rather than regional policy; after all, a new national regime of support for the agricultural industry was about to be established. It could also have been the presumption that the social value to be attached to more homes and jobs could not conceivably be outweighed by the loss of any amount of the region's agricultural output. Whatever the explanation, it is clear that in place of the cost-benefit technique the Plan chose to depend on more or less conventional mechanisms to determine the boundary between urban and agricultural land uses - mechanisms which, from the standpoint of resource allocation, can arguably be described as arbitrary.

Establishing the Boundary between
Agricultural and Urban Land Uses

Two mechanisms were employed in the Plan to contain urban expansion and to limit agricultural losses to those which were "necessary": the "avoidance of high quality land" mechanism, and the Green Belt mechanism.

The primary recommendation of the agricultural chapter was to minimise interference with agricultural land of high fertility - specifically land of grades A and A+ in the Department of Agriculture classification scheme. (By "fertility" was thus meant a composite index of geological, topographical and man-made features; in keeping with other classification schemes this essentially stresses soil quality, rather than current or historical productivity). However, there was no reference to this grading scheme in other than the agricultural chapter of the Plan, or to the need to avoid land of these particular qualities, or explicit evidence that the mechanism had operated in relation to any of the proposed urban developments.

Land fertility is an unsatisfactory basis for an allocative mechanism. First, fertility is not synonymous with usefulness - or more specifically the potential private and social value of the land in a particular agricultural use. This is partly because it is not an immutable physical characteristic of a piece of land, but is to an extent the resultant of particular patterns of use. Of course "natural" or other physical influences do condition land values, but they are not the sole determinants. "Inherent fertility" is a potential to be realised through hard work and is only one of the factors expressed ultimately in the profitability of control of the natural environment implicit in agricultural production. The other factors such as costs and prices, willingness to invest and relationships such as available technology and location also play their part. There are two corollaries. Present fertility is a poor intimation of its potential value; fertility can change, though slowly, while the present way the capacity of the land is exploited only gives expression to current expectations of economic conditions of the relatively near future. The second corollary is that to place a dividing line between particular types of fertility is a wholly arbitrary device, inadequate as a basis for distinguishing between that land which can be given up and that which should be retained in agriculture. One basic danger is that the line may be drawn ridiculously close to the "best" end of the spectrum so as to constitute no hindrance to urban expansion; the opposite may also be a possibility. And what happens when the poor quality land has all been transferred to urban use? Is the remainder, the "best" land, inviolable? That is clearly another matter to which reference will be made later.

Second, an allocative mechanism based on land fertility is of doubtful practicality given the typical disposition of land of the various grades of fertility. On the one hand, if a town is virtually encircled by land of a uniformly high grade of fertility then strict application of this mechanism precludes urban expansion; on the other hand, if fertility of the surrounding land varies considerably from locality to locality then the mechanism implies piecemeal transfer to urban use, which is probably unsatisfactory from both the developers' and the farmers' point of view. Taking these factors together it would appear that rigorous operation of this mechanism would be impracticable and not in the interests of efficient use of scarce resources.

The alternative mechanism to limit non-agricultural

166

development set out at length in the other parts of the <u>Plan</u> was the Green Belt. Not an innovation in principle - the <u>Plan's</u> consultant, Patrick Abercrombie, had of course been a principal architect of London's Green Belt - the conception for the Clyde Valley was distinctive in that it was

'... essentially one of agricultural preservation' (para. 66).

This conception was endorsed in the agricultural chapter:

'The general thesis ... that Glasgow and the neighbouring towns should have a green belt which should be reserved from urban exploitation is sound' (para. 1296).

Significantly, this general thesis appeared in Chapter 3 of the <u>Plan</u>, 'Open Space and Recreation'. But, as noted already, the <u>Plan</u> contained proposals for several large new urban developments on land which was then in agricultural use. In short, the extent of productive agricultural land in the proposed Green Belt was essentially a residual after the satisfaction of urban development requirements; seeking to preserve what is left is not the same thing as passing a balanced judgement as to the amount which should be left.

The Green Belt mechanism is essentially zoning for broadly-defined purposes. On the surface this has greater potential than determining land use on the basis of fertility. Reserving areas for particular categories of uses at least implies some reduction in uncertainty about the future, the avoidance of piecemeal development, and the satisfaction of both farmers and developers, notwithstanding the implied constraints on the operation of the land market. Conflict with efficient use of land is not excluded, however, and much depends on how the dividing or limiting lines are drawn. So the issue of criteria is not resolved by Green Belt zoning: it is only a mechanism by which criteria, whether arbitrary or purposeful, are put into effect.

Can farmers legitimately be given assurances that their agricultural pursuits are inviolable once they are within a Green Belt, or are located on the "best" agricultural land? The long planning periods which are necessary in agriculture to ensure an adequate return to investment in equipment and improvement have to be borne in mind. To give a watertight guarantee that agriculture will not be disturbed throughout the duration of such periods implies that the prospect of more land being required for future urban expansion can be ignored, and that future generations will remain bound by past zoning decisions. This would seem to be an impracticable assurance to give, partly because future urban growth within a region may prove to be inevitable, and partly because it is not politically expedient to commit future planners to a particular course of action.

Yet the Regional Planning Staff simply proposed that:
'... the hinterland of the great Clydeside conurbation, after the long-term housing needs are met, should be _permanently_ safeguarded for agriculture up to the moorland edge' (para. 572, underlining added).

The _Plan_ took the optimistic view that the possibility of subsequent pressure for further urban expansion could be entirely discounted, on the grounds that in the contemporary context the proposed urban developments reflected the saturation level of population in the region:
'We recommend that ... [the Green Belt's] use be primarily of an agricultural character; that no other use be allowed after the long-term housing and industrial needs, proposed by us, are met;...' (para. 577).

It is significant that, notwithstanding these long-term proposals, Manson emphasised the necessity of taking steps to improve the confidence of farmers on the urban fringe or within the envisaged Green Belt. In this respect he expressed a principal post-war concern of the agricultural community:
'... if some means can be devised to give security of tenure there should be confidence to proceed with long-term plans to increase the efficiency of the [agricultural] units' (para. 1296).
'It is essential to the dairy farmer that he can be reasonably certain of the future ... Too often, dilapidated equipment is found in the vicinity of towns because no-one is prepared to furnish the necessary capital' (para. 1297).

In other words, from the agricultural point of view, the attractiveness of the proposed Green Belt was associated with the assurance which could be conferred on farmers within it that they would not subsequently be disturbed. But Manson gave no consideration to particular means whereby he felt that this assurance could be provided. The only specific proposal was made elsewhere in the _Plan_:
'... it is plain that progressive agriculture is an impossibility until security of tenure to the farmer is assured... [It] is clear that what is badly needed is public ownership with a policy devoted to planned intensification of agricultural production' (para. 572).
'We... recommend that the whole of the Green Belt land should be acquired by public funds; that its ownership be vested either in the State or in the

Regional Authority...' (para. 577).
In fact, the agricultural implications of the recommended public ownership of farmland comprising the Green Belt was not discussed at all in the Plan, even although nationalisation of land (particularly agricultural land) was a live issue in planning circles at the time. Surprisingly, Manson did not mention public ownership of farmland in the section of his chapter entitled "Agricultural Observations on Proposed Plans". It is possible that he evaded it to avoid involving the Department of Agriculture in a political issue about which the farming lobby had strong views, or indeed because he was not aware of the presence of this controversial recommendation in the Plan at the time of writing his chapter; he was not, after all, a member of the Planning Team. But possibly it was because he had reservations about the relationship between public ownership and security of tenure. Certainly to make all farmers in the Clyde Valley (apart from those beyond the "moorland edge") tenants of the State in order to solve the problem of uncertainty confronting the farmer, confuses uncertainty due to the type of decision-maker with uncertainty due to the prospect of future decisions being made. It seems immaterial whether the farmer is the tenant of a private land-owner, or the tenant of a Government agency, or indeed an owner-occupier himself, if he is confronted with the uncertain possibility of future disturbance of production due to a land use change over which he has no control. Thus the total exclusion of future urban incursions, with all that is implied about the capacity of planners to anticipate land requirements for generations ahead, and the willingness of politicians to abide by past decisions, is an indispensable feature of the Green Belt as an agricultural reserve.

As far as the Green Belt proposal itself was concerned, both Manson and the Planning Team were agreed as to its potential usefulness. But this agreement may have been due to their different viewpoints, rather than a common assessment of the situation. As Robert Grieve said eight years later, "It may mean different things to different people..." (Grieve 1954, 21). The urban planners' justification of the Green Belt concept was its capacity to contain peripheral urban development, as well as its aesthetic and recreational potential, while the agriculturalist saw its attraction as the inviolable status which it could potentially accord agriculture. Both viewpoints are in themselves entirely valid, but neither pertain to the central problem of determining the wisest allocation of land between competing uses, that is, the most appropriate extent of the Green Belt.

Looking in greater detail at the "long term housing and industrial needs" for land as determined by the writers of the

Plan, there is little evidence as to just how the particular allocation of the available land between agricultural and non-agricultural uses was to be established. Estimated overall acreage requirements were provided for only four out of the seven new urban developments proposed, and no indication was given of their qualitative composition in terms of grades of agricultural land. Nor was there discussion of the problems of avoiding or minimising the transfer of the highest quality land. This may well have been regarded as a matter for detailed planning, rather than for the Plan itself. This applied even where the impact was to have been the greatest: the combined effect of development of Houston and Bishopton, together with the projected Clyde Estuary integrated steel plant at Erskine, would have created a nearly continuous urban development from Houston to the Clyde. Virtually all of this land was of very high agricultural quality, but specific technical considerations left little room for manoeuvre:

'... suitable land for industry between the river Clyde and Bishopton ... comprises some of Scotland's finest agricultural land, and we are not prepared to see this sacrificed, unless for some exceptional project, such as this steel unit, for which no comparable site is available' (para. 320).

Of course, the difficulty is that technical considerations can be and are overtaken by advances in the technology on which they ultimately rest; for example, access to deep water is relative to the size of ship and growth in tonnages of vessels subsequently led to Hunterston replacing Erskine as the site with incomparable potential for a new steel unit. Yet it raises the wider issue of the extent to which it is the function of the planners to temper contemporary expediency with an unprejudiced awareness of the dynamics of the actual situation - which necessarily falls short of the ability to foretell the future.

Considerable emphasis was given to the need to avoid the truncation of farms, either through taking away economically vital parts of units, or the impairment of several units by the bete-noir of planners, linear development. Manson advocated the transfer of entire units, rather than partial changes affecting a large number of farms. The wisdom of this suggestion can be appreciated, though the argument could have been extended to include avoidance of undesirable encirclement and isolation of entire farms by urban development. This was particularly relevant given the nature of the urban development proposals in the Plan: development of new towns as opposed to the extension of existing urban areas runs the risk of isolating farms in corridors between old and new settlements. Some attention was paid to issues of this nature; for example, in the summary of recommendations the statement was made that it was, "...essential to prevent wasteful cutting up of farmland and units by straggling urban extension" (para. 1888). But the plans for the proposed new towns could not be sufficiently detailed at that stage to indicate if this awareness had borne fruit in terms of steps being taken to avoid the problem.

One notorious truncator of agricultural holdings appears to have been ignored altogether, namely developments in communications. The Plan proposed substantial modifications in the pattern of communications in Central Scotland, some of which impinged on the agricultural community. But the Plan did not provide estimates of land required for this purpose, nor was there any discussion of how particular proposals were designed to avoid high quality land, or at least to minimise their impact on the agricultural economy. This issue was not mentioned at all in the agricultural chapter.

A further factor not dealt with at any length is the impact on agriculture of sheer proximity of urban development. On the immediate boundary between farmland and the urban area the phenomenon of "peri-urban erosion" of land quality is in evidence. This has been defined as,
    '... trespass by people and animals, destruction of
    hedges and fences and the possibility that the
    suburban population will regard the farmland as a ...
    convenient method of disposing of unwanted
    perambulators, bicycles and indestructible plastic
    containers and bottles, ...' (Ormiston 1973, 83).

This is, of course, a serious matter in the context of a livestock-based agricultural economy. Limited consideration was given to this issue in the agricultural chapter, but the view was expressed elsewhere in the Plan that this was not a serious problem:
    '...it has been stated that such impairment as exists
    from trespass is of a negligible character, ...'
    (para. 562).
On the basis of current observation this would now be an unwarrantedly optimistic view of a discomfort additional to the normal uncertainties of farming on the urban fringe; clearly it has been made worse since the 1940s through increased mobility, changes in packaging and similar developments (OECD 1979). No mention whatsoever was made of impairment to farming of its industrial counterpart, pollution, although dust and smoke were recognised as a detriment to urban development (para. 905). Again this is evidence of a static approach to long-term planning.

171

One of the few positive recommendations for the agricultural sector was the nucleation of agricultural labourers' residences, into villages. For Manson this was a necessary response to the poor standard of amenity offered by the then-existing accommodation, and independent of more radical contemporary opinions in favour of the "collectivization" of agriculture:

'As the first necessary step in the reconstruction of the countryside the State will have to take over the ownership of the agricultural land... One must however go further ... A more drastic reform is needed ... the State purchase of land must be followed by its division into suitable [i.e. large scale] economic holdings ...' (Hall 1942, 25).

Manson was aware of these views but did not subscribe to them himself (Manson 1945, 124). But the anticipated advantages of nucleation - enabling the provision of much-needed social and cultural facilities - implied a considerable agricultural population. The post-Plan and post-war level of employment in agriculture was expected to be much the same as pre-war in 1938, though Manson accepted that this was "conjectural". As it turned out, employment in agriculture declined rapidly, and currently is less than one third of the immediate post-Plan level.

Yet, the practicality of the rural housing recommendation rested entirely on the level of employment. Fortunately for the majority of researchers, the failure to predict accurately the future level of employment of a resource is not in itself a fault. But the failure cannot be easily dismissed if virtually no attention has been paid to the dynamics of the industry concerned, particularly possible trends in technology and investment, on which the level of employment ultimately depends. An omission of this nature is further evidence that the Plan took an excessively short-run view of the industry, a view fundamentally inconsistent with the needs of regional planning in general, and the reorganisation of rural housing in particular.

In the immediately preceding paragraphs a number of particular aspects of the Plan's treatment of agriculture have been examined in some detail; there are others which could be dealt with in a similar manner. However, in the present context it is the broad issues which are relevant rather than the details. The substance of the matter is the presumption implicit in the Plan that reallocation of the resources of a region can be justified without acknowledging the fundamental economic nature of the exercise. This type of physical planning owes its existence to the technical ease with which farmland can be turned to other uses. But the fact that resources have alternative mutually exclusive uses - including use now as against use in the future - obliges any argument for or against their reallocation to struggle with the problems of comparing their respective benefits and costs, and to portray a socially desirable allocation of resources as a particular balance between costs and benefits of individual uses. This should direct effort to purposefully creating flexibilities to allow particular combinations which would otherwise be incompatible. The Plan essentially acknowledged agriculture as the occupier (rather than the user) of the residue of land left after urban requirements had been met. And there is little evidence of flexibility. No trade-offs between urban and agricultural uses were contemplated; that is, no marginal reductions in the planned urban requirements to benefit agriculture. And after the long-term urban needs had been met the effect of the envisaged Green Belt was to eliminate any trade-off in the opposite direction: no marginal reductions in rural uses to permit future growth of urban use, which would have to take place outside the region. In a sense it is ironic that "overspill" into other regions was proposed as part of the solution to the Clyde Valley's housing problem, without forcing explicit consideration of this land allocation issue, because the supposition that population in the Central Urban Area of the region had reached 'saturation level' involves a hidden trade-off between further urbanisation and retention of rural land uses.

The planning technique implicit in the Plan was first to determine land requirements for urban growth, by subtraction thereby determining the land available for agriculture; second, to place urban developments where possible on lower quality land, paying attention to amenity and recreation, those useful externalities of agriculture for which it does not in general receive payment.

Agricultural and Land Use Planning:
A Closer look at the Problems

In the preceding sections of this chapter it has been argued that the Plan made no significant contribution to the debate on how to achieve the "correct" balance between agriculture and other uses of land. Yet it was published only a few years after the Barlow Report and the Scott Report (Royal Commission 1940, Scott 1942) which together comprised a serious statement of the relevant issues. It should be noted that Abercrombie was a member of the Barlow Commission, which

'... had taken the view that agriculture was outside
its Terms of Reference; and consequently that it was
precluded from considering the effects upon

173

agriculture of the decentralisation and dispersal of
industry and population which it recommended ...'
(Scott 1942, iv).
With some reservations this could equally well be applied to
the Plan. The Scott Report endeavoured to redress the balance,
but it can scarcely be said that the issues were resolved, or
that guidelines were established which could free subsequent
planners from the responsibility to consider the issue afresh
in particular contexts. The nature of the problem is such as
to encourage the expression of extreme views which generally
reflect vested or sectional interests - and not only
agricultural interests. This discourages the emergence of an
agreed body of land use planning principles, even although
reference to such a body has - at least superficially - the
potential to reconcile opposing vested interests. One may
share the Scott Report minority viewpoint of Professor Donnison
that to claim, as the majority did, that
'... whatever conditions may be imposed,
constructional developments in country areas must be
inconsistent with the maintenance of agriculture and
the well-being of rural communities ...' (Scott 1942,
60),
placed agriculture "in a specially privileged position". But
equally one can disagree with his recommendation that
'... it should be incumbent upon the agricultural
occupier, or other agricultural interest, to show
cause why land should not be diverted to some other
use' (Scott 1992, 120)
on the grounds that in context it places the other uses in an
equally privileged position, in view of the difficulties of
evaluating the social costs and benefits of different uses of a
piece of land.

Since then the issue seems rarely to have surfaced as an
unresolved problem. The Plan may have established a precedent
in this respect, with its inconsequential chapter on the
agricultural economy, and its omission of any material
discussion of the issue of land transference. Certainly a
review of regional plans and related Scottish material
published since the Plan reveals no substantial change either
in interpretation of, or response to the problem of determining
an appropriate balance between agricultural and non-
agricultural land uses. Structure plans have been developed,
and the more specific land capability classification has become
available but there has been no reappraisal within the
documents themselves of this central issue of balance.

In 1977, the Scottish Development Department published the
first National Planning Guidelines which defined the land based
resources of national significance and suggested safeguarding

policies for regional reports, structure or local plans.   The
guidelines were revised in 1981, but they remained inexplicit
about   the criteria by which those preparing plans might   judge
the   point   of   balance   in   agricultural   land   transfer.   The
Guidelines   were perhaps less explicit than Manson had been   in
1946   – they extended the presumption against development   to
include B+ as well as A and A+ farmland, and they conceded that
sites   of   under   2 ha.   in area would not be   regarded   as   of
national   significance.   They   required local   authorities   to
justify   the   use of prime farmland in relation to   alternative
land, but there was no guidance on the criteria to be measured.

In these circumstances of inexact Government   guidance,   most
strategic   reports,   structure and local plans avoid a detailed
treatment   of   the   issue,   and   some   parallel   the   apparent
redundancy   of the Plan's treatment of agriculture by   devoting
little space to it,   in some cases none at all. For example, a
discussant   at a Royal Scottish Geographical Society   symposium
in 1979 said of the Strathclyde Structure Plan:
    'A   quick   glance   ...   would leave   an   outsider   to
    believe that Argyll, Lanarkshire and Ayrshire didn't
    exist. Admittedly there are five short paragraphs on
    Remote Rural Areas – but no mention of agriculture or
    land. Similarly, in the Chapter entitled Environment
    there   is no reference to rural land,   per   se.   And
    finally,   the   important   section on   Resources   only
    deals   with land in terms of area of   derelict   land"
    (Boyle 1980, 115).
And   yet,   the   Consultative Draft version of   the   Strathclyde
Structure Plan contained figures provided by the Department   of
Agriculture and Fisheries for Scotland (DAFS) which showed that
between 1971 and 1976 some 60 per cent of the agricultural land
lost   to   urban   development   in the Region was   in   the   prime
categories   of   A+,   A   and   B+   – those   to   be   avoided   by
development.

The   Lothian Structure Plan,   supposedly   demonstrating   a
"different   approach   to   policy   making" (Lyall 1980,   117)
received   favourable   comment   from   those   concerned   with
agriculture;   but   the Report of Survey contains only   a   brief
assessment   of   agriculture   under   the   general   heading   of
Environment, and records the fact that 80 per cent of land lost
from   agriculture   in   recent years is in the   highest   quality
categories.   As   it   happened,   the downward revision of   the
region's population forecasts reduced the land requirements and
meant   that   more land could be left   in   agriculture.   But   a
downward revision of population forecasts does not constitute a
different   approach to the matter of establishing the   boundary
between land uses.   Of course, it has already been pointed out
that   given   the disposition of agricultural land of   different

qualities in relation to urban areas some loss of high quality land is inevitable. Moreover it is a difficult matter to test whether or not the recorded levels of transfer are lower than they would have been in the absence of the present machinery of evaluation in which the DAFS is involved. One other report set its face firmly against considering the issue at all:

> 'We do not propose to embark on a discussion of the net advantages and disadvantages of using land for agriculture or industry or housing, etc.' (Campbell and Lyddon 1970, 25).

It is worthwhile endeavouring to identify the main components of the issue, in order to establish its complexity. First there is the matter of the loss of agricultural production due to urban expansion. This can be decomposed into a number of separate issues. To start with there is the sheer loss of output, shorn of any locational consideration. The contribution of Alice Coleman (Coleman 1977) has ensured that planning circles are aware of the debate (Edwards and Wibberley 1971; Centre for Agricultural Strategy 1976; Wise and Fell 1978) about the adequacy of our food production capability, but it would be fair to say that there are few signs of general agreement that this loss of output is a matter of concern. This is partly because the area of land transferred from agricultural use in any one year - or even in a decade - is small in relation to the whole, and partly because the argument that

> '... The increase in efficiency in ... agriculture far more than outweighs the effect of loss of land to non-agricultural development ... [so] ... it is fair to assume that the increase in efficiency will continue to outbalance the loss of land ...' (Select Committee on Scottish Affairs 1971, Question 24)

can be made to yield the specious conclusion that there has not been a loss of output, but only concentration of production on a smaller acreage. Therefore it needs to be stressed that there has been a loss of output and moreover a loss of a prospective increase in the agricultural productivity of the land transferred from agriculture; consequently the loss of output could be regarded as "growing" with the passage of time even if no more land were to be lost from agriculture. The loss of output should not be in dispute - it is a fact, unlike the assumptions on which a judgement of the social significance of the loss is based: the assumption as to the degree of self sufficiency in temperate foodstuffs which is in the national interest; the assumption as to the future growth in agricultural productivity which should be attained (with its attendant assumptions about the willingness of producers to invest and of society to make available the complementary resources); the assumption as to the appropriate time horizon –

176

the year 2000 or the year 2200?

Next is the locational dimension. Issues such as the nation's future food supply appear to relate to the national rather than the regional situation. Yet attainment of national policy targets, such as an increasing degree of self-sufficiency in agricultural products, depends on the performance of the constituent regions; lost output in one region means that the contributions of the others must be increased further if the overall target is to be attained. Thus there is a regional dimension to national policies, and a national consequence of regional policies. Ironically, a principal justification of the particular treatment accorded to agriculture in and after the Plan is that agriculture is the subject of national rather than local policy, in contrast to much of the urban development process. If the national policy is never translated into regional terms then the regional planner may legitimately presume that making good the loss of agricultural output due to urban growth is not the responsibility of the agricultural industry left within his region. Could all regions simultaneously plan for urban expansion with no consideration of the combined outcome of their actions? Could one region be required to limit its urban growth to enable its agriculture to compensate for the loss of agricultural land in other regions - a kind of agricultural "overspill"?

The assessment of the loss of output consequent upon urban expansion has yet another dimension. It has already been implied that evaluation of the loss should take into account the fact that productivity of land left in agriculture will increase over the years; after all, this is the same process which, it is argued, provides the compensation in other areas for the loss of a particular plot of agricultural land. But there is a further dynamic factor which should also be considered. The flexibility of agricultural uses of land, which enables the farmer to change his tools and techniques readily in search of improved productivity, is in marked contrast to the rigid and specific uses and technologies of urban activities. This flexibility can yield a further benefit where the inevitable uncertainty about the future is encountered: agricultural land not used for urban development today is still readily available for urban development tomorrow. If it is committed to a particular urban use it will most probably have to remain in that use for some considerable time, irrespective of what the passage of time will reveal about the wisdom of the initial decision. Indeed, once it is conceded that agricultural land is not an unlimited supply of "white land" on a development plan (i.e. not allocated for early development, but without the protection of being included in a Green Belt), it becomes even more apparent that the most important cost of the urban use of a particular piece of land is the other urban uses of the future which are thereby excluded - the so-called 'user cost'. Thus the lost output of today's urban expansion is not necessarily agricultural; and even although future urban uses are conjectural their incorporation in the assessment of the social desirability of urban expansion could well put a quite different complexion on the calculation. It could even be argued that one of the most important benefits of a Green Belt is the preservation of land for conversion to urban use at some time in the uncertain future - though the inflexible permanent zoning of the type proposed in the Plan ruled that out. Alternatively, the depletion of energy sources and the accompanying rise in energy costs may require preparation for an era of dependence on vegetative sources of energy - either through a return to horse-drawn farm vehicles and implements, or through the conversion of biomass more directly to energy. Preparation for such a situation - perhaps no longer far-fetched - would entail leaving more land in agriculture and oblige increased urban output to come from increased productivity of existing urban areas. In turn this would require the identification of low productivities within the urban area and their re-development without additional agricultural land being required.

The second main consideration is the "amenity" provided incidentally by the agricultural industry by virtue of its open air technology, and the risk that it will be impaired by urban expansion. Frequently in planning documents the only mention of agriculture and its role in the region comes under the heading of amenity, recreation or landscape, with the most pressing problems identified as conservation (or preservation) of these qualities and guaranteeing access to agricultural land for recreational purposes.

   'If the countryside is seen only as a source of food
   or wood, functional changes may be wholly desirable,
   but if it is also regarded as a necessary complement
   to urban living, it becomes very relevant to the
   broader context of planning' (Scottish Development
   Department 1968b, 9).

This, on the face of it, is an unexceptionable statement. But the issue is one of balance, and the general conclusion of a review of the literature is that at the moment the balance is tipped in the direction of a concern for amenity and recreation rather than a concern for agricultural production. As one representative of the farming community has put it,

   'A new approach to rural planning is needed.
   Emphasis on recreation has become an obsession; we
   have forgotten to look at the countryside as whole'

(Hellard 1976, 44).

It is true that the amenity of the agricultural landscape can reside in features which successive generations of occupiers have introduced or modified specifically for reasons of private amenity value, features which should be preserved from both urban and agricultural development, rather than features intrinsic to modern agricultural production. However, there is little discussion of the problems of the agricultural producer, together with a perhaps uncritical assumption that what is an amenity to a planner is an amenity to the general public; witness the emphasis on education:

> '... wooded farmlands are a valuable visual and cultural asset. Wherever possible, the land should be planned for multi-use to alleviate and control the pressures at present on it. Much of the countryside could be recreational open space if the public were educated to respect it' (Scottish Development Department 1966b).

In the context of marginal agriculture this is a familiar line of approach, particularly in situations where recreational use of land could constitute an alternative economic use of land. But it appears to be applied without further consideration to the entire agricultural economy, and without any analysis of the most obvious problems which would be raised by increased access to farmland. One argument which has been advanced (Weller 1976, 131-141) entails the more carefully considered distinction between factory farmland and amenity farmland, with the former being regarded as '... sacrosanct against urban development ...', and to which there would be no public access. Some level of subsidisation would be necessary on the latter, where the objective would be '... caretaker management to keep the landscape from dereliction, but without hope of economic return'. In addition, it is more generally accepted that buffer zones should exist between urban and agricultural areas to absorb the pressure which otherwise would lead to the peri-urban erosion of agricultural activities. But in essence these are only variants of the familiar policy of avoiding high quality agricultural land.

Third, amongst the main considerations, the precise siting of urban expansion rather than the determination of its extent appears to have become the dominant issue related to agriculture. And here again the 'high quality land avoidance' mechanism continues to be applied, in the manner suggested in the Plan'.

> 'Housing sites have been chosen from the best available, but with due regard to conservation of the best agricultural land' (Jack Holmes Planning Group

1968).

In other words, morphology becomes the final safeguard for the agricultural industry, as urban blocks of pre-determined size are moved about to find the "best" layout. This amounts to only a vestige of flexibility, as it is evident that town planning considerations exert considerable influence by this stage in the planning process. Even "moving" high quality land, by improving the quality of remaining agricultural land, has been considered to be an alternative to resiting urban developments, though with no accompanying cost estimates:

'The long term importance of agriculture as a land use must be considered very carefully. Positive planning for the long-term improvement of land is necessary. This can be carried out by extending the limits of the different qualities of land out into the adjacent poorer land. The aim should be to improve the latter to compensate for the good quality land lost in development.' (Scottish Development Department 1966b, 57).

This clearly leads into more difficult issues, even although on the surface it seems to offer the possibility of an engineering solution to the allocation problem, allowing the particular region to have both urban development and good-quality agricultural land. But the resource cost has once more to be considered against the benefit conferred, and there are no intuitive grounds for the presumption that this is worthwhile.

Finally, there is the problem of the phasing over time of urban development. Perhaps the most intractable of the difficulties of planning is the projection of rates of change of land uses and planned rates of transference of land from one use to another. The establishment of target populations or levels of employment related to particular dates in the future appear to be generally unaccompanied by any attempt to prescribe how many hectares per year should be reserved for urban expansion. Closely related to this is the more general issue of the co-ordination of the efforts of local authorities in determining their specific land requirements for the future. According to the West Central Scotland Plan Team too much land too soon, and too much land of the wrong type has been reserved for urban expansion, at least in West Central Scotland:

'... the total regional resources of underdeveloped housing land allocated in Development Plans or the approved plans for the new towns at the end of 1970 were sufficient to ... accommodate a residential population of about 300,000 [more than the highest estimated population growth between 1972 and 1991]... As regards industrial land, the overall amount

180

allocated by local authorities and new towns is even
more in excess of possible needs ... [But] not all of
[the housing land] is equally suitable ... [and] the
sites reserved are not necessarily those which it
would serve the best interests of the region to
develop for housing, [while] in and near the
Clydeside Conurbation there has been a shortage of
good industrial sites, and it is necessary to make
more good sites available for early building' (West
Central Scotland Plan 1974a,52, italics added).

Despite an obvious difference in scale the situation brings
to mind Cullingworth's comment that
'... in 1937 there was sufficient land zoned for
housing to accommodate 350 million people'
(Cullingworth 1974, 22)
and one is tempted to ask if the progress which has been made
in co-ordination of land requirements is sufficient. Since
much of this land is agricultural it is likely that the
prospect of future development for urban purposes has already
had a significant effect on the productivity with which it is
used, one manifestation of planning blight. The view has been
expressed that
'... most land zoned for development is agricultural,
and will not be blighted rather it will increase in
value' (Select Committee on Scottish Affairs 1972,
56).

However, this would appear to confuse present use value,
based on current agricultural productivity, with potential use
value; the latter may well appreciate with the passage of time,
but it cannot be presumed automatically that this provides the
regional community with compensation for the loss of
agricultural output during the possibly long period before
development takes place. In the English context, the proposal
has been put forward that
'Where agricultural land ear-marked for development
is not required immediately, it should be a condition
of planning consent that the developers produce
within a specified period an acceptable plan for
farming the land in the interim' (Advisory Council
for Agriculture and Horticulture in England and Wales
1978, 21).
Whether this is a practicable suggestion remains to be seen.

So much, then, for the main features of the problem of the
planned transfer of land from agricultural to urban use, and
some of the responses which they have evoked. Now we try to
draw the various strands together to account for the
distinctive treatment of agriculture.

Planning and the Treatment of Agriculture - the Central Issue

The distinctive treatment accorded to agriculture derives at least partly from the very difficult problem of achieving an "efficient" allocation of resources by administrative means, given the present mixture of private and public control over resources in Britain. Planners are not unaware of the problem, but perhaps do not appreciate the extent to which its influence can lead to questionable stewardship of land resources. The refinement of planning techniques and procedures which has taken place since the Plan is welcome, but it seems the presumption still exists that there can be a simple physical planning solution to a problem which has exercised economists for some considerable time.

Let us illustrate the problem by first developing a stylised form of planned resource allocation. Suppose for the moment that private freedom of choice with regard to resource use is prohibited (noting en passant that at least one concept of allocative efficiency has consequently to be discarded) and that a central planning authority exists. Its first step in planning the future state of a region could then be a detailed listing of all the particular activities or "outputs" which might be pursued in the region, including many different specific types of industry, housing, recreation and amenity. Suppose further that the technology appropriate to each activity or output is known and is inflexible, and that, as part of the technology, the land (or area) requirement of a unit of each output is known. Given the total area of the region it should be apparent that the actual deployment of that land depends on the particular combination of output targets which is chosen. However, at this stage there will be many possible solutions to this exercise in programming, many different combinations of outputs or land uses which fit physically within the overall area constraint. The introduction of minimum land requirements to make some particular uses technically viable will not enforce a single solution, not even if the region is planned as a closed economic system (a contradiction in terms?). Thus the physical dimensions of the problem are not sufficient to generate a solution; there are still choices to be made by the central authority, juggling with the "social benefits and costs" of particular uses, to compare relative worth and to allow a particular combination of activities or outputs to be designated "optimal".

Now of course a command economy, entailing highly detailed planning by a centralised authority, is not a reality within the British context. Much decision-making is decentralised and fundamentally private. As a consequence this stylised scheme of resource allocation proves to be deficient and impracticable. It is impossible for existing planning authorities to specify in advance and in the necessary detail precisely which outputs could be produced and with which technologies - in short there is insufficient "physical" information; and even if all the physical information was available choices still would have to be made by the non-existent omnipotent Central Planning Authority. Nevertheless, this stylised form appears to be the antecedent of the present planning approach, though it has been grossly simplified to make it operational.

A degree of aggregation of individual land uses is introduced to avoid the problem presented by the inability to determine the future output levels of each of the multitude of specific land uses with the necessary detail and precision. The crux of the matter is then the particular aggregative structure which is employed, the particular categories of uses of land which remain after specific activities have been grouped together. Three groups typically remain: residential use, industrial (non-agricultural) use and agricultural use. The difference between residential use and the other two categories is probably sufficiently qualitative to justify that division. But agriculture, insofar as it yields output, employment and incomes, and requires an extent of land, is like any other form of production. Why should it be distinguished from "industry"? Certainly its density index (i.e. output or employment per unit area of land) may be lower than other "industrial" uses, but there presumably exists a spectrum of densities - albeit obscured by the use of industry-wide average densities as a result of the aggregation process - and the drawing of a dividing line on such a spectrum requires the application of some other criterion. The implicit criterion supporting this aggregative structure seems to be simply the prior occupancy of land by agriculture.

But while that may explain the aggregative structure employed for planning it does not of itself explain the treatment of agriculture as a residual, that is with no output target of its own but instead with a boundless ability to look after itself. The reason for this appears to lie once more in the planning approach. Aggregation is used as a way round the extremely difficult (if not impossible) problem of setting sufficiently precise targets for specific activities. And if there are degrees of impossibility the more specific the activity being examined the greater the problem. Yet the adopted structure defines one highly specific activity, namely agricultural production. It is a complex issue to set targets for agriculture, either in terms of output or employment. The second best approach, then, is to treat the agricultural industry as a residual user of land, left to its own devices. Justification for this is provided by the fact that, by and large, agricultural development on agricultural land is outwith the ambit of planning controls. Moreover, the planner may reasonably expect that the ostensibly powerful Department of Agriculture and Fisheries for Scotland will protect - or at least represent - the agricultural interest. The irony is that in a particular sense the DAFS is in an even weaker position in relation to agricultural development than is the local authority in respect of private housing and industry. While the nationalisation of the right to develop achieved by the Town and Country Planning Acts left the intention to develop still very largely a private matter, the legislation did provide the local authority with a system of controls, albeit negative in nature, entailing the granting or withholding of planning permission. There is no equivalent, however in terms of agriculture; the DAFS is not similarly empowered in respect of agricultural pursuits on individual farms. The nature of agricultural policy is such that individual farmers are left to their own devices within the sphere of influence of broad national agricultural policy. This has important implications for land allocation:

> 'While the decision to take land for mineral extraction or a motorway may be based on national priorities, land for farming is not related to any accepted national food plan. Thus farmers can never argue that any particular hectare should be inviolate, especially since food production increases in spite of farmland losses. Indeed they argue from a weak brief against any encroachment' (Weller 1979, 95).

It is therefore not unexpected that Scottish development plans and in particular structure plans have shared the wider tendency to be "... without exception ... negative with regard to food production planning"; moreover it is difficult to see how to implement the recommendation of the Agriculture and the Countryside report that

> '... structure plans should clearly specify the priorities attached to agriculture and horticulture ... and not merely assert a policy for safeguarding the better quality agricultural land' (Advisory Council for Agriculture and Horticulture in England and Wales 1978, 21).

or to accommodate the view of one writer that

> '... There should be a clear policy of land use in which each hectare should relate to a strategy of food production,' (Weller 1979, 13).

In the absence of a clearly defined role for each farm,

agriculture must inevitably be treated as a residual user of land.

Of course, the point is that without a residual user of land the planning technique virtually disintegrates. If only two mutually exclusive uses remain (residential and all-industry) there might be no solution to the allocative problem, due to the complementarity of these uses: the trade-off would have to be between houses and jobs. But irrespective of this the technique is a mere shadow of its initial promise, since the use of industry-wide (excluding agriculture) employment densities derived elsewhere removes the need to consider the future composition of the region's industry at all (e.g. Lothian Regional Council 1977, 8) - although the densities can always be adjusted on an ad hoc basis to allow for impressions about the future structure in a particular area.

This degeneration of the planning technique from the stylised form set out above introduces a surprising but inevitable degree of inflexibility into the land allocation issue. The "ideal" technique implies a large number of potential trade-offs between uses, in which choice of different activities with their unique but differing densities could play an active role in permitting the simultaneous attainment of particular aggregate output targets. For example, an agricultural objective and an industrial employment objective could be made compatible by planning for high employment density of industrial land use, so that the transfer of land from agriculture would be minimised. However, through aggregation and the use of average densities this opportunity is excluded.

It is worth noting that there appears to be virtually no consideration of possible flexibility of densities in published Scottish regional planning documents, either with respect to industry or residential development. Indeed, the latter seems to be regarded as quite inflexible:

'Given that the land is available I do not think a county council could resist a burgh's wish to extend its ground with the argument that they could build up instead of building out. If the local authority could make their case for the need for more ground at an accepted level of density, that would be a valid argument for getting the extension' (Select Committee on Scottish Affairs 1971, Question 24).

Inflexible maximum residential densities related to considerations such as public health in its broadest sense would be one thing, but density standards related to architectural norms or "style" are quite another matter. As far as private residential developments are concerned densities are presumably inversely related to property values and so present further opportunities for complex trade-offs. The use of industrial densities from elsewhere seems to involve the assumptions not only that what has arisen in one industrial stucture is of direct relevance in planning another, but also that an average based on an unspecified but probably substantial area is of relevance for marginal changes in land use.

The Influence of the Clyde Valley Regional Plan

From the Plan onwards, Scottish regional planning documents appear to share a common conceptual framework. On the surface there has been a significant refinement of technique over the years, which to some extent obscures the basic continuity of approach. It would seem that the Plan made its impact by setting a precedent which later studies could improve on technically but not replace with something materially different. The impact is more implicit than explicit, and there was little need for attributions to appear in later planning documents. The gradual evolution of concepts such as green belts and new towns, and changing emphases on these as solutions to "the planning problem", have also helped to conceal the underlying and unchanged philosophy, set out in the preceding sections of this chapter.

It is important to stress that to set out to achieve a planned balance between agriculture and urban use of land does raise a methodological and conceptual problem. It is not simply a matter of the relative "importance" of agriculture and other activities, even although the assertions and counter-assertions in the literature would make it appear so.

The real issue has two components: the intrinsic difficulty of planning future resource use in the context of a significant degree of private and public decentralisation of control over decision-making, and the difficulty of achieving a desirable outcome, in terms of the balance between private and social benefits, of that planning process. "Agriculture versus the rest" is only a distinct case of the general issue insofar as the farmer already occupies a resource of potential greater flexibility of alternative use, compared with the occupier of urban land; but it is a distinct case which reveals that the presently developed planning approach to land allocation has severe shortcomings.

Predicting the future course of an economy with decentralised decision-making, where the behaviour of each component may depend on its anticipations of the behaviour of each other component, is an impossible task - at least in any precise manner - and one from which economists in general have shrunk, setting a precedent for planners to do the same. It is all the more impossible to plan such a course, and for the planners to insist on the attainment of certain public targets as may be represented by the so-called national interest or social benefit. To set out to achieve this presupposes a degree of administrative control which would rarely be tolerated in Britain. That does not exclude the possibility that in particular circumstances there can be sufficiently general agreement as to what is the public interest in a particular area to warrant the presumption that private and other conflicting national interests can be ignored or over-ruled where appropriate. It may well be that the housing and employment needs of post-war reconstruction were sufficient for such a case to be made for the Clyde Valley. If so, it is to be expected that this would be reflected in the relevant planning documents. As Manson wrote in the Plan

'Planning authorities are naturally obsessed with the importance of housing...' (para. 1295).

However, this would not absolve those concerned with the planning process of the responsibility to develop subsequently a generally applicable approach to the central problem of planned resource use, rather than one which was critically dependent on contemporary circumstances which might well prove to be subject to radical change. The National Planning Guidelines (1981) signify Government's acceptance of its responsibility for guidance and decisions on the transfer of agricultural land. Yet the Guidelines of 1981 are no more explicit on the economic issues involved than were Manson's First Principles of 1946. Decisions over land transfer continue to be resolved in the physically orientated manner reflected in the Plan.

Thus, in retrospect, it may be justifiable to view the Plan as a particular response to the pressing needs of the immediate post-war situation. Being first in the field inevitably made it a blueprint to some extent for later contributions relating to quite different circumstances, but in terms of establishing a method adequate for planning an efficient allocation of resources such as land in the national interest, it appears to have had little positive impact. And unfortunately there has been little subsequent methodological development. The balance between agricultural and urban uses of land continues to be resolved in the same physically-oriented manner set out in the Plan. It is perhaps not in itself an issue of overwhelming significance for this generation (or even the next few), but it does serve to reveal the core problems of planned resource allocation more clearly than many other related issues.

8 Recreation and Open Space

VERONICA BURBRIDGE

CONTEMPORARY APPROACHES TO RECREATION AND THE COUNTRYSIDE

The Plan's Setting

The Clyde Valley Regional Plan was prepared during a period of growing interest in recreation and countryside matters. The need to provide open space within cities had long been recognised, but the desirability of providing recreational access to open country was a relatively new issue. The provision of recreational space was closely linked with attempts to create new urban forms, to prevent urban sprawl and to protect areas of high landscape value. These issues demanded attention within a regional context, and their consideration became inter-twined with wider land use planning matters and programmes for post-war reconstruction.

Concern for health, welfare and environmental standards within urban areas may be traced back to the Victorian Health in Towns movement. In Glasgow, an important step in the provision of public parks was taken when Kelvingrove Park was acquired by the City in 1854, followed by Queens Park in 1864 and Alexandra Park in 1870. Private philanthropy provided much needed if inadequate open space in the rapidly growing city. Within Glasgow, parks such as Rouken Glen and Cathkin Braes were given to the City and in 1906 the Ardgoil Estate in Argyll was gifted to Glasgow Corporation.

The Victorian era also witnessed the growth in popularity of the Scottish landscape and holidays at the seaside. Visits to Scotland by Queen Victoria and the royal family as well as the writings of Sir Walter Scott did much to make Scottish tourism fashionable. By the 1880s, the 'coasting season' had become a recognised feature of life in the West of Scotland and the annual 'Glasgow Fair' holiday provided the opportunity for a mass exodus to Clyde resorts by river steamers and railway. The wealthy took seaside houses for the summer whilst the vast majority of city inhabitants made do with day trips "doon the watter" to escape the grim struggle of Victorian urban life.

During the late nineteenth century, shorter working hours and the introduction of free time on Saturday provided workers with more opportunity for leisure. The holidays with Pay Act 1938 was an official milestone in the movement towards paid holidays for all workers. In 1937, only 4,000,000 insured workers in Britain had received holidays with pay; by 1947 this figure had reached 14,000,000. The nature of holidays began to change. Working-class seaside visitors tended to be day-trippers, but by the 1940's they were able to go further afield and to stay for longer periods. However, for the masses the day-trips continued to offer the only affordable form of holiday.

In the inter-war years there was increased interest in recreation in open country around major urban agglomerations such as Glasgow. Hiking and cycling were popular. The Scottish Youth Hostels Association was formed in 1931 and opened its first hostel at Inverberg on Loch Lomondside in 1932. By 1946, the Association had 38,000 members and over seventy hostels, fifteen of which were in the Clyde Valley.

The National Trust for Scotland was formed in 1931 and within six years had acquired large tracts of land in Glencoe and the Balness Estate in Argyll. These areas were to be maintained as 'national parks' with unrestricted access for the public. The Forestry Commission was also active in providing access to country areas. In 1936, the Ardgoil Estate was combined with land owned by the Forestry Commission to form the Argyll National Forest Park. These lands provided significant mountainous areas with no restriction on public access. Elsewhere in the uplands strong sporting interests led to conflicts between ramblers and landowners.

The international movement for National Parks gained support at this time. The Addison Committee, appointed in 1929 to consider the concept of National Parks based on experience in Canada and the U.S.A., reported in 1931. It stressed the need for countryside conservation and envisaged a nation-wide scheme of parks, open spaces and playing fields. It noted that

Scotland required "special consideration", but no action was taken on the report and it was not until the impetus for post-war reconstruction in the 1940's that further steps in recreation planning were achieved.

Between 1940 and 1947, a series of outstanding reports provided blue-prints for post-war development. Two which had implications for recreation planning were those of the Scott Committee on Land Utilisation in Rural Areas and the Uthwatt Committee on Compensation and Betterment. Although Scotland was not included within the terms of reference of the Scott Committee, the Secretary of State, Tom Johnston, did appoint a number of Committees to investigate rural matters including hill sheep, land settlement, hydro-electric development and the herring industry. It was not thought necessary to appoint a new committee on land use. This was indicative of the different conditions which prevailed in Scotland, where there was only one conurbation and population pressure on the countryside was less intense than south of the border. The Scottish National Parks movement came later and was less active than its English counterpart. In Scotland, greater stress was given to rural economic development than to recreation and conservation. In addition, the administrative arrangements adopted by the Scottish Office provided a different policy context for the emergence of rural and recreation planning.

In 1942, the National Parks movement in Scotland gained some momentum with the formation of the Scottish Council on National Parks, which submitted proposals for Park administration to the Secretary of State. In response, the Scottish Office was cautious and unenthusiastic; it saw more problems than benefits and pointed to overlapping and conflicting interests (Cherry 1975). However, in January 1944, stimulated by progress on the Dower Report on National Parks in England and Wales and disquieted by the growing activity of the Forestry Commission in this field, Tom Johnston appointed the Scottish National Parks Survey Committee. The Committee was chaired by Sir Douglas Ramsay of the Scottish Council on National Parks and was asked to advise on areas which might be suitable park sites. The report of October 1944 recommended five National Parks, including the Loch Lomond-Trossachs area which had been suggested to the Committee by the Clyde Valley Regional Planning Advisory Committee. A further three areas including St. Mary's Loch were placed on a reserve list.

The Clyde Valley Regional Planning Advisory Committee had just commenced work on the preparation of the Plan and subsequent events saw close links between national and regional developments in recreation planning in Scotland. A Scottish National Parks Committee was appointed in 1946 to consider and report on the administrative, financial and other measures necessary for the provision of National Parks in Scotland. The Committee was again chaired by Sir Douglas Ramsay and included past members of the Survey Committee as well as Robert Grieve from the Plan.

The Committee's report was submitted in July 1947, a year after the completion of the Plan. It recommended that a National Parks Commission for Scotland should be established, with local committees for each park including representatives of the local planning authorities. The Commission would be concerned with the preservation of natural amenities and provision of access, holiday accommodation and recreation facilities, the maintenance of rural life and the fostering of suitable rural industries. It also recommended that land required for specific National Park purposes should be acquired by outright purchase, by agreement or compulsorily, and that as large a part as practicable of the uncultivated land within the designated area should be purchased. The Scottish Committee went further in its advocacy of public ownership than did its English counterpart. Land in mountainous and upland areas was relatively cheap, but in advocating a policy of public acquisition the Committee came up against land owners and sporting interests.

The climate within which the Plan was prepared was one of optimism for the future of National Parks in Scotland and for a central authority for their administration. National Parks constituted one element in the centralised planning system envisaged at the time. However, when legislation was finally passed in 1949, provisions for National Parks and their administration only applied to England and Wales, although the Nature Conservancy was established on a nation-wide basis.

During the 1940's recreation planning also achieved new importance at the regional level. The need for more open space within cities and the preservation of open space for agriculture and recreation were basic considerations in the search for new approaches to urban form. Abercrombie's Greater London Plan completed in 1944 recognised a hierarchy of different types of recreational and open space needs, and proposed a park system for its region. The Plan reflected this concern for all aspects of recreation; the different physical, social and economic conditions prevailing in the Greater London and Clyde Valley regions led to different approaches and resulting recreation strategies. In a physically more diverse region, the Plan was faced with a wider spectrum of resource opportunities for recreation. In attempting to deal with a regional continuum of recreational need, the Plan embarked on a new and difficult venture clearly linked to emerging national policies and changing social conditions.

THE PROPOSALS OF THE PLAN AND THEIR IMPACTS

Recreation Planning

The recreation planning proposals of the Plan were part of the over-riding concern for the reduction of high densities and were complementary to policies for the protection of agricultural land and the establishment of a green belt. The Plan covered a wide spectrum of recreation including open space in urban areas, centres for active sports and games, general access to open country and National Parks. It was concerned with the need to plan and manage the Clyde Coast as a regional and national holiday resource, to conserve areas of high landscape value and to protect sites of nature conservation interest.

The Plan's proposals related to land use aspects of recreation provision and were primarily concerned with public recreation space. The difficulty and expense of providing open space within built-up areas was recognised, but the Plan followed already established practice in the definition of standards of provision as measures of need. The Plan advocated "minimum" standards of seven acres per 1,000 population and "desirable" standards of ten acres per 1,000 population, but noted that even the minimum standards would be difficult to achieve in many parts of the Conurbation. Detailed surveys and the application of such standards suggested a vast deficiency of public recreation space in the industrial basin of the Clyde, amounting to 7,800 acres or over 12 square miles. The attempt to achieve uniform standards was not practical, and given the crowded conditions of much of the conurbation and the proximity of open country, it was inevitable that the community should look to the urban fringe and open country for the satisfaction of its recreational needs.

The Plan anticipated that recreation pressures would affect upland areas of high scenic quality close to the Conurbation. The physical structure of the Clyde Basin and the comparatively narrow extent of agricultural lowland allowed a different approach to a Green Belt from that adopted in the earlier Greater London Plan. The Clydeside Green Belt was defined for the protection of agricultural land and had only a minor recreational role. It was suggested that some of the narrower wedges and corridors between built-up areas would not be suitable for normal agricultural use and could be used for facilities such as allotments. A novel proposal was that urban public institutions could be moved to fringe areas to free

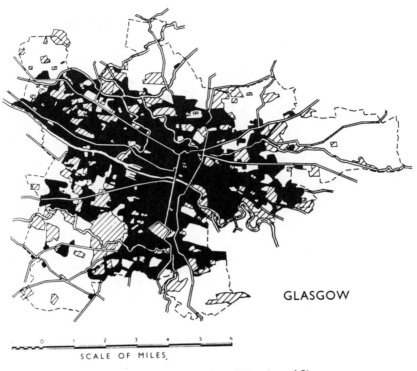

GLASGOW

SCALE OF MILES.

48. Open Space deficiency in Inner Urban Area of Glasgow

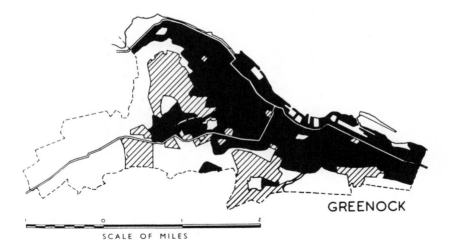

GREENOCK

SCALE OF MILES

Figure 8.1 The Plan's illustration of Open Space deficiency in
Inner Urban Areas of Glasgow and Greenock

193

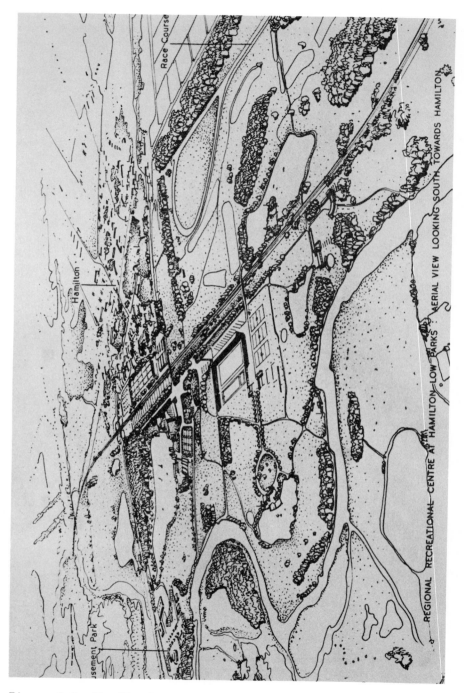

Figure 8.2   The Plan's proposed Hamilton Low Parks Recreation
Centre

inner city sites for recreational open space.   This policy was
only feasible within the context of contemporary proposals for
public ownership of development rights and Green Belt lands.
The   potential   conflict between recreation   and   lowland
agriculture was recognised by the Plan but was not considered
important.   The need to educate townsfolk in matters such as
the shutting of gates was noted, but the level of disturbance
and vandalism faced today by farmers in the urban fringe was
not anticipated.

A regional approach was taken to formal recreation and sports
facilities.   Strategically placed Regional Recreation Centres
were recommended at Killermont,   Pollok,   Drumpellier and
Hamilton Low Parks.   These would provide urban areas with a
wide range of recreation facilities over and above the open
space provided within local planning units,   and were to be
maintained by the Regional Authority.   Numerous reports were
prepared for the Plan by recreational and scientific bodies
concerned with informal recreation and the countryside.   Areas
of interest to naturalists and geologists and areas of scenic
value were identified and contributed to the proposals for open
space preservation.

The provision of access was seen as the crux of the problem
of informal recreation in open country, where it was proposed
that there should be access to all moorland.   Access already
existed in many areas but was denied in important areas such as
the Kilpatrick Hills, the Campsie Hills and the Renfrewshire
Hills.   A system of walkers' paths was suggested as an
alternative to "heavily trafficked" roads in popular areas.
The Plan also drew attention to the recreation potential of the
Antonine Wall and recommended footpath access along its length.

The Plan considered that the new Regional Authority should
deal with the problem of footpath access in a comprehensive
manner.   This could only be achieved on a regional basis where
funds could be made available and local authority efforts could
be co-ordinated.   The area immediately north of Milngavie was
used as an example of how this might be achieved in practice.
The area was proposed as a Regional Park to be managed by the
Regional Authority with sites for chalets, camping and picnics
to be managed by a warden service.   It was assumed that
agriculture and forestry would remain viable and that there
would be little change in the existing character of the
landscape.

The Plan's treatment of the Clyde coast also exhibited the
dual concern for strategic planning and detailed design.   The
Clyde coast was the traditional holiday area for people from
Clydeside.   A detailed coastal survey was carried out and

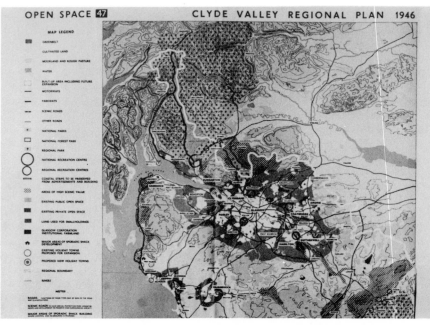

Figure 8.3 Clyde Valley Regional Plan 1946. Open Space

Figure 8.4 'Maid of the Loch' on Loch Lomond, 1980

strategic proposals were made for the definition of conservation areas.

New holiday towns were proposed at Rosneath and Hunterston, similar to the Butlin's holiday camp which had been erected near the Heads of Ayr before the Second World War. Detailed design proposals were made to guide the coastal planning authorities, and the construction of a yacht centre by reclaiming part of Hunterston Sands was recommended. Hunterston remained zoned as an area for recreational use and of high scenic value until 1970, when the Oceanspan Report sealed its fate as a site for heavy industrial activities.

A detailed approach was also taken to the proposed improvement of unsightly holiday shack developments which had grown up in open country and along the Ayrshire coast in the 1920's and 1930's. The Plan drew up guidelines for the future siting of chalets and recommended that no more than twenty should be permitted on any one of the widely distributed sites, in locations determined by topographical and amenity factors. Local Authorities would be encouraged to set high standards of design and to prepare layouts for individual sites. In later years caravans were to be the subject of similar studies. However, although the first factory production of trailer caravans had taken pace in 1922, their impact had not been felt in the Clyde Valley by the 1940's.

The Plan supported the move to create a National Travel Holidays and Catering Board and stressed the national dimension of problems associated with the provision of tourist and holiday facilities. The national dimension of recreation planning had also been stressed by the National Parks movement. The close involvement of the Clyde Valley Regional Advisory Committee and Planning Team in the Scottish National Parks discussions drew regional and national proposals together. The Plan supported the proposal for a National Park in the Loch Lomond-Trossachs area, but suggested that the Park should be larger than the 320 square miles outlined by the Scottish National Parks Survey Committee and should include the approaches to the Park. A National Recreation Centre at Balloch was proposed as a reception area for tourists and a gateway for visitors to the Highlands. The Centre would help to rehabilitate the Balloch area which was an eyesore at the entrance to the Park, and would provide all-year-round recreation facilities for the 2,000,000 people living within twenty-five miles. The Balloch Centre would have an important regional role and the concentration of facilities would enable strong conservation policies in the rest of the Loch Lomond area.

The Immediate Impact of the Plan

The immediate effect of the Plan was limited by the failure to establish a Regional Authority and by the continuation of fragmentary planning. This was compounded by the lack of National Parks legislation in Scotland and the lack of any national level arrangements for recreation planning.

The Ramsay Report was submitted in 1947 but a climate of opinion was already forming against National Parks in Scotland. A Department of Health Working Party considered the matter, but in 1950 it was decided not to pursue a National Parks Bill for Scotland. There were several reasons for this turn of events. The Scottish problem was certainly different from that in England. Recreational pressures were less intense in the Scottish countryside, and greater attention was being given to rural industries and tourism to support rural economies rather than to issues of access and conservation. Doubts were expressed about the need for another commission and local authorities and the Scottish Office argued for the use of existing machinery wherever possible. The central government response was apathetic. The Secretary of State, Arthur Woodburn, showed no enthusiasm and did not regard the need for legislation "as one of pressing urgency" (Cherry 1975). The proposals for public ownership of land were strongly opposed by landowners who were able to voice their opposition through positions in local councils and countryside associations.

In 1945, opposition from local landowners had been voiced against the Plan's proposal for a National Centre at Balloch. Sir Iain Colquhoun, Baronet of Luss and Chairman of the National Trust Council and Executive Committee, speaking at the official opening of the Loch Lomond Youth Hostel at Auchendennan protested against the project, which he thought would turn Loch Lomond into a 'joy park' or 'fun fair'. In this he was supported by the Lord Provost of Glasgow, who pointed to the Kelvin Hall and Glasgow Green as providing all the enjoyment of that kind that people desired.

There was no political will for National Parks in the 1950's and local authorities lacked finance and manpower for the task of running and developing parks. A National Park scheme for Scotland would be difficult to achieve and ineffective in practice. The Department of Health preferred to work directly through the local planning machinery, and in 1948 the Secretary of State had introduced National Park Direction Areas for the five areas proposed as National Parks. All planning applications in these areas had to be notified to the Secretary of State, who had the option of calling-in the application for his own decision. This represented a rudimentary system of control but there remained a lack of any administrative or financial framework for positive implementation. In 1955, Dumbarton County Council expressed interest in a Loch Lomond-Trossachs National Park, and in 1959 the District Councils Association passed a resolution urging National Parks for Scotland, but no action was taken.

At the regional and local levels, priorities lay with housing and employment. Little finance or planning manpower could be made available for recreational and countryside matters. However, the influence of the Plan may be seen in the continuing concern for urban open space standards expressed in local authority development plans in the 1950's and early 1960's. The 1953 Development Plan for Part of Lanark County referred to the Clyde Valley Regional Plan and applied the standard of seven acres of open space per 1,000 population to the planning of built-up areas.

In 1960, the survey report for the City of Glasgow's Development Plan Quinquennial Review showed that it was impossible to achieve the optimum standard of 13 acres per 1,000 people, set by the National Playing Fields Association and the Department of Health for Scotland. A standard of 7.2 acres per 1,000 people was adopted, similar to that advocated by the Plan for the Conurbation as a whole. The Quinquennial Review, noting the uneven distribution of open space in Glasgow, identified a deficiency of about 2,455 acres, which it concluded could not be met in the built-up area but would have to be provided on the periphery of the Conurbation. Since that time, planning for recreation has become concerned less with the definition of crude open space standards and more with the definition of needs for different types of recreation and the positive planning of space for particular activities.

Development in the Period 1960-1974

The early 1960's saw a resurgence of interest in countryside matters and in the recreational use of open country. Increased affluence, longer holidays and increased car ownership led to further growth of recreational pressures on the countryside. The inability of existing planning machinery to deal with these problems was rapidly being recognised. The 'Countryside in 1970 Conference' (1965) presented a new view of problems associated with the pressures of urban population on the countryside, and advocated a more co-ordinated approach to rural planning and development. Study Group 9 of the Countryside in 1970 (1965) Conference was appointed to consider countryside planning and development in Scotland. The Group was chaired by Robert Grieve, then Professor of Town and Regional Planning at the University of Glasgow. The Group's report to the Second

Countryside Conference in 1965 recommended the establishment of a Countryside Commission in Scotland to determine countryside standards and policy, to make grants to other authorities and to carry out with its own executive powers those projects which could not be handled by existing agencies.

In the early 1960's, two unsuccessful attempts were made to prepare Scottish Countryside legislation. The draft Countryside (Scotland) Bill of 1961 proposed Exchequer grants to be paid, on the recommendation of a new Scottish Countryside Advisory Council to local authorities, voluntary organisations and individuals, towards the cost of minor works which preserved or enhanced the natural beauty of Scotland. The Bill was unpopular with the Association of County Councils who feared the role of the Advisory Council and preferred to deal directly with the Secretary of State. In 1965, a Countryside and Tourist Amenities (Scotland) Bill took up these proposals and extended them to include a Scottish Tourist Fund, financed by a levy from the Scottish hotel industry. The Fund had been proposed by the Scottish Tourist Board, but the Bill was strongly attacked by the British Hotels and Restaurants Association and the British Travel and Holidays Association. There was also conflict between amenity society and local authority interests concerning the powers to be given to the proposed Amenities Council. Opposition again led to the abandonment of the Bill.

At this time, concern for the countryside was expressed in two Scottish Departmental Circulars. Circular 40/1960 (Department of Health) encouraged the designation of green belts and gave official justification to the presumption against new housing in open country. Circular 2/1962 (Scottish Development Department) encouraged local authorities to prepare surveys of recreation facilities, to submit development proposals for tourism and to define areas of great landscape value which would enable the development of a comprehensive national scheme for the preservation of the countryside and the development of tourism. The circular encouraged local authorities to work together in a regional context and this approach was taken up by Ayr, Bute, Argyll, Renfrew and Dumbarton, who joined together with the aim of producing a regional plan for tourism. However, little was achieved and the lack of financial resources inhibited development. Further action awaited the Countryside (Scotland) Act 1967, which established the Countryside Commission for Scotland and provided long awaited machinery and finance for recreational projects in the countryside.

The Countryside Commission for Scotland was given the statutory duty to keep under review "all matters relating to the provision, development and improvement of facilities for the enjoyment of the Scottish countryside, the conservation of its natural beauty and its amenity and the need to secure public access for open air recreation". The establishment of the Commission was followed by the granting of statutory duties and new funding powers to two other agencies concerned with recreation and tourism. The Scottish Tourist Board had actively promoted Scottish tourism since its formation in 1946 and was given statutory duties to encourage and finance tourist facilities by the 1969 Development of Tourism Act. This was followed in 1972 by the formation of the Scottish Sports Council, which brought together the Scottish Council of Physical Recreation, active in Scotland since 1945, the Advisory Council for Scotland, originally appointed in 1953, and a section of the Scottish Education Department previously responsible for grant aid to sport and physical recreation. Within a period of five years, three central agencies for the development of recreation and tourism had been created and were to provide the framework for further development in this field.

The Countryside Commission for Scotland saw the establishment of country parks as its immediate priority. Three of the first four country parks in Scotland were sited in Strathclyde, at Culzean, Muirshiel and Palacerigg. Later, Strathclyde Regional Park was sited within the Clyde Valley in the area of Hamilton Low Parks, the site of one of the Plan's major recreation recommendations:

> 'It (the Park) is strategically placed to serve a great industrial population within easy reach and it was an obvious choice, particularly in view of the fact that it entailed a certain amount of rehabilitation in the shape of reclamation and river training which is badly needed in any case' (para. 732).

No immediate action had been taken by the local authorities and it was not until 1964 that the idea was revived by the Scottish Development Department, when the construction of the M74 northwards from Larkhall provided the opportunity of rehabilitating this area using spoil from the road works. Under the Countryside (Scotland) Act 1967, grant assistance was made available to fund the development of the park. A joint park authority was established with representatives from Lanark County and Motherwell and Hamilton Town Councils. Work began in 1973 and was substantially completed by 1976. A further park established during the 1960's was the Clyde/Muirshiel Regional Park, based on the country parks at Muirshiel and Lochwinnoch. The Plan had recommended improved access to these areas in the Renfrew Hills, but again the project was only realised when development funds became available.

Figure 8.5   Strathclyde Park under construction at Hamilton Low Parks

Figure 8.6   Sailing on Strathclyde Park

In the late 1960's, a series of regional plans for recreation and tourism was commissioned by the Scottish Tourist Board including a study by Travis (1970) of the Firth of Clyde. This report identified locations for country and national parks and returned to the Plan's proposal for intensive recreation developments in the Craigend/Mugdock and Balloch areas. Progress on one of these proposals was made in 1980 when Sir Hugh Fraser gifted land at Mugdock to Central Regional Council, and a joint committee of representatives from the Central and Strathclyde Regions and the Stirling and Bearsden and Milngavie Districts was formed to consider a joint country park project.

The West Central Scotland Plan (1974) also echoed many of the Plan's proposals. Loch Lomond, the A74 and the Clyde coast were identified as areas with particular needs for tourist facilities. It was suggested that an urgent task for the new Strathclyde Regional Council was to draw up a countryside and coastal strategy, and to prepare a co-ordinated regional programme of country parks and conservation proposals. The West Central Scotland Plan pointed to the plethora of public and private agencies involved in rural and recreation planning, and considered that the lack of satisfactory administrative arrangements remained a major problem. Particular concern was expressed about the Loch Lomond area, for which it was suggested that a management board should be established with responsibility for management plans, recreation centres and ranger services and with effective powers of planning control. These features had been recognised by the earlier Plan as part of the essential framework for park development.

The administrative problems of rural and countryside planning also concerned the Parliamentary Select Committee on Scottish Land Resource Use, which in 1972 recommended the preparation of a national structure plan and the closer consultation of agencies responsible for aspects of the economy and use of the countryside. In its observations on the Committee's report, the Government felt that the shortcomings of land use planning could be largely rectified by better use of existing administrative machinery. A Scottish Standing Committee on Rural Land Use was established with representatives of major public agencies concerned with rural activities and environmental issues.

Development 1975-1980

The re-organisation of local government in 1975 and the introduction of new planning machinery provided a new context for developing recreation at Region and District levels. In addition, as the 1970's advanced, changing social and economic conditions and greater emphasis on the problems of urban deprivation brought new considerations and priorities to recreation planning.

The Local Government (Scotland) Act 1973 had placed a statutory duty on Regional Authorities to ensure adequate provision for people's enjoyment of coast and countryside. New departments with specific responsibilities for leisure and recreation were set up in the new Regions and Districts. The new Regional Department of Leisure and Recreation for Strathclyde was initially headed by Arthur Oldham, formerly Director of the Glasgow Parks Department, whose creative management had encouraged greater use of urban parks and brought countryside walkways into the City. However, the new management structure for leisure and recreation in the Regional Council was not successful. Lack of political support, no specific working remit and failure to define satisfactory differences in functions between regional and district levels, were all factors which contributed to the lack of success in the arrangements.

During the 1970's, urban deprivation and the creation of employment became major issues. Strathclyde Regional Council (1977) identified derelict and degraded land and poor housing environments as among the main strategic issues to be faced by its forthcoming Structure Plan. Provision of recreation facilities became linked with matters of urban environmental improvement and the rehabilitation of outworn areas within Glasgow and on the urban fringe. The over-riding need was for environmental improvement to increase the attractiveness of the region for investment. Recreation issues were secondary to more pressing economic problems and received only slight attention in the first Strathclyde Structure Plan completed in 1979. However, at this time there were numerous national developments which had important implications for regional and local planning.

In 1974, the Countryside Commission for Scotland, the Scottish Tourist Board, the Scottish Sports Council and the Forestry Commission embarked on a joint programme of Scottish Tourism and Recreation Planning Studies. The programme was designed to assist in the evolution of strategies for sport, outdoor recreation and tourism for each new Region and Island Authority Area in Scotland, co-ordinated within a broad national framework. The studies sought a corporate approach to recreation planning in common areas of concern. However, they were not as successful at regional and local levels where the changing economic climate and different priorities and pressures led to slippage in a complex and ambitious programme.

At this time, the Scottish agencies published a number of

documents concerned with strategic planning for recreation and tourism. The Scottish Tourist Board's Preliminary National Strategy (Scottish Tourist Board 1975; 1977), stressed the role of tourism in generating employment and the importance of urban based facilities for the joint use of tourists and local people. Travis's report for the Scottish Tourist Board (1974) suggested the establishment of a Maritime Museum in Glasgow and a Museum of Emigration at Greenock.

In 1974, the Countryside Commission for Scotland advocated "A Park System for Scotland" in a report which proposed a hierarchy of parks and new machinery for their administration. Special Parks with individual authorities were proposed for areas including Loch Lomond and the Trossachs. Issues concerning the balance of administrative and planning powers were again raised but, in any case, the report coincided with local government re-organisation when other concerns were paramount and little could be achieved.

The new planning system had established Structure and Local Plans as principal statements of planning policy. The Secretary of State now sought to disengage central government from day-to-day involvement with the planning work of local authorities. A series of National Planning Guidelines was published by the Scottish Development Department to assist in the definition of proposals which raised national issues and which should be notified to the Secretary of State.

Earlier, in 1974, the Scottish Development Department had issued coastal planning guidelines which identified preferred development and conservation zones for the guidance of oil-related developments. Conservation zones along the Clyde from Cloch Point to north of Largs and from south of Ayr to Dipple, coincided with those identified by the Plan as areas of high scenic value to be preserved from buildings and advertisements. The new preferred development zone at Hunterston marked a strong divergence from the proposals in the Plan, which had envisaged this area as a holiday village.

The National Planning Guidelines were followed by the Countryside Commission for Scotland's review (1978) of the national framework for landscape conservation and outdoor recreation. The Commission's report identified landscapes of national importance, and provided the basis for changes in the system of development control and referral to the Secretary of State which had operated since the definition of National Park Direction Areas in 1948. Within the newly defined and more extensive areas of scenic importance, only limited classes of development were now to be referred. The new referral system gave an important role to the Countryside Commission for

Scotland. However, it did not receive universal support and was criticised by local authorities for its agency involvement and for acting as a brake on economic developments in remote areas. Under the new system, Loch Lomond and the Trossachs were redefined as National Scenic Areas.

However, by the late 1970's, the local authorities were moving towards the kind of comprehensive planning for Loch Lomond which the Plan had proposed thirty years earlier. A Local (Subject) Plan was prepared for recreation, tourism and landscape conservation through the Loch Lomond Planning Group representing Dumbarton District Council, Stirling District Council, Central Regional Council and Strathclyde Regional Council. In 1980, the draft Local Plan identified "policy areas" and proposed a system of management by a joint committee of the two District and two Regional Councils with responsibilities in the Loch Lomond area. The Committee would have executive powers for management and implementation and advisory functions, but would not have local planning powers. The compatibility of local planning decisions would be ensured by statutory adoption of the Local Plan and through consultation. The Committee would include representatives from national interests appointed by the Secretary of State.

In 1980, preparatory work on the first Review of the Strathclyde Structure Plan gave attention to recreation and landscape isues within a wider countryside strategy. A typology of three major areas for countryside policy was recognised: (1) Areas of Rural Stabilisation, (2) Remote Landscape Areas, and (3) The Countryside Around Towns. Strathclyde included a wider geographical area than the Clyde Valley, and the Structure Plan gave more attention to the need to reinforce the unstable base of rural communities than had appeared necessary to the Plan in the early 1940's. The Plan had not anticipated a reduction in agricultural labour from prewar levels, but had proposed a redistribution of population from farm cottages to small villages. It noted the disadvantages to the agricultural community of creating large rural settlements, and advocated housing for rural workers at an intermediate village level between farm and small town. The villages would look to local centres for services, but would maintain their individuality. In fact, the decades since the 1940's witnessed further large reductions in farm employment, and the organisation of rural services became a major issue in many areas. Other factors such as increased numbers of holiday and retiral homes in rural areas were altering basic social and economic conditions, and had implications for stabilisation policies. Rural Districts considered that the new Strathclyde Regional Council's concern for urban deprivation underestimated the problems of remoteness and low income in Argyll, Southern

Lanarkshire and the peripheral parts of the Region, which were also of highest landscape and recreation quality. The preparation of the Review of the Structure Plan questioned the appropriateness of key village strategies to conditions in the Region and proposed the identification of functional settlement groups. The emphasis was again on the needs of the community rather than the concentration of facilities and development.

The Regional Council's policy on Remote Landscape Areas was based on the designation of protected areas for development control purposes. In a similar manner, the Clyde Valley Regional Plan had identified areas where developments should be restricted and where detailed design guidelines should be enforced. The designation of protected areas for control purposes has become an important planning tool. In dealing with countryside around towns, the Regional Council's broad aims of protecting agricultural land and preventing the merging of settlements were similar to the earlier intentions of the Plan. However, since the 1940's the conflict between recreation and agriculture had grown in intensity. Informal recreation pressures were difficult to police and solutions could not be found in the delineation of zones of exclusive land use. Additional problems of waste disposal and industrial pollution had arisen, which demanded new solutions which tended to lie outside the control of regional planning policies. An urgent need was for local urban fringe management schemes and the co-operation of a wide range of agencies and local interests in practical experiments on the ground.

The Plan had taken a positive approach to the provision of recreation facilities, including design guidelines. In the new planning system after 1975, matters of detailed management and design became primarily the concern of District Councils and of their Local Plans. The Strathclyde Regional Council managed the two country parks for which it had taken responsibility in 1975, but new initiatives in management and design were subsequently taken only in conjunction with groups of District Councils. A Local (Subject) Plan for the Forth and Clyde Canal was published for discussion purposes in January 1980, having been prepared jointly by the District and Regional Authorities through which the Canal passes. This type of inter-authority enterprise was supported by the availability of funding from the Countryside Commission for Scotland and the Scottish Development Agency. The Plan had regarded the Canal as a disadvantage to development and an obstruction to road and rail communications, concluding that it was in the public interest to discontinue and fill in the Canal. This proposal was never implemented, and the Canal lay derelict until its archaeological and recreation potential was recognised in the 1970's.

Elsewhere, the _Plan_ had recognised the Region's archaeological heritage in recommending comprehensive planning treatment for the Antonine Wall. A study of the recreational potential of the Wall was not undertaken until commissioned by the Countryside Commission for Scotland in 1973, to be subsequently partly taken up by individual Districts. A more considerable recreational development anticipated by the _Plan_ was the creation of a footpath system in the region. This remained a dormant proposal until riverside walkways were established in Glasgow on Arthur Oldham's initiative and the first designated long distance footpath, the West Highland Way, from Milngavie just north of Glasgow to Fort William was officially opened on 6 October 1980. The West Highland Way had involved the co-operation of three Regional Councils and was funded by the Countryside Commission for Scotland.

THE PLAN IN RETROSPECT

The _Plan_ was chiefly concerned with the needs of the congested and outworn urban areas of the Clydeside Conurbation. The reduction of densities and the re-organisation of space to serve society's changing needs had profound land use implications, which could only be tackled on a regional basis. Within this context, the two related matters of recreation and open space were seen as vital elements in the improvement of living standards and creation of new patterns of land use. The _Plan_ was not constrained by limits of departmental or agency responsibility. It dealt with the total complexity of recreation needs and foreshadowed work which would later be undertaken by Government, specialised agencies, District and Regional authorities. Its treatment of recreation and open space as an integral part of the Region's complex activities still has valuable lessons for planning today.

During the thirty-five years since the _Plan_, recreation planning has reacted to changing social and economic conditions and has matured in approach, techniques and administration. The _Plan's_ proposals for recreation and open space were advanced in their anticipation of recreational needs and in the comprehensive strategy which they proposed. The proposals did not achieve immediate success because of the failure to establish any suitable administrative and financial framework. It was not until the early 1970's that Government had created recreation funding agencies and a new local government structure and planning machinery, which could provide a workable framework for the developments foreshadowed in the _Plan_. The evolution of arrangements for recreation and countryside planning between 1945 and 1980, was marked by definition of the extent to which administrative responsibilit·

208

should be vested in central and local government or specialised agency, and by the pragmatic solution of making the best use of existing machinery wherever possible. The Clyde Valley Regional Plan recognised the full extent to which recreation and countryside matters were interwoven with other activities and land uses, and pointed to the role of the Regional Authority as effective co-ordinator. It is doubtful that any one specialised agency could deal with the total complexity of recreation and countryside planning. At the same time, the lack of any departmental or economic focus demands the co-ordination of recreation and countryside matters with other sectoral considerations. The Clyde Valley Regional Plan's basic assumption that this should be tackled on a regional basis holds true today.

The lack of an effective framework for regional and recreational planning was a major constraint on achieving the Plan's proposals. Renewed interest in countryside matters and positive political will in the 1960's combined to mark this period as one of renewed activity and interest in countryside and recreational planning. During the 1970's, economic recession and severe cuts in budgets for recreation provision inhibited the expansion of recreation planning and development. More emphasis was given to the management of existing facilities than to the planning of new projects involving large amounts of public expenditure. In the 1960's, recreation planning had aimed to meet the needs of an increasingly affluent, mobile and leisured society, but by the late 1970's this image had substantially changed. Inflation, mounting unemployment and increasing petrol prices were all factors which influenced the use of leisure time. Greater emphasis was given to facilities close to urban areas, to recreation projects as part of urban and environmental renewal programmes and to less capital intensive projects linked to informal community development schemes. These events may in turn require the further evolution of flexible administrative and agency solutions.

Changes in social and economic conditions and developments in administration and legislation alter the context within which Scottish recreation planning is carried out. Nevertheless, within the period 1945-1980 the Plan remained a remarkable document. It foreshadowed later approaches to recreation planning and its strategic appraisal of recreation needs produced a pattern of proposed facilities which substantially withstood the test of time. However, the achievement of these proposals had to await the evolution of new and complex planning machinery at all levels of government.

9 Robustness in Regional Planning: An Evaluation of the Clyde Valley Regional Plan

URLAN WANNOP AND ROGER SMITH

THE IMPACT OF THE PLAN

Was the Plan Fulfilled?

There has not been an exact fit between the recommendations made in the Clyde Valley Regional Plan and what has happened 'on the ground'. Despite the level of detail given in the Plan, it is doubtful whether those working on it saw it as a precise blueprint. Even so we can be impressed by the formidable degree to which the Plan was realised. We can be equally impressed with the influence that the Plan exercised over a long period of time.

This influence can be quantified in a simple but informative way. Figure 9.1 is based upon the seventy-six items contained in the Summary of Recommendations and Conclusions of the Plan (reproduced in the Appendix). It attempts, within broad chronological bands, to show when recommendations and conclusions were implemented. This is a matter which cannot always be done with any precision and it cannot be assumed that the implementation of any given recommendation was necessarily attributable to the influence of the Plan. But with these qualifications, three important conclusions stand out:-

> (1) Out of seventy-six recommendations and conclusions some fifty can be judged to have been realised;
>
> (2) Of the fifteen items subjectively judged as of

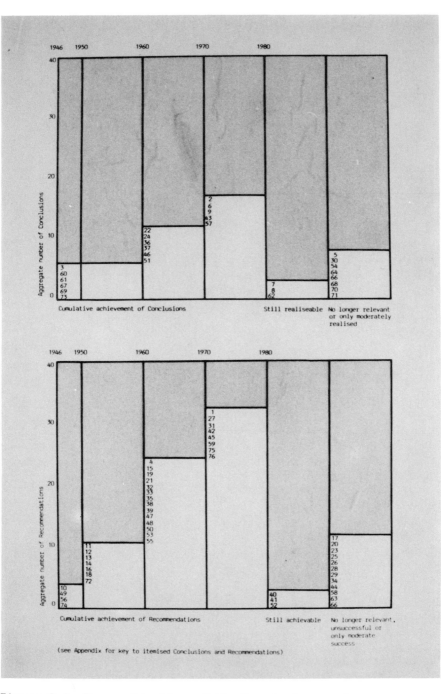

Figure 9.1   The realisation of the Conclusions and
Recommendations of the Plan

higher importance, only four might be said to have failed to be implemented;

(3) Most items implemented came about over fifteen years after the Plan had been published.

The major strategy that dominated the Plan was that of decentralisation. It was to that end that the regional planners related the more significant of their other recommendations. Until the early 1970's, such a philosophy dominated the planning of the region with two persistent areas of concern - (1) the decaying physical fabric of much of the region's housing stock, especially within Glasgow, and the attendant heavy-overcrowding and congestion, and (2) the poor condition, measured in terms of high unemployment and low productivity, of the region's economy. The housing problem was seen as the more important, at least until the early 1960's. This accords with the priority given in the Plan. Thus, the designation of East Kilbride, Cumbernauld, Livingston and the subsequently abandoned Stonehouse, combined with the town expansion programmes following the 1957 Housing and Town Development Act, may not have followed the Clyde Valley Regional Plan recommendations to the letter, but they did realise the spirit of the proposals of decentralisation which were intimately linked to the redevelopment of the Glasgow slums.

The rationale of overspill depended upon the preservation of a Clydeside green belt or, more precisely, a green envelope. There were immediate major encroachments on the proposals set out in the Plan, but here again the spirit gained respect and high quality land which might have been used for development has been kept in agricultural use.

As for the region's economic base, the Plan saw the need to revitalise traditional heavy industries as well as to draw in new plants. An important element of the thinking was also bound up with decentralisation. Three of the four new towns recommended in the Plan were to act as magnets drawing growth industries from the more prosperous parts of Britain - and indeed the world. The fourth new town depended upon the relocation of the Lanarkshire steel industry. The new towns, in absorbing smaller firms from the congested parts of Glasgow, were also to provide them with space for expansion. In fact, the Scottish Office extended the scope of the Plan's proposals to a considerable degree, and by 1963 Government was arguing that new towns, and the economic growth that was to be encouraged within them, could be used to reconstruct the economy of the central belt of Scotland. The Clyde Valley proposals were enlarged to such a degree that in 1966, Irvine was designated to play a purely economic role in which

overspill from Glasgow played no part. Indeed, the Development
Corporation was antipathetic to links with Glasgow's planning
problems.

   Associated with economic development, the Plan also made a
strong plea for a national economic plan for Scotland and for a
Regional Authority charged 'to secure and hold industry for the
benefit   of   the   whole   Conurbation' and to regulate   the
distribution and location of industry.   The founding of the
Regional Development Division and then of the Scottish Economic
Development Department in the Scottish Office can be seen as an
alternative   realisation.   More   significant   was   the
establishment in 1975 of the Scottish Development Agency.
However, although the Agency drew in streams of argument
previously flowing within the Scottish Economic Development
Department, it was immediately associated with the analysis of
the West Central Scotland Plan of 1971-74 rather than with its
predecessor Plan of 1944-46.

   The proposals of the Clyde Valley planners for housing and
industry   had   major   implications   for   transport   and
communication.   The Plan was anxious to speed traffic flows
into and out of the region, from Glasgow to the decentralised
settlements and within Glasgow itself. These are matters which
have been to the fore within West Central Scotland since the
war.   Certainly there has been a strong and continuing
influence of the need to establish motorways from England into
the region, even if manifested only in the short M74 motorway
linking with the dual carriage highway (A74) to England and the
M8 linking the East Coast of Scotland with the West - integral
to the 1963 White Paper on Central Scotland and the Oceanspan
reports.   We can also see, at least in principle, the motorway
and dual carriageway proposals linking Glasgow and the new
towns which were powerfully advocated in the Greater Glasgow
Transportation Studies of the 1960's.   Within Glasgow itself,
the need for a series of ring roads was a principal element in
Glasgow's planning until the early 1970's, when only the inner
of three rings was retained in a strategy now dominated by
radial routes into the City.   The Plan's anticipation of
traffic growth was well-judged.   Rejecting the Ministry of
Transport's multiple of x4 for traffic growth in twenty years,
the Plan assumed a multiple of x6 for growth to the 'long-
term'.   The number of cars in Great Britain actually grew by a
multiple of x6 from 1946 to 1968.

   As with so many of the proposals in the Plan, there was a
hiatus between 1946 and the 1960's before the recommendations
for open space and recreation were either implemented directly
or absorbed into other plans and policies.   Thus, it was not
until 1973, for example, that work began on the Plan's proposal

for Hamilton Low Parks - now Strathclyde Park. Similarly, it was not until the 1960's that the Clyde/Muirshiel Regional Park was established. At a more ambitious level, the schemes in the Plan for a national recreational centre at Balloch as an entrance to a proposed National Park for Loch Lomond and the managed development of the recreational amenity of the coast of Ayrshire, have yet to be implemented. But the robustness of the proposals is seen by their recurrence in the strategies of local authorities, commissions, the West Central Scotland Plan and the Strathclyde Structure Plan.

The extent to which what the Plan wanted was achieved 'on the ground' or in the development of planning thought and policy is less easy to discern in community planning standards and architecture. The Plan loathed the overcrowding in the tenements of Clydeside. It noted the work of Mackintosh and a few notable West of Scotland architects of the late 19th century as exceptional by contrast with the mediocrity and architectural despoliation of the general run of Victorian and post-Victorian building. What was thought to be most evidently worthy of preservation were examples of eighteenth century architecture, especially within the planned and industrial villages of the period. This enthusiasm was later taken up by the 'conservation' societies which became prominent in the 1960's. In terms of new developments, the Plan's advocacy of neighbourhood units was immediately realised in the new town of East Kilbride.

The Plan recognised that its principal proposals would immediately cut across the established pattern of local government. The concluding chapter discussed the underlying issue of how its package of proposals could be implemented. The solution was unequivocally represented as the setting up of a regional authority, and it can be demonstrated that the 1975 reform of Scottish local government with its regional emphasis and the creation of the Strathclyde Regional Council derive considerably from the Plan. The continual emphasis of the Plan upon organisation and programmes was to be as significant an influence on Scottish affairs as its physical proposals were for the Clyde Valley.

So far, recommendations which were either achieved or remained alive as ideas have been isolated without passing judgement upon the degree to which the Plan exercised influence. In many instances the spirit rather than the letter of the recommendations was realised. East Kilbride and Cumbernauld were located precisely where the Plan proposed; the other new towns to serve the region were not. The green belt became a permanent part of regional strategy, but encroachments were made into some of the key areas suggested in the original proposals. The regional authority and a national industrial agency were achieved, but the Strathclyde Region and the Scottish Development Agency were in significant respects different to what had been originally anticipated. The list could be extended.

Some recommendations in the Plan have been abandoned. The arguments for a great international airport in the region, and for the substantial commercial redevelopment of the Glasgow docks, have ceased to be seriously discussed. And some recommendations, like the need for community planning in relatively low density schemes were effectively ignored, as the peripheral housing estates of Glasgow and the comprehensive redevelopment schemes demonstrated.

Even so, we must return to the good fit between proposals and achievement in the Plan, which becomes the more striking when seen against the modest size of the planning team and the short period in which the Plan was compiled, and also against the undeveloped state of the art of regional planning and the lack of experience of planning in the intellectual disciplines on which the team could draw.

Factors for Failure and Success

The contemporary student of regional planning, who understood how the Plan was prepared but who was unfamiliar with the subsequent history of West Central Scotland, might be tempted to deduce that the Plan's assumptions of a total population continuing at a level similar to that existing for the next 40 or 50 years would cause it to miss the tide of events – like the contemporaneous regional plan for Central and South East Scotland. This population assumption at the core of the Plan was to be overtaken by birth rates contrary to the declining trend of the pre-Plan period. The Plan had no contemporary evidence by which to anticipate the substantial natural increase of population which would be generated within Glasgow and the substantial exodus from the City without official encouragement.

As fundamental as were the difficulties of foreseeing post-War demographic trends were the difficulties of anticipating the progress of the Clydeside economy. Although the Plan noted the vulnerability of leading industries, the industrial proposals concentrated on the need to relieve congested industrial employment and to divert new industries from declining districts of high unemployment to expanding areas and were a reflection of the Barlow philosophy without adjustment to Clydeside conditions. The then conventional planning policy was set beside the primitive state of regional economic theory.

British Universities had hardly even familiarised themselves with the modest advances that had been made in regional economics across the Atlantic. Furthermore, regional statistics and survey data was limited.

The initial hostility of Glasgow to the Plan did much to retard its implementation. Support from successive Secretaries of State for Scotland was never assured. Indeed, lacking the local impact of a regional authority for Clydeside with strong executive powers, the Plan's progress depended upon the changing strength of economic conditions and a favourable balance amongst the several kinds of political force, the relative strength of which fluctuated over time.

What then were the forces ranged against the Plan which delayed or countered it? Initially, the objections lay primarily with the local authorities of the Clyde Valley. The Plan as a whole was neither rejected nor approved by the Clyde Valley Regional Planning Advisory Committee, which in 1947 recommended to its constituent local authorities that they instead support a long list comprising the majority of conclusions and recommendations including the principle of a Green Belt and an Inquiry into the case for a Regional Authority. A shorter list of the Plan's proposals dealing with the sharp political issues of policy for the new towns and population and industrial relocation was presented without any recommendation, as representing a cleavage of opinion on the Committee. The Scottish Office accepted the necessity for new towns to help reduce Glasgow's congestion, but Bruce, the City Engineer, remained adamant that the City could and should be rebuilt largely within its boundaries without resort to new towns. Westwood, the first Secretary of State in the Labour Government elected in 1945, designated East Kilbride against Glasgow's objections and the Development Corporation began work in 1947. Glasgow withdrew from the Committee and was not to rejoin until Bruce's influence on City policy disappeared. The Westwood commitment to the other three new towns and the Green Belt proposed by the Plan also disappeared when he was succeeded by Arthur Woodburn, who conceded Glasgow's expansion southwards at Castlemilk into the Green Belt where his predecessor had resisted the City's wishes. The nucleus of the Plan staff was now in the Scottish Office and was directly responsible for advising the Secretary of State. A peak of national financial difficulties and, perhaps, an acceptance that Glasgow's independent planning preparations offered the probability of more rapid housebuilding than new towns would offer, over-rode the conservation of Green Belt at Castlemilk. Later, the scale of building at Drumchapel and Easterhouse would also reach further into the Green Belt than the Plan had recommended.

Before Woodburn was in turn succeeded as Secretary of State
by Hector McNeil, moves within the Scottish Office were in the
direction of proceeding with a new town at Houston, in lieu of
that at Bishopton which the Plan had proposed to be directly
associated with overspill from Greenock, for which McNeil was
Member of Parliament. Houston was suspect to McNeil's
political colleagues in Greenock as East Kilbride had been
suspect to Glasgow; overspill was a mark of diminished status,
lost political and social strength, the diversion of new
industries and a possible draw upon established industries from
older towns. McNeil stopped the move to add Houston to the new
town programme. In 1951, the election of a Conservative
government antipathetic to new towns brought a halt to the
programme of further designation in England and Wales and
accompanied the prolonged delay before Cumbernauld was
designated in 1956.

Within these first five years of the Plan's life, changes in
emphasis in Government attitude to the contentious issue of new
towns, expansion of Glasgow into the Green Belt and industrial
location, were associated with successive individuals in the
post of Secretary of State for Scotland. Westwood's commitment
to the Plan and McNeil's rejection of Houston were personal
acts; Woodburn's role was less markedly personal.

Thus during the period of almost 30 years in which the Plan
was to remain the outstanding appraisal of the region's
condition and the most comprehensive declaration of policy, it
lacked the fundamental support of a Regional Authority for
Clydeside. Without that internal regional impetus, the Plan's
progress depended upon the changing strength of economic
conditions and a favourable balance amongst the several kinds
of political force whose relative strength and attitude to
components of the Plan fluctuated over time.

The Politics of Regional Planning and Development

Political pressures in regional development in the Clyde Valley
have come from sources characteristic of metropolitan planning
and change elsewhere in Great Britain. Party politics has
tended to be less obvious a factor of stress in regional
planning within British metropolitan regions than has been the
institutional politics of relationships between the great
Cities and their surrounding Counties. In the territorial
battles of the 1950's and early 1960's between Manchester and
Cheshire, or in the 1960's between Birmingham and neighbouring
Worcestershire and Warwickshire, the politics of status and
administrative boundaries overshadowed issues of party
advantage even if these were also inherent in the
redistribution of electors between the areas of separate

217

Councils.   Institutional politics were similarly prominent   in
the Clyde Valley.   Even so, party politics and decisions   in
planning   taken   with   strong   political   motives   cannot   be
discounted;   interest   includes the degree to which motives may
rest   with   an individual politician – as with McNeil   or   some
subsequent Secretaries of State,   or may lie collectively   with
an   elected   political   majority – as   perhaps   with   the
Conservative administration in Renfrewshire in their aggressive
period of development of new communities in the County.

Glasgow   was   not   in sustained   dispute   over   proposals   to
encroach   on adjoining Counties,   as was notably the case   with
Manchester   in   North-West England and with Birmingham   in   the
West   Midlands.   The restraint of Glasgow and its neighbouring
authorities on an issue which was so contentious in England   in
the   1950's   and   1960's   can   only   be   explained   against   a
background of several distinctive Clydeside   factors.   Glasgow
retained   considerable   unbuilt   land   within   its   boundaries,
including   Green Belt in which the City Council and   Government
were   both   prepared to concede sites for   building;   all   five
Counties   in the Clyde Valley were willing to accept new   towns
or   to   themselves institute overspill expansion   schemes;   the
City   Council   enthusiastically   negotiated   further   overspill
schemes   right   across Scotland.   From the   early   1950's   the
balance   of inter-authority politics and the general acceptance
of   Glasgow's housing problems accordingly favoured the   Plan's
principles   of   dispersal   to   an   exceptional   degree.   The
significance   of institutional politics in regional development
was   notably   characterised   in   1975,   when   the   same   local
government leaders from Lanarkshire who only three years before
had supported the designation of Stonehouse new town,   were   to
lead the campaign against it when they took over the leadership
of the new Regional Council.   The successful change of emphasis
in   regional   development policy of the mid 1970's   accordingly
depended   upon   a   coincident   but   separately   inspired   reorganisation   of   local   government.   The   Plan's   dispersal
strategy   was   not   significantly   impeded   by   the   old   local
government pattern which the Plan had sought to replace.

Until 1975,   local authorities and the Scottish Office tended
to   a more intimate relationship than is customary in   England.
Relations frequently combined   an excessive dependency   by   the
local   authority   with some condescension on the part of   Civil
servants.   After 1951 and the retreat by Government from overt
regional planning,   the Scottish Office re-asserted its assumed
responsibilities   in   the   designation   of   Cumbernauld,   the
subsequent   incorporation   of regional growth area policy   into
the Plan's metropolitan strategy of dispersal and the formation
of   the   Regional   Development   Division   of   the   Scottish
Development   Department.   In   the   absence   of   a   regional

authority, the Government carried into its own organisation the principles which the Plan had sought to apply to local government. The peak of Government dominance in regional planning was held between 1963 and 1973.

Local authorities climbed up from their subordinate position in regional planning only when the West Central Scotland Plan was being shaped between 1972 and 1974. Although the Scottish Office welcomed the new plan's proposals for economic policy, for an Economic Development Corporation and an Environmental Improvement Task Force, the plan's open reservations about Stonehouse challenged deep-rooted convictions in the Scottish Office about the inevitable pre-eminence of new towns in Scottish industrial development. The West Central Scotland Plan, for whose beginnings the local authorities had had little collective enthusiasm and in which none had been prepared to be seen to share in Government's lead, finally became an assertion of the new regional responsibilities of local government.

The position of the Secretary of State for Scotland in the political administration of the United Kingdom has incorporated a degree of independence in planning policy and - until the late 1970s - a distinct advantage in competition for public expenditure between UK regions. The ability of the Scottish Office to press on Whitehall a sustained case on Scotland's behalf has customarily been reinforced by the willingness of Scots groups to cut across party, social, industrial, cultural and administrative divisions in support of a collective Scottish interest. The Scottish lobby and the weight of Scotland in electoral considerations, went in hand with the achievement of relatively more new towns for the Clyde Valley than was granted to any other British conurbation. Cumbernauld had been designated in 1956 by the initiative of a Conservative Secretary of State for Scotland, as the first exception to the antipathy to new towns with which the Conservative Government had entered office in 1951; the Conservative Government would delay the designation of a further new town in England until they had been in office for ten years. In 1976, a Labour Scottish Secretary of State would take steps to end Stonehouse's short life before the English new town programme would be curtailed by the Secretary of State for the Environment, and the GEAR project in Glasgow would precede by almost five years the initiative of the succeeding Conservative Government to establish Urban Development Corporations in the docklands of Liverpool and London. The force of the Scottish lobby had also been evident when the West Central Scotland Plan had published its proposal of 1974 for a Strathclyde Economic Development Corporation, to be enacted as the · Scottish Development Agency.

McNeil's influence as Secretary of State in stopping the move to establish a new town at Houston followed Bruce's equally personal intervention in the progress of the Plan as City Engineer. Twenty-five years later, Millan's actions as Secretary of State to terminate Stonehouse and create the GEAR project would similarly reflect local personal experience and political circumstances. Although the preparatory negotiations which led to the commissioning of the West Central Scotland Plan began during the office of Ross, whose occupation of the post of Secretary of State for Scotland was the longest since the inception of the office in 1885, his personal influence on regional planning in the Clyde Valley was perhaps most notably borne on the developing relationship of Irvine New Town to the rest of North Ayrshire and to his own constituency of Kilmarnock.

The colour of party politics was not consistently attached to particular emphases of policy nor was it constantly evident in regional planning in the Clyde Valley. New Towns had been a party political issue in England when the Conservative opposition strongly opposed arrangements for the designation of the earliest new towns for London in 1946, but party issues were less obvious in Scotland until 1975, when the electors of the new towns of Strathclyde were showing a collective tendency to move in support of the Scottish National Party. The Labour Party acutely resented the disruption which Scottish Nationalism caused to the Party's established base in industrial Scotland. The successful campaign of the Regional Council to terminate Stonehouse and bring the other regional new towns under the influence of its strategic plan, ran parallel to the Council's concern at the electoral threat of Nationalism which the new towns epitomised. But here again, Labour Ministers' willingness to terminate Stonehouse did not extend to stringent restraint on the other new towns, so that the regional political concern of the Strathclyde Labour Party was not shared equally by the national Party leadership in Government.

The change in 1974 from a Conservative to a Labour Government which followed the publication of the West Central Scotland Plan was important to the creation of a Scottish Development Agency on the lines anticipated in that plan. The popular advantage to the new Government in quickly capturing an initiative in Scottish economic affairs by creating the Agency, combined with the electoral advantage of seizing political ground from the Scottish National Party. The quick succession of the Labour Party to government in Whitehall and in Strathclyde created a climate in which the West Central Scotland Plan's proposals of 1974 could be accepted and, crucially, be effected at a speed impossible for the Clyde

Valley Plan of 1946.

Was the Plan Right?

In measuring the influence of the Plan we have not so far
evaluated its 'rightness'. Riding the tide of events over a
long period may or may not be desirable. But if greater
attention in Government initiatives had been paid to Glasgow,
if high density development had been avoided, if greater
investment had been made in community facilities and if the new
towns programme had been dovetailed into policies for the inner
areas, then many of the problems later facing the Government
and local authorities would surely have been lessened. If
slum clearance had been dovetailed more closely into overspill,
if greater care had been taken to avoid socio-economic
discrimination in the official overspill schemes, and if more
attention had been paid to social services in Glasgow, the
problems of the Clyde Valley might have been less acute than
they became. Considering the accumulating influence of the
Plan as an advisory document, perhaps it could have been more
influential if a regional authority had been quickly
established during the late 1940's. But this would have
depended upon the officers and elected officials having a
sensitive appreciation of what the Plan was about and a
commitment to implement it.

The simple enumeration of the high proportion of the Plan's
proposals which have been adopted does not confirm that it was
right, unless it can also be shown that no alternative courses
of action would have better met its objectives. Nor would the
failure of underlying assumptions have denied the quality of
the Plan if it had proved flexible to change. On these tests,
what has been the quality of the Plan?

If the Plan is viewed as one whose proposals were
cumulatively adopted over a period of thirty years, its
influence was carried through times in which the economy of the
West of Scotland was initially protected by the industrial
expansion of the United States from the worst consequences of
its own decline, but subsequently increasingly suffered from
the dwindling of external investment and the worsening
competitive position of its domestic industries. Population
within the region grew from 1945 to a peak in the mid-1960's,
from which a sustained decline became firmly established.
Within ten years of publication of the Plan, the region had
already experienced a growth of some 50,000 population; because
the Plan had assumed that there would be no growth, events in
the following decade had actually generated a potential need
for another new town in addition to the four envisaged by the
Plan. This potential would disappear within a further ten

years, and in the early 1980's the Plan's proposals for new
towns and urban growth can be seen to be much more in scale
with a balanced strategy for a time of falling population than
was the programme of growth areas by which the Plan was
extended in the mid 1960's. The Plan was simultaneously right
about the size of the long-run scale of demand for new towns,
wrong in its underlying demographic analysis, wrong to assume
the acceptance of its proposition that the Clyde Valley was
saturated with population and - perhaps - right to propose that
a major displacement of people from the West to the East of
Scotland should begin in the 1940's, rather than almost twenty
years later as was to occur.

These events highlight the dimensions of programming and
resources which are part of contemporary regional planning.
The Plan did not detail any phased programme for action or
affirm the feasibility of its proposals by a supportive
appraisal of resources. The Preamble to the Plan represents a
different but perhaps not contrary attitude -
    'It is not too much to say that, if a reasonable
    standard of decency of living is to be aimed at, the
    major proportion of the communities of the region
    require complete replacement within the next twenty-
    five years' (para. 4).
The Plan thus set objectives for change and development in the
region on a horizon beyond the reach of any convincing
financial appraisal. The matter of resources was dealt with in
what the Plan regarded as the prior issue of organisational
arrangements, whereby the longer-sighted of the Plan's
proposals would be fulfilled. Thus,
    'The Regional Plan - which of course is a long-period
    plan - should be under constant review in order to
    meet and provide for ever-changing circumstances and
    conditions' (para. 1794).
    'We point ... to the urgent and clamant need for a
    review of the administrative problems facing
    Clydeside and the Conurbation, if a real solution of
    the major difficulties which stand in the way of a
    sane and sound Regional Plan is to be arrived at. In
    the absence of such a review we believe Regional
    Planning will be futile' (para. 80).

A later Principal Planning Officer for Glasgow would give his
view of subsequent history in evidence to the Parliamentary
Select Committee on Land Resource Use in Scotland of 1971-72,
    'We have had the Clyde Valley Regional Advisory
    Committee since 1946, but it has not been able to
    achieve anything as such because it does have no
    teeth at all. It cannot dictate to the local
    authorities, it cannot force on the local authorities

its views about regional matters, and therefore, although a lot of the Clyde Valley Plan proposed by Abercrombie has been realised, do not let us have any doubt about it, it was because it was realised later that these were good things to do, it could not be imposed at all. The Regional Plan was advisory and gradually became accepted but it took a long time to be accepted.'

The urgent and clamant need for a review of administrative problems asserted by the Plan was not satisfied until the Wheatley Commission, twenty years after and almost at the horizon of its proposals. A partial review of regional planning strategy was incorporated in the Central Scotland White Paper of 1963, but no review of complementary depth was completed until the West Central Scotland Plan of 1974; no administrative change was fulfilled until 1975. The major issue of resources raised by the Plan was therefore not resolved until its time horizon for physical action had been overrun. It may reasonably be said that the Plan was failed by its clients and not by its omission of an analysis of the financial component of resources. If this is a fair judgement, it is perhaps equally applicable to the Plan's omission of any consideration of alternative strategies for decentralisation, having rejected the alternative strategy for Glasgow's reconstruction presented by the City Engineer in the First Planning Report of the City.

THE PLAN AND ITS SIGNIFICANCE

The Special Case of the Clyde Valley in British Politics and administration.

It is insufficient to explain the influence of the Plan on the Clyde Valley by the fact that it rode tides of ideas and events, although that may have been a central factor. Clydeside has represented something of a special political case in Great Britain. The existence of the Scottish Office with a Secretary of State having a place in Cabinet has given peculiar political leverage to Scottish affairs. In addition, the political and economic history of Clydeside between the Wars had led all political parties to accept the depth of its social problems and to respect demands for their relief. Bad housing and high unemployment rates of West Central Scotland have been a continuing pressure on political consciences. Of course, this has also been true of the depressed regions of the North West, the North East of England and South Wales, and what gave West Central Scotland its edge for so long was its coupling of potential and actual support for a Labour Government to a coherent regional lobby, which perhaps nowhere else in the

223

United Kingdom so easily ignored internal, factional interests. The Conservatives were anxious to erode the Labour support by showing themselves sympathetic to the needs of Scottish industrial areas. After 1966, this quest by the two major parties for the Scottish vote was increasingly complicated by the growing strength of the Scottish Nationalist Party, which at least until 1978 was making inroads into Parliamentary, Regional and District seats in West Central Scotland. So for reasons of genuine concern, as well as for electoral considerations, Governments placed a high priority on easing the great social and economic problems of West Central Scotland. Furthermore, this concern was given greater purpose and direction because of the existence in the Scottish Office of the Scottish Development Department and the Scottish Economic Planning Department.

These concerns needed to be underlain by a strategy for which the Plan provided an inspirational basis. This gave the Plan early political strength, reinforced by an emerging and sympathetic flow of ideas for social and economic reform in the fields of education, housing, social welfare and economic development. Certainly, the first post-war Labour Government could see the Plan's views as consistent with its conception for change in Britain. Indeed, in terms of the Government's attitude to regional development, it accorded with the philosophy of the Barlow Commission to which the Government subscribed. By the mid 1960's, the Barlow philosophy was being reinterpreted to meet conditions of economic and population growth but of sustained disparities between the quality of life and standards of living enjoyed by the various regions. Although a continued policy of decentralisation of population and industry and commerce from Greater London was advocated as late as 1970 in the Government's Study for the South East of England, new and reinvigorated regional policies had emerged with regional planning boards and councils, tightened policy over industrial location and extended amounts and scope of public financing of firms in development areas and regions. Within this freshening climate, the Plan still underlay the additional physical and economic policies and developments introduced to West Central Scotland in the 1960's. The analysis was that the Plan remained correct in most essentials, but had to be extended because there was now no sympathy for its argument that population growth in the Clyde Valley should be restrained. It could be argued that instead of drawing on the 1948 Plan for Central and South East Scotland, the programme for development and growth in the 1963 White Paper on Central Scotland stretched the Clyde Valley Regional Plan to meet the requirement of the whole central industrial belt. The seeds of growth area philosophy allied to new towns could be found in the Plan, and Livingstone and Glenrothes were to

224

become recognised as both growth points and reception areas for emigrants from the West of Scotland.

Thus, the Plan can be seen as a package of physical and economic planning concepts which became increasingly enlarged by Government. But these developments were associated with the essential factor of individual administrators and planners working in Scotland and keeping the ideas of the Plan alive when planning was not in favour. The two key personalities were J H McGuinness and Robert Grieve, whose importance lay in:

(1) their intimate involvement in the preparation of the Plan. McGuinness, as an administrative civil servant within the old Department of Health in the Scottish Office, played a major role in the setting up of the regional advisory committee. Grieve, as leader of the full-time team working on the Plan, assumed most of the responsibility for interpreting Abercrombie's broad strategy to meet the needs of the region;

(2) their commitment to the broad proposals of the Plan throughout the 1950's and 1960's;

(3) their position of influence in government planning policy as far as it was concerned with West Central Scotland. McGuinness moved from the Department of Health to the Scottish Development Department when it assumed responsibility for planning. He subsequently founded the Regional Development Division which grew into the Economic Planning Department. Grieve, who had been recruited by Abercrombie from local government, joined the Department of Health, subsequently taking charge of affairs in West Central Scotland and later becoming Chief Planner for Scotland in the Development Department. These two men combined in positions of strength to develop policies grounded in the Clyde Valley Plan.

In isolating the role of individuals, account has also to be taken of the Chairman of the Clyde Valley Regional Planning Advisory Committee, Hugh MacCalman. MacCalman kept the idea of a regional authority alive, and as a member of the Wheatley commission was to be profoundly influential in recommending a reformed Scottish local government based upon a regional structure throughout Scotland and in the Clyde Valley in particular.

Summarising the influence of the Plan, it may be said to have grown within a framework of planning attitudes that dominated government thinking from at least 1939 and can be characterised as Barlow and Neo-Barlow policies. A range of national legislation over matters such as new towns and industrial

location was passed to realise these policies. The Clyde
Valley exhibited an acute form of the problems to which Barlow
and Neo-Barlow philosophies addressed their solutions. There
was perhaps an inevitable progression from this to the fact
that the Plan's recommendations were couched in Barlow-like
terms, because both Abercrombie and Sir William Whyte, the
Clerk to the Clyde Valley Regional Planning Committee, had been
members of the Barlow Commission. Although Abercrombie had
declined to sign the main report and Whyte had done so only
with reservations, their differences lay not with Barlow's
direction but essentially in their fuller view of the role of
the proposed National Industrial Board, which they thought must
control industrial development in all parts of Britain and not
only in the London area. Abercrombie considered that the Board
must have executive powers embracing planning as well as
industry, and here lay the basis for the Regional Authorities
which he proposed both for the Clyde Valley and for Greater
London. The continuity of Barlow's philosophy rested upon
Abercrombie's pre-eminence in metropolitan and regional
planning and his choice by the Regional Planning Committee as
consultant to the planning team. Moreover, much of the
influence of the Plan stemmed from the dedication of the few
men who had been completely involved in the preparation of the
Plan, and who remained in Scotland to foster and modify it
according to changing circumstances. Although some of the
recommendations in the Plan were separately adopted by local
authorities and government-appointed bodies with planning
responsibilities, the most powerful body in having the
recommendations implemented was the Scottish Office.

The Vision of the Plan

In its maturity, the reputation of the Plan remains that it was
visionary. It anticipated policies which would prove
increasingly irrestible as time passed, as their logic was
borne home to those initially unable to recognise their
inevitability or unable to immediately carry them against other
priorities. Its sweep of recommendations was of a boldness
appropriate to the swelling spirit for social change which
arose in Britain during the middle and later period of the war
of 1939-45. With a large national programme of social and
economic reconstruction in hand, it is understandable why
legislation and energy for internal regional administrative
changes could not be spared in the early post-war years. The
Plan's visionary reputation in Scotland lay in its panoply of
proposals for Clydeside and in the continuing commitment of
MacCalman, McGuinness and Grieve in their mutually supportive
but distinctive roles.

Three aspects of the vision are worth examining briefly. Was

226

the Plan influential outside Scotland, was it peculiarly
Scottish, and for which Scots was the vision shaped?

Followed only by Abercrombie's collaboration with Jackson in
the West Midlands Plan of 1948 - which looked to evolutionary
regional change associated with decentralisation but without a
programme of new towns - the Plan was succeeded by a vacuum in
the United Kingdom until regional planning was revived in
Scotland in the Central Scotland White Paper of 1963, and in
England through the series of regional studies commencing with
that for the South-East in 1964.   The Scottish revival brought
a more sophisticated and creative linkage between economic and
physical planning than had been evident in the Plan; as late as
1970 in England, however, the Strategic Plan for the South-East
still demonstrated the classic methods of Abercrombie.   Only
with the Strategies for the North-West in 1974 and the North in
1977 was there a new cast to English regional planning,
translating to a larger scale the style of sub-regional
planning emerging in England under the influence of the
Teesside Survey and Plan (1968) and in Scotland after the
Grangemouth/Falkirk Regional Survey and Plan (1968),   and
reflecting the major developments in regional planning of the
West Central Scotland Plan (1974).

The reputation of the Plan outside Scotland probably lay in
its underpinning of the structure of regional planning for
which Scotland was to gain an increasing and   rightful
reputation, rather than in any direct impact on practice in
England or in countries with developing economies, where
techniques of economic planning were introduced rather than the
essentially physical planning techniques of British practice.

Abercrombie worked from London and travelled to meet his team
intermittently; Matthew was nominally Deputy Consultant, but
his other responsibilities left scanty time to assist the Plan.
Grieve was leader of the working team and effectively the
masterhand in shaping the detail of the Plan.   However, any
Scottishness in the Plan's character probably lies in
particular facets and in its depth of local knowledge rather
than in any uniqueness of its vision.   The detailed economic
proposals of the Plan foreshadowed the weight which would be
given to problems of employment and industrial change in
Scottish regional planning from 1960 onwards.   England would
lag some ten years behind in putting economic proposals at the
centre of its revived regional planning, just as the Greater
London Plan had found less necessity than had the Plan to
elaborate the industrial functions of the Regional Planning
Authority which each proposed.   Although there are common
threads to the two published reports, the sense of social and
physical geography on Clydeside is closer and richer.   The Plan

leaves an impression of life in the Clyde Valley more vivid
than the Greater London Plan leaves of life in the London
Conurbation. Both plans describe and detail topography and
local conditions in a manner now uncommon in regional planning,
but it is hard to justify a marked Scottishness in the quality
of the Plan except in the hard landscape of Glasgow and the
physical conditions representative of the bitter economic and
social history of Clydeside.

For whom was the vision held up? There is a vivid sense in
the Plan of a communal rejection of the squalor and deprivation
of Clydeside's legacy of Victorian tenements and failing
industry. The Plan's representation of deprivation as
comprising bad housing and the risk of unemployment is less
complete than would be customary in 1980. The dimensions of a
latter-day radical analysis of urban and regional problems were
absent in the Plan as they would be from all subsequent major
metropolitan and regional plans in the United Kingdom.
MacCalman had written in his preface to the Plan that 'The
proof and test of any plan is whether it meets the needs and
requirements of ordinary folk.' This is the language of
politics and was the language of socially committed planners
until about 1968. It would be too simple a view for many
contemporary analysts of the motives and consequences of
planners and of politicians.

The Plan and the Nature of Regional Planning

What can be learned about the nature of regional planning from
the Plan? Since the early 1960's there has grown a distrust of
plans in the Master Plan idiom, especially those of an advisory
nature. The Planning Advisory Group of 1965 analysed the
performance of the statutory Development Plans following the
Town and Country Planning Act of 1947 and found them
inflexible, too frequently irrelevant and too quickly obsolete.
The major advisory Regional Plans prepared for the metropolitan
regions of Britain in the late 1960's and early 1970's
emphasised that effective regional planning was a sustained
process and not the result of spasmodic major statements of
strategy. The Plan had said this in 1946, and in 1967 Robert
Grieve would contain the strategy of the Highlands and Islands
Development Board in only a few paragraphs of the Board's first
annual report; the Board's policies were developed continuously
and not in any Master Plan. For the Highlands and Islands, the
creation of a development agency allowed Grieve to carry the
Plan's conception of regional planning to its logical
conclusion. Yet, the Clyde Valley Plan over a period of 30
years and the West Central Scotland Plan over a period of five
years, have shown that - in the same region - an 'end state'
plan and a 'rolling' plan could each profoundly influence

regional development in the periods of their currency. Furthermore, this influence was exercised within the context of a multiplicity of local authorities and of government departments and agencies.

A number of factors have been isolated to account for this influence. The first point is that the recommendations will draw strength if they reflect the direction and persistence of 'accepted' planning ideas, and these ideas must be translated to meet the circumstances of the region. Then come the elements of political environment and chance. Of course, if the specific plan is persuasively prepared, it will influence the drift and respectability of ideas.

An important element in the exercise of a plan's influence is the quality of the planners and their ability to secure positions of influence to work for its implementation, especially within government. The influence will be the greater if there are intimate relations between central administration and the local authorities. The Scottish tradition has been of benign intervention in general and direct challenge in particular instances. In terms of the plan making process, the planners must have the qualities to anticipate the possible directions of events. This awareness or good fortune is of paramount importance, especially where empirical data and predictions are so imperfect. Indeed, the detail may be of no great significance. This point is worth making following the debate of the 1970's on British structure plans, on their scope and the level of detail they should contain. Although most of the very detailed work of the Plan was irrelevant to its future influence, that detail did not prejudice its broader strategic recommendations. Its detail may even have added to its authority.

The Plan and the Theory of Regional Planning

The long view of 25 years which the Plan took and over which an accumulating number of its policies were adopted or fulfilled, allows an important test of the principal theories of plan and policy-making debated in the 1960's and 1970's, characterised at the extremes by the disjointed incrementalist approach associated with Lindblom (1959) and by approaches variously described as static by Cherry (1970) and as unitary by Foley (1963). Foley described the Greater London Plan as almost a classic unitary plan, which subsequently became adaptive in the way of the political and administrative process of government into which it was absorbed. Adaptive planning on a systematic, recurrent cycle has alternatively become known as iterative planning.

By this categorisation, the Plan would ostensibly stand as a unitary plan which became adaptive as it was transmitted into the developing regional strategy of the Scottish Office. Certainly, the Plan is built on a framework like that of the Greater London Plan, but it would be misleading to describe it as unitary - with an implied rigidity - if the Regional Authority which features in both plans is considered to be central or at least equal to their proposals for new towns, regional recreation centres and other 'static' components. The role of the Regional Authority was clearly to foster dynamic, adaptive planning, and both plans tended towards stasis only in other's failure to activate their recommendations for continuous planning. The two plans were certainly comprehensive, but the degree to which both were to be fulfilled in particular sectors of their vision denies that these lay within an indivisible, unitary framework.

Without any Regional Authority for Clydeside, Government intermittently adapted and extended the Plan to particular changes of circumstance. Taking Hart's (1976) description of an iterative process of planning, there were perhaps four major iterations of the Plan at irregular intervals. The period 1948-56 was an initial, long period, in which Government pursued a holding strategy until Glasgow accepted both its need for overspill and its responsibility to financially support the programme of resettlement beyond the City boundaries; the addition of Cumbernauld to the working strategy marked the second iteration of policy and the opening of the period 1956-1963, encompassing Glasgow's full acceptance of the logic of the Plan as well as the City's initiatives to negotiate overspill reception schemes throughout Scotland and to establish 29 Comprehensive Development Areas within the City; the third iteration arose from the expectations of rising population and economic growth which substantiated the growth area philosophy dominating Government planning strategy for Central Scotland from 1963-1974; the fourth iteration commenced with the West Central Scotland Plan and was still continued in the Strathclyde Structure Plan of seven years later.

Do these iterations of policy and the performance of the Plan accord with Hart's account of the nature of adaptive, iterative planning, and with some of the features which distinguish it from disjointed incrementalism? A principal characteristic of incrementalism is its short-view of the future, recurrent reaction to events and disinclination to assume a normative horizon towards which it sustains long-run policies. On these counts the Plan was clearly not incrmentalist, being normative to a visionary degree and notwithstanding the expectations of adaptation incorporated in the concept of a Regional Authority. Lindblom's protaganism of incrementalism is based upon the advantages of 'muddling-through' which lie in reduced need for information, theory and objectives, and in the supposedly greater likelihood of this approach being adopted in practise with associated economy of resources and greater emphasis on action.

No one plan can corroborate or deny either the rational-deductive or the disjointed incrementalist hypotheses. However, the Plan stands as a notably successful version of the rational-deductive model, not necessarily right because successful but certainly effective by its anticipation of what the physical and political topography of the Clyde Valley would make either inevitable or acceptable. Its detailed knowledge of the urban and rural landscape of the Clyde Valley represented a notable depth of information of a particular kind, but in the absence of the full array of contemporary statistics now expected in regional planning, its knowledge of existing social, economic and physical conditions was intuitive rather than exact. Equally, the iteration of the Plan's strategy which occurred in 1963 with the adoption of growth areas, represented a normative policy which was to prove vulnerable because it depended upon impracticable economic and demographic assumptions. By good fortune or judgement, the Plan's rationale was to stand up to events; the growth area rationale was to be found out and, in retrospect, might have been more robust if pursued by smaller, incremental steps.

A parallel theory of regional planning lies in the analysis of the function of its principal forms. Gillingwater and Hart distinguish the three core forms of policy-making, control of developments by action and communication of knowledge. Policy-making was to be embraced in England by the Strategic Plans for the North-West and for the Northern Region, but neither was to have their policies made effective across their full front of attack because Government would not offer the means of control. Even so, these two plans were important means of communication of regional issues both within their own regions and within Government and the field of interest in regional planning. The Regional Economic Planning Councils of the period 1964-1979 would represent the most clearly defined example of regional planning as a form of communication.

The Plan was to represent regional policy, control and communication. The commissioning of a plan from consultants by an Advisory Committee, held the possibility that either the Committee or Government could completely reject the policies which would be presented. Prepared at a remove from the machinery of control, the Plan was guaranteed the opportunity to communicate only so far as its policies would be within the bounds of expectation or credibility. It can be shown that the political climate for communication was sympathetic, but the Plan's policies did not so quickly coincide with established means of control as did those of the White Paper on Central Scotland in 1963. Control was, however, a central issue of the Plan in its conviction over the necessity for regional administration. Subsequently, the Plan's vision was to represent a means of communication by which Government sustained the will to pursue a regional strategy and to foster collective support for it amongst the institutional interests of the Clyde Valley.

The Government assumed partial control in applying the Plan in the absence of a Regional Authority and took responsibility for extending its policies in the 1960's, rather than to again delegate the job to the Advisory Committee or to Consultants. The West Central Scotland Plan was initiated in conjunction with the local authorities and an advisory committee, as the Plan had been, but it was to be passed to the authorship of consultants only after its initial surveys and analyses had been made. The West Central Scotland Plan was to combine policy with issues of control in policy for economic aid for industrial restructuring and the expansion of environmental action. Unlike the Plan, however, a Regional Authority awaited the West Central Scotland Plan which could share the job of control with Government, who yet remained responsible for essential regional policy in relation to the Scottish Development Agency, the new towns and the allocation of capital finance for housing, transport and the other components of regional structural change and development.

The Plan in the Perspective of Regional Planning

The Plan was profoundly influential within the Clyde Valley and in Scottish planning. Too many recommendations were achieved in spirit and in the letter to argue that there was not a wide connection between the Plan and subsequent developments. However, this hits upon one of the most difficult problems of historical inquiry. How can a real and a merely apparent causal connection be distinguished? The historical process cannot be reconstructed by leaving out some of the apparently key elements, one by one, in order to provide a rank ordering of significance and to eliminate those which have no significance at all. All that can be sought is a mixture of clear inference and circumstantial evidence.

It will be clear from earlier chapters that many later initiatives in matters of concern to the planning of West Central Scotland acknowledged their debt to the Plan. It is fair to argue that the Plan was the catalyst for the Green Belt and the vigorous and extensive overspill policy, and that these two factors influenced the way that Glasgow went about its redevelopment policies. It can also be argued that there was a causal link between what the Plan had to say about a regional authority and the way in which local government reform eventually proceeded. How was the influence in these and other directions exerted?

The strategic planning climate stretching from the early 1940's to the mid 1970's was dominated by the twin concepts of decentralising population from the great industrial cities – particularly to facilitate redevelopment schemes – and of injecting new industry into the economically declining regions. These policies gripped the imagination of postwar governments until the early 1970's, apart from a retrenchment in England and Wales during the first half of the 1950's. There was a ground swell moving in the direction of the Plan's recommendations before they were made. The Plan was the product of a movement which also incorporated the Barlow Report and the Greater London Plan. The ubiquitous Patrick Abercrombie ensured the lineage.

It would be wrong, however, to see the Plan simply as a summation of advanced planning thought. It interpreted the ideas of its lineage to meet the needs of a specific region, and in so doing added to, reinforced and enhanced an emerging planning tradition. F J Osborn's (1950) contemporary review of the Plan for The Spectator regarded it as the peak of Abercrombie's achievements in metropolitan and regional planning in the United Kingdom.

Osborn's critique was especially valued by the Plan team; his historical perspective of planning and his qualities as 'the quintessential common man' combined in a commitment to dispersal of the Conurbations to new towns, but yet he could be critical of policies to achieve this. The Greater London and Clyde Valley Regional Plans were importantly related here. In 1943, Lewis Mumford (1946) had written sadly in the Architectural Review of Abercrombie's County of London Plan published in that year that 'Regrettably, the planners have not fully lived up to their vision;... the superstructure they have created denies their fundamental convictions ... I must ask if a plan for London – or any other British city – can proceed without taking its place in a larger scheme of regional and national development ... What is lacking is not planning skill but .... urban statesmanship ... The effort to retain London's existing population was a major decision. The whole plan depends upon it; in fact the whole plan falls by it.'

Mumford disapproved of what he considered to be a caricatural and dismissal of dispersal in the Preamble to the County of

London Plan. A year later, in 1944, Abercrombie had produced his plan for the wider area of Greater London which now accepted much larger dispersal and a programme of new towns. In its Preamble, the Greater London Plan set out five underlying assumptions which nearly correspond to the preconditions for replanning London with which Mumford had concluded his critique of the County of London Plan.

Two years later, in 1946, the Clyde Valley Regional Plan more fully met and considered Mumford's preconditions for regional planning and development. Although not speaking of birth rate and population replacement as a dominant element of planning faith - as Mumford had done - the Plan undoubtedly considered decline an adverse trend, against which it was considered prudent to plan for a constant population. The Plan represented this as the 'saturation' level of the Clyde Valley. In the heart of the Conurbation, the Plan urgently sought to continue the outflow of population 'now apparent in every great city in the United Kingdom', but it rested its case primarily upon the intolerable living conditions of an abnormally congested urban area, rather than upon Mumford's view of the city as a reproductive machine by which 'the reproduction of children ... is now a primary condition for the good life.'

In retrospect, Mumford's fear of 'biological failure' was representative of the period but - despite the evidence of nationally declining birth rates - appears to have been less conscious of social and spatial variations and the still vigorous national increase of congested inner cities. The Plan also better met the rising spirit of its time and of Mumford's pre-conditions in its proposals for land. Whereas the Greater London Plan had assumed 'that new powers for planning will be available, including powers for the control of land values', proposing a regional Planning Authority with power to acquire land, it did not envisage land nationalisation to liquidate the existing structure of urban land values as Mumford did. Nor did the Plan go so far as Mumford. Equally with the Greater London Plan, it had no proposals on the issue of urban land values, but it forthrightly recommended that ownership of the whole of the Green Belt should be vested in the State or in the Regional Authority, whereas in Greater London Abercrombie envisaged that except for land of outstanding beauty or for recreation, the predominantly agricultural area of the Green Belt could be safeguarded 'by other and equally effective methods.'

Post-Barlow Economic and Planning Policy

Influential as the Plan became, in specific respects its policies failed to 'bite', and were long deferred or were not

matched by the quality of detailed planning by others. The
Scottish Office could not prevent Glasgow City Corporation from
building modified versions of the old tenements and high rise
towers in inner parts and on the outskirts of Glasgow, at
higher densities than those recommended in the Plan. New
industry could not be attracted to the region on a scale
sufficient to offset the unemployment caused by the decline of
indigenous industry. Glasgow Corporation did not heed the
Plan's warning of the need to provide a full range of services
in new municipal estates and so exacerbated the range of social
problems in Easterhouse, Castlemilk, Pollok and Drumchapel.
Many of the recommended centres for leisure and recreation
remained unprovided, as did much of the transport strategy. By
the beginning of the 1970's, the failure to adopt the Plan's
proposal for continuous regional planning became no longer
acceptable to political opinion. West Central Scotland was
moving into a post-Barlow phase. What factors were responsible
for this?

Of the factors surrounding the reassessment of neo-Barlow
philosophies during the early 1970's, perhaps the most basic
was the growing weaknesses of the British economy, particularly
keenly felt in a region of low economic growth where policies
of relatively high public expenditure had become a widely
accepted and expected solution.

During the late 1960's there was an increasing questioning of
policies aimed at dispersing population from metropolitan
areas. A series of studies documented the social and economic
ills which had arisen in conjunction with urban renewal
programmes, and the urban wastelands that these could create
were becoming increasingly evident. New towns, it was being
argued, were adding to the problems of the inner cities by
drawing their youngest and most able people. Similarly,
industry was no longer congested in the urban cores. The call
now came for rehabilitation of the inner areas rather than
demolition and rebuilding. These ideas strengthened when it
realised that national population growth was slowing down.

Government could be more readily converted to these ideas
when the need was to cut the growth of public expenditure.
Rehabilitation was seen to be socially desirable and cheaper
than renewal and decentralisation. Furthermore, because
economic growth was limited, the arguments for siphoning off
economic growth from the prosperous to the less prosperous
areas became less convincing. The stress was now placed on
stimulating indigenous industries in regions where unemployment
rates were high and the inflow of new industries was slowing.

Obviously, this Post-Barlow philosophy tended to work against

235

the indefinite pursuit of some of the fundamental recommendations of the Plan. Indeed, it might be argued that just as the Barlow philosophy was pioneered in West Central Scotland by the Plan, so the Post-Barlow philosophy was pioneered there too by the West Central Scotland Plan, published in 1974. This new plan was tentative in respects, but on the basis of the precarious state of the region's economy, the experience of unexpectedly rapid movement of population away from Glasgow and the region and the declining birth rate, it challenged whether a further new town was needed at Stonehouse and, also, whether the economic salvation of the region could be based upon the attraction of migrant industry.

Anticipating the tide of thought in the United Kingdom as well as in the region, these partly tentative proposals were strengthened and significantly implemented during the subsequent two years. The remaining old tenements whose worst cases had been so criticised in the Clyde Valley Regional Plan were now seen as artifacts worthy of preservation for social as well as architectural reasons. Stonehouse was abandoned and overspill agreements with the older of Glasgow's new towns and expanded settlements were drawn to a close. A conscious attempt was made to attract people back into Glasgow. Stress was placed on revitalising the indigenous industries of the city. An Urban Renewal team based upon staff of the abandoned Stonehouse Development Corporation came together in 1977 to co-ordinate action by the Scottish Development Agency, the Scottish Special Housing Association, Glasgow District and Strathclyde Region, in the Glasgow Eastern Area Redevelopment Project (GEAR). This substitute for a new town development corporation for an inner sector of Glasgow aimed to co-ordinate programmes for housing, industry, transport and social facilities. The policies of the West Central Scotland Plan were transposed first to the Strathclyde Regional Report and then to the Structure Plan for the region.

In an atmosphere of national economic uncertainty, the need in the 1980's to promote industrial activity in regions which had earlier dispersed industries to Clydeside meant, of course, that what was left of the growth area extension to the Plan's strategy was no longer buoyed by the high hopes of the early 1960's. Further, growth area theory had been much reduced by criticism of its relevance to advanced industrial economies and by experience of its practice in Western Europe.

It might be thought that recognition that the policies of the Plan have matured signifies the end of its influence. Yet, there are elements of the Plan which are timeless or are likely to endure. The new towns have still to be completed. The recommendations for leisure and recreation facilities are still valid. It might be that any further reform of local government would take a form in West Central Scotland even closer to the original scheme in the Plan than the one instituted in 1975 following the 1973 Local Government (Scotland) Act. If Strathclyde Region were reduced in size it might embrace the smaller metropolitan area suggested in the Plan.

Planning for the Clyde Valley Under a Regional Authority

In the 1980's, when events were moving beyond the horizon of the Plan's view of the future, the existence of a regional authority for the Clyde Valley provided the opportunity for regional public administration which the Plan put at the centre of its ambitions for planning in the region. The first intervention of the Regional Council in regional development was its political campaign of 1975/76 to terminate the new town of Stonehouse. The unstated cause pursued in the campaign was the Council's authority as the new regional administration for Strathclyde. The Stonehouse issue represented a precisely defined test of the influence of the Council in an aspect of regional development in which authority was divided between central and local government. Although there was sympathy for Strathclyde's case in the key figure of Millan, as Minister responsible for planning for Scotland and subsequently as Secretary of State, some influential Civil Servants were opposed to the stopping of Stonehouse. The termination of Stonehouse early in 1976 coincided with the presentation of the Strathclyde Regional Report, sought by the Secretary of State after the first year of work of the new Regional Councils. The Regional Report linked the issue of the claim of Stonehouse for resources with the Council's concern for the condition of Glasgow and older parts of the Clydeside Conurbation, where it identified a concentration of areas of severe social, economic and physical deprivation exceptional by British comparisons. In moderating this deprivation, the raising of local government revenue on a region-wide base and the ability to redistribute it within Strathclyde according to priorities such as those implicit in the Regional Report, was potentially an even more significant opportunity in regional development than the physical planning strategy of the regional Report and the Regional Structure Plan.

Under Strathclyde Regional Council, the largest concern of planning in the region in the late 1970's and the early 1980's was no longer the necessity for new land for new housing and new towns and the prospects of growth areas, but had shifted to the issue of resources for urban renewal and change. Yet, although a regional authority could better distribute certain parts of public expenditure, in a local government system in which the Regional Council lacked direct responsibility for

237

housebuilding and action to rehabilitate housing, it was intimately concerned but not directly capable of making policy for this largest single urban use of land and still the largest problem in the physical improvement of the Clyde Valley.

The Plan as a Resource in Regional Development

Whereas resources had become a central issue in the West Central Scotland Plan and the Strathclyde Structure Plan of the 1970's, the Plan of the 1940's had been concerned with the issue of resources primarily in its arguments against the feasibility of Bruce's proposals for the renewal of Glasgow. Even so, the argument implied rather than explicitly stated the issue of resources. The Plan did not expect its proposed regional authority to directly undertake urban renewal or housing action, and it examined the amount and distribution of unfit housing only in the course of calculating the population overspill required from the Clydeside Conurbation. Densities of existing and proposed housing were discussed and portrayed at some length, but the Plan's pre-occupation was with clearance of unfit houses and relief of overcrowding. Issues of rehabilitation and the management of housing improvement are as absent from the Plan as they would become dominant in plans of thirty years later. In the Greater London Plan, the discussion was entirely in terms of density without even an estimate of the spatial distribution and quantity of unfit housing as the Plan recorded in an Appendix. Between 1945 and 1975, finance would replace land as the principal resource which shaped regional plans.

By 1970, the City of Glasgow would have come to issue successive ultimata to Government on the scale of special financing required to overcome its deficiences of community facilities and housing standards. By 1980, Government would have come to fund nearly half of public expenditure on housing in Glasgow through their appointed agencies of the Housing Corporation and the Scottish Special Housing Association, rather than through the City Council. The exceptional Government dimension to the renewal of Glasgow and its economic and physical environment through these agencies and the Scottish Development Agency was not sought nor thought necessary by the Plan. In 1979, the Regional Structure Plan would consider these issues of financial and organisational resources essential to its objectives. Yet, the Plan had been more concerned about the necessity for collective public intervention in the development of the Clyde Valley than had been the Greater London Plan, and the Plan had presaged a scale of Government intervention by agencies in which Scotland has been exceptional in Great Britain for over 40 years.

The Plan's recognition of the issue of the management of resources and the subsequent active participation of Government in Scottish urban and regional development, perhaps infer the truest judgement on the Plan's place in the history of regional planning in the United Kingdom.

The Plan was perhaps not original in any significant individual proposal. Its scope had been embraced by the vision of more than a decade of political, professional and intellectual discussion and analysis in Scotland and elsewhere in Britain, Western Europe and America. The Greater London Plan had anticipated the technical methods central to the Plan as it had foreshadowed the nature of its proposals. But the Plan carried the logic of this approach to regional planning further, and in the special vigour of its presentation and its colour, extra depth and extra width, it had repaid its professional debt to the Greater London Plan in excess. Collectively, the proposals of the Plan were radical. For the Clyde Valley, the Plan had translated polemics and the deep concern of individuals into recommendations of policy directly commissioned by an Advisory Committee of Government and local government. The Plan made formidable demands of private and governmental energy and self-interest. The British Government was simultaneously making other overwhelming demands of itself in the early years of post-War reconstruction and of reforming social and economic legislation. It might be judged that resources of political will and administrative organisation were a greater constraint than finance in proceeding with the Plan's proposals for physical change. Seen from London, the Plan dealt only with the Clyde Valley, even if it housed one third of Scotland's population. Indeed, Greater London and the Clyde Valley together comprised under a fifth of the Cabinet's concern for the population of the United Kingdom as a whole. Even so for none of the other five conurbations were there plans with such inherent authority or which envisaged such sweeping new measures in administration and regional change.

The Reith Report which preceded the New Towns Act of 1946, combined with the Clyde Valley Regional Plan and the Greater London Plan to bring new towns of the initial national programme to only those two amongst the seven British conurbations. The other significant proposals originating in the Plan were not to be taken up until a decade later, but it cannot be supposed that a convincing and acceptable costing of the Plan's proposals would have significantly accelerated its whole strategy. There was cleavage in the Clyde Valley Regional Planning Advisory Committee on the Plan's central proposals for new towns, for population and industrial relocation and for control on the location of new industry. Yet it was in these acutely contentious issues of local

239

politics that Government immediately moved with measures directly supporting the Plan. For the remaining majority of the Plan's conclusions and recommendations the Committee assented. This public and political acceptance of the vision and inevitability of the Plan was itself a resource for planning, reinforced after 1950 when the City of Glasgow came to fully accept the necessity for dispersal beyond its boundaries.

If the Plan itself became a resource in the coherent development of the Clyde Valley, its weight was considerably due to the special intimacy between the Scottish Office and local authorities which has been characteristic of Scottish public administration. For thirty and twenty years respectively, McGuiness and Grieve were continuous in this influence which drew from and sustained the Plan's vision in the Clyde Valley and transmitted selected elements to the rest of Scotland. In the failure for twenty years of Government to institute reform of local administration, the regional initiatives of the Plan to secure better development were applied by the Scottish Office through the Scottish Industrial Estates Corporation and the Scottish Special Housing Association. Elsewhere, the Highlands and Islands Development Board (HIDB) was the translation by McGuiness and Grieve of the Plan's administrative vision to the other great problem region of Scotland, and to the form of an agency closer to the Scottish Office than to local government.

Ten years after the HIDB had been established under Grieve's chairmanship, the Scottish Development Agency was created to extend the industrial and land renewal roles which the Plan would have placed with its regional authority. The Agency had arisen with strong supporting arguments for a Strathclyde Agency from the Plan's successor plan for West Central Scotland, but the separation of the Agency's functions from those of the new Strathclyde Regional Council was only partly attributable to the Agency's Scotland-wide role and its adoption of powers from established government agencies including the Department of Industry - which had been answerable to a United Kingdom rather than a Scottish Minister. However, the Agency also confirmed a further major advance in the direct participation of Government agencies in urban change and economic development in Scotland. The Plan's proposals for new towns in the Clyde Valley had marked a similar advance thirty years before.

The Plan's significance for Government initiatives and the modern history of Scottish planning and development was on this analysis as great as it was for the Clyde Valley. It did not explicitly anticipate all the measures which other plans or new issues would stimulate. It did not anticipate Glasgow Corporation's 1960 programme of 29 Comprehensive Development Areas or the 1976 GEAR initiative, but it was the sure and massive base for all that followed in the development of planning and strategic administration in Scotland. Forty years later, it had not been surpassed in authority in any case of regional or metropolitan planning in the United Kingdom.

Appendix

Summary of Conclusions and Recommendations of the Clyde Valley Plan

(This is a verbatim reproduction of Chapter Thirteen of the Plan. References refer to the <u>Plan's</u> chapters.)

(1) The physical planning of the Clyde Valley Region, to be fully effective, must go hand in hand with Economic and Social Planning. (Preamble.)

(2) The Region is an economic unit, and must be considered as a whole. (Preamble.)

(3) Socially and Industrially the Region has reached a critical point in its history; the inevitably far-reaching changes in basic industrial structure, combined with the urgent necessity for the reconstruction of obsolescent housing and industrial buildings, present a unique opportunity for the progressive replanning of the Region in accordance with the highest standards of efficiency and amenity. (Preamble.)

(4) The need for detailed social studies throughout the Region - beyond the scope of this Report - is fundamental to the successful implementation of the Plan. The establishment of a Chair of Town and Regional Planning in Scotland is suggested to provide the means of organising and co-ordinating this hitherto neglected aspect of planning survey. (Preamble.)

(5) It has been assumed that, immigration and emigration apart, the population of the Region will remain, over the next 40 or 50 years, substantially as at present, but will have a higher proportion of the older age groups. This does not, however, presuppose a static distribution of population. (Chapter 1.)

(6) Population movement has been a dominant feature in the past History of the Region, and a further great shift of population is anticipated in future. The Region, and particularly the City of Glasgow, has grown principally by immigration. To-day, the Central Urban Area of the Region is at saturation point. It is only within the framework of a National Policy of Decentralisation that the inward drift to the industrial belt can be checked. On the other hand, the Regional plan provides for an increase in the existing movement of industry and population away from the congested urban areas. (Chapter 1.)

(7) The two major factors affecting industrial change are
(a) The decrease of mining in Lanarkshire.
(b) The re-orientation of the steel industry.
With regard to (b), no definite information is, at this date, available. We have forecast the possible effects on Lanarkshire and on Renfrewshire of such a development as far as we have been able to do so with the limited information available, but it is clear that considerable revisions and amplifications of the Plan will be immediately required if a decision to re-locate the major steel plants is made on the lines anticipated. (Chapter 2.)

(8) New industry is urgently required in the Region,
(a) for the purposes of diversification and balance;
(b) to absorb anticipated unemployment in the declining basic industries. (Chapter 2.)

(9) Research is required into types of new industry best fitted for the Region's economy, and into the best Regional location for the planned expansion of existing industry. (Chapter 2.)

(10) A strengthening of the Distribution of Industry Act, 1945, is required, to give positive powers of control over the location of industry throughout Scotland, coupled with the implementation of the Barlow Committee recommendations for the prohibition of further industrialisation in congested areas. (Chapter 2.)

(11) The migration of miners should be encouraged from the declining Lanarkshire Coalfield to the expanding coalfields in the East of Scotland, and in Ayrshire. (Chapter 2.)

(12) The opportunity should be seized to develop the increasing Ayrshire coalfield in such a way as to avoid the errors of the past. For this purpose a social as well as an economic programme is necessary.
A grouping of population to meet the needs of expanding production in this Sub-Region in a limited number of small towns, as opposed to isolated mining settlements, is proposed. (Chapter 2.)

(13) A series of planned industrial Estates, to provide the Region with modern factory accommodation, and to attract suitable industries, is proposed.
Comparatively few new factories were built in the Region for war-time purposes; much existing factory accommodation is out of date and unlikely to attract the modern industrialist. (Chapter 2.)

(14) The decentralisation of industry and population from the congested central urban area must be planned together. The new towns proposed must be fully provided with local employment. It follows that new industry, to meet anticipated unemployment in the urban areas, should be steered to the new towns in accordance with a timed schedule.

(15) The industrial development of the new towns should also include a limited amount of industry decentralised from the congested areas. (Chapter 2.)

(16) The careful regulation of new industry into the central urban area at the present time, when congestion is at its maximum, is essential, if planned decentralisation is to be successful. (Chapter 2.)

(17) It follows that the development of the new towns proposed must be undertaken with the utmost speed. (Chapter 2.)

(18) Further zoning of individual sites by Local Authorities for industry should form part of a general development plan. (Chapter 2.)

(19) A comprehensive programme of physical rehabilitation of the derelict areas is essential, not only in the interests of the people, but in order to attract new industry. This will include control of future spoil heaps and the

244

clearance of disused industrial buildings and structures.
(Chapter 2.)

(20) As   a short-term measure for   smoke abatement, smokeless
urban   zones are proposed,   coupled with the encouragement
of scientific use of coal and the ultimate prohibition of
its combusion in the raw state.   An inquiry should be made
into the large scale development of district heating,   and
in particular the use, for this purpose, of the waste heat
from existing and proposed electric power stations on the
River Clyde.   (Chapter 2.)

(21) A   limit should be put to the further   continuous   outward
spread of the conurbation by prescribing an inner line to
the Green Belt: this line is not determined by the
existing boundaries of local authorities.   (Chapter 3.)

(22) The   preservation of a permanent green belt both as a
corridor between communities and as a general enclosure of
the conurbation is essential to provide for recreation,
fresh air and protective foods.   (Chapter 3.)

(23) The green belt extending to the moorland edge contains
practically all agricultural land in middle and lower
Clyde Basin: it is recommended that all this land not
required for building,   be bought by Regional Authority or
State.   (Chapter 3.)

(24) The chief recreational and rambling area lies outside the
Agricultural Green Belt and has three main requirements:
(a) Access to all moorland;
(b) Limited access to certain areas;
(c) A comprehensive system of Walker's Paths. (Chapter 3.)

(25) The coast requires protection against continuous building:
at the same time accommodation is to be increased by two
new holiday towns and holiday camps for family use: the
positions of the latter require careful study.   (Chapter
3.)

(26) Two areas are recommended as National Parks
(a) Loch Lomond-Trossachs District;
(b) St. Mary's Loch District.
A proper entrance, combined with a National Recreational
Centre, is planned for (a) at Balloch and the expansion of
villages on the fringe of (b) for holiday and tourist use.
(Chapter 3.)

(27) A Regional Park should be made at Craigend, north of
Milngavie: Regional Recreation Centres at Killermont,

Pollok, Drumpellier and Hamilton Low Parks; and Recreational Halts on main roads at Douglas and Balloch. (Chapters 3 and 5.)

(28) A most unsatisfactory position obtains as regards the area and distribution of open space, particularly in county urban areas in the Clyde Basin. Standards of local open space according to distribution of the population are recommended. (Chapter 3.)

(29) Maximum densities for urban areas should be prescribed: in no case should density exceed 140 persons per net residential acre. This figure must lead to a general policy of housing decentralisation. It is not considered feasible or desirable to redevelop recent housing schemes at higher densities in order to reduce the decentralisation problem. (Chapters 4 and 7.)

(30) A re-integration of urban communities is essential to prevent general sprawl and the coalescence of the conurbation. Ultimately a progressive redistribution of ribboned housing should be undertaken. (Chapter 4.)

(31) Decentralisation of population should be provided:
(a) by building up a limited number of existing towns in the Region e.g., Kilmarnock, Beith and coastal resorts urgently in need of increased facilities. This can only be done (apart from the special problem of the Coastal Resorts) by encouraging new industry to settle in such towns;
(b) by building new towns in the Region;
(c) by encouraging the growth of industry in other parts of Scotland, in accordance with a wider plan to relieve the over-balance of population in the Industrial Belt. (Chapter 4.)

(32) The local decentralisation of certain towns on the fringe of the conurbation may be dealt with by additional peripheral development in a direction away from the City of Glasgow. (Chapter 4.)

(33) In North Lanarkshire the recommendation is to group together small and scattered communities round nodal points. (Chapter 4.)

(34) In the City of Glasgow, additional peripheral growth within the inner line of the Green Belt should be limited to 250,000 people; a balance of 250,000 to 300,000 people should be located away from the existing conurbation. (Chapter 4.)

(35) Three new towns are recommended at East Kilbride, Cumbernauld and Bishopton, the latter to take overspill from Greenock. A further large new town at Houston will be required if the steel industry is relocated below the River Cart. (Chapter 4.)

(36) The conclusion is arrived at that the Clyde Valley has reached saturation point as regards population: the relief of central congestion and overcrowding should be considered in relation to the balance of population and industry in the interests of Scotland as a whole. (Chapter 4.)

(37) A regional report does not attempt to make detailed proposals for individual towns: each town has to be subjected to detailed analysis and the general conclusions of the report require to be worked out in detail. A sample of such detailed application is given for the Leven Valley. (Chapter 4.)

(38) The treatment of Roads, Railways, Water-routes and Airways, as combined communications is essential. The fundamental principle behind the co-ordination of all forms of transport should be the concentration and canalisation of traffic into the type of transport most fitted for the purpose. Our proposals for electrification, given below, presuppose such canalisation in accordance with a comprehensive Regional Transport Plan. Detailed survey for such a plan is urgently required, and should be undertaken by the Ministry of Transport in close consultation with the planning authorities concerned. (Chapter 5.)

(39) A sharper segregation of road traffic is advocated: rapid through traffic is to be canalised in a limited number of one-purpose motorways. Associated with motorways is a system of arterial and sub-arterial roads: where these pass through areas of high amenity a parkway treatment is recommended. (Chapter 5.)

(40) A thorough reorganisation of road intersections is required to bring these into conformity with the different types of road traffic. (Chapter 5.)

(41) Introduction of service roads on all existing or proposed arterial roads within built-up areas, with access at long intervals, is recommended. (Chapter 5.)

(42) Improvement for cross-river communication is proposed by tunnels and bridges. (Chapter 5.)

(43) The counterpart of the canalisation of the through traffic on motorways and arterial roads is precinctal planning for residential, industrial shopping and other areas. (Chapter 5.)

(44) In addition to the main road from the South with its connection to the New Forth Bridge, four other routes in relation to the central conurbation are planned as motorways, an outer ring road with three spurs and three radials. The two inner rings proposed by Glasgow are agreed to, but there is some doubt whether they can be constructed as one-purpose motorways. (Chapter 5.)

(45) It is suggested that an attempt should be made to convert the existing new road between Glasgow and Edinburgh into a one-purpose motorway. (Chapter 5.)

(46) In adapting existing roads or constructing new ones through open country for one-purpose motorways, the needs of the farming and village communities for local traffic must not be neglected. (Chapter 5.)

(47) Much more attention should be given to the landscape designing of roads, both in regard to their general layout in relation to the country or town and in regard to their detailed treatment and planting. (Chapter 5.)

(48) Electrification of certain railway lines is recommended, i.e.,
Glasgow, via Paisley, Port Glasgow and Greenock to Gourock, and from Port Glasgow to Wemyss Bay with short spur to Crookston.
The Cathcart circle, with spurs to East Kilbride and Burnside.
Bridgeton Cross to Dalmuir and Dumbarton with forks to Balloch and Helensburgh.
Bridgeton Cross to Rutherglen, with the possibility of extension to Hamilton and Motherwell.
Investigation of the possibility of electrifying the lines to Ayr and Ardrossan with a diesel service from the latter to Largs, and of the canalisation of traffic on one line from Edinburgh to Glasgow with the view to electrification is also suggested. Where electrification is introduced, care must be taken to avoid wasteful competition with road transport. (Chapter 5.)

(49) A committee of enquiry is suggested to investigate how redundancy and overlapping may be avoided, particularly in view of the grouping of the railway companies and the changes in mineral line and industrial traffic.(Chapter 5.)

(50) It is suggested that serious consideration should be given
to the terminal stations in Glasgow, with a view to
establishing a Central Inter-change Station for passenger
traffic. A subsidiary Interchange Station is also
suggested at Merklands (Partick) where both railway
systems intersect Glasgow Corporation Subway. (Chapter 5.)

(51) Improvement is called for in rail transport of
merchandise. This must be co-ordinated with road
transport. Road haulage for short distance and railway
haulage for long distance and heavy tonnage are generally
the most appropriate. (Chapter 5.)

(52) The Prestwick Airport should be equipped in every way for
its international role and first-rate rail and road
connection with central Scotland and the South is
proposed. (Chapter 5.)

(53) The Regional Airport of Renfrew should be preserved from
interference by building: the possibility of an East
Glasgow Airport should be again examined. (Chapter 5.)

(54) The possibilities of helicopter flights should be kept in
view, particularly for connection with National Park
areas. (Chapter 5.)

(55) The Clyde improvements recommended follow in general those
of the Cooper Report: these include new road bridge and
ferry and tunnel crossings: alternate berthage to
Broomielaw for passenger steamer services: the improvement
of dock facilities: new graving docks: naval dock:
improvement of junction of Cart and Clyde with special
reference to the new steel plant at Inchinnan and
Paisley's docks on the Cart. (Chapter 5.)

(56) In order to co-ordinate all these requirements - some of a
conflicting character, it is urged that the Clyde Port
Authority recommended in the Cooper Report be set up at
the earliest possible moment. (Chapter 5.)

(57) The scale of operation in the improvement of Terminus
Quay, required anyhow for immediate production, should be
closely related to the long-term proposals for the
transference, over a term of years, of the principal
coking and steel plants to the Inchinnan site.(Chapter 5.)

(58) It is recommended that the Forth and Clyde canal should be
done away with. (Chapter 5.)

(59) The Monkland Canal should be filled in except in certain

short portions for amenity reasons. (Chapter 5.)

(69) The Mid Scotland Ship Canal does not appear to be a practicable or economic proposition: it would gravely interfere with road and rail communications running north and south. (Chapter 5.)

(61) The great importance of the agricultural areas of the region is stressed, especially for dairying: in 1938-39 it produced nearly half the total milk handled by the Scottish Milk Marketing Board. It is therefore essential to prevent wasteful cutting up of farm land and units by straggling urban extension. (Chapter 5.)

(62) Village and country planning are essential: the villages should be supplied with sufficient houses for agricultural workers and should be grouped suitably for social, educational and shopping facilities. (Chapter 6.)

(63) The fruit production from the Upper Clyde Orchard country should be increased so that the Region should no longer be dependent upon Covent Garden. (Chapter 6.)

(64) With so much of this valuable and limited farm land unavoidably required for housing and urban decentralisation, it is necessary that the remainder should be regarded as inviolable. There must be security from the further possibility of urban extension: stability of tenure, especially in the Green Belt round the conurbation is essential. (Chapter 6.)

(65) The principles of Community plananing are enunciated and standards of density, accommodation, plot planning, industry, open space, community buildings, schools, shops, etc., are recommended for adoption in the preparation of detailed schemes of development. (Chapter 7.)

(66) The sample detailed study of the Vale of Leven illustrates the application of the principles in the above recommendation. The redevelopment of Alexandria is used as an example of the way the work may be carried out by progressive stages. This principle should be applied elsewhere. (Chapter 8.)
Notes upon individual places, described as Vignettes, give general indication of the lines upon which detailed studies should be prepared. (Chapter 11.)

(67) Special study should be given to the examples of good architecture in the region: these range from great churches, castles and houses, to the smaller farm

buildings, town houses and country cottages. Some of these should be preserved intact; others are useful as indicating treatment which may influence modern design. Reference is made to the use of colour in some of these older buildings. (Chapter 9.)

(68) The marked topography of the region should give scope for variety of treatment in building and for imaginative site planning. Some examples of this are illustrated. (Chapter 9.)

(69) A high degree of architectural design in the new building schemes is called for, especially in the new towns: in place of the picturesque accident of historic groups, a broad treatment of house design, in which emphasis is not laid on individual blocks but on the architecture of the whole, is called for. (Chapter 9.)

(70) A higher standard of design is to be demanded, not only for houses but for bridges, roads, factories, street furniture, and every single object that goes to form the regional picture. (Chapter 9.)

(71) Public services in general require regional in place of local provision. The combination of many plants in the different services will not only prove economical but should create a higher standard of efficiency. (Chapter 10.)

(72) As regards water, the Department of Health has already made surveys with a view to devising suitable areas for combination. It is strongly advised that the water resources of the Region should be used to the best common advantage irrespective of county or local authority boundaries. (Chapter 10.)

(73) As regards gas, the report of the Committee of enquiry of 1944, is endorsed: suitable and efficient groupings should be brought about in this region in conformity with the Committee's recommendations. (Chapter 10.)

(74) As regards electricity, combination of generating undertakings is already effected by the Board: the hydro-electric plant on Loch Lomond and two other power stations have been located: it is urged that an equalisation of prices and a uniform supply of current should obtain. (Chapter 10.)

(75) A Regional Authority of a permanent character, in order to ensure a continuous policy of positive planning, is

recommended. The area for convenience of administration might be limited to that portion of the Region which is contained within the outer line of the Green Belt surrounding the central conurbaiton. (Chapter 12.)

(76) It is recommended that within this area certain major functions should be shared by all the local authorities under a suitable administrative scheme: these would include the acquisition and control of land required for the Green Belt; Regional Parks; conservation of water resources; the distribution and location of industry; rehabilitation of derelict areas; the establishment of New Towns* and the oversight of the local planning schemes. In general the supervision and control, in an advisory capacity, of the Regional Plan on behalf of the local authorities should be done by the Regional Authority. It is recommended that the Local Authorities should request the Secretary of State for Scotland to undertake, along with the Local Authorities concerned, a full enquiry into the question of the establishment of a Regional Authority. (Chapter 12.)

*Since secured under the New Towns Act.

Bibliography

Abercrombie, Sir Patrick (1943), Town and Country Planning, Oxford University Press, London.

Abercrombie, Sir Patrick (1945), Greater London Plan, HMSO, London.

Abercrombie, Sir Patrick and Forshaw, J.H. (1943), County of London Plan, Macmillan, London.

Abercrombie, Sir Patrick and Jackson, P. (1948), West Midlands Plan, Ministry of Town and Country Planning.

Abercrombie, Sir Patrick and Matthew, Robert H. (1949), The Clyde Valley Regional Plan 1946, HMSO, Edinburgh.

Advisory Council for Agriculture and Horticulture in England and Wales (1978), Agriculture and the Countryside, A.C.A.H., London.

Allan, C.M. (1965), The Genesis of British Urban Redevelopment with Special Reference to Glasgow. Economic History Review, 2nd Series, Vol.XVIII, No.3.

ASB Study Group No.1 (1946), Journal of Royal Institute of British Architects, Vol.53, No.10.

Bagwell, P.S. (1947), The Transport Revolution from 1770, Batsford, London.

Baird, Robert (1958), Housing, The Third Statistical Account of Scotland. Ed. Cunnison, J. and Gilfillan, J.B.S., Collins, Glasgow.

Board of Trade (1932), An Industrial Survey of South West Scotland made for the Board of Trade by the Staff of the Political Economy Department of the University of Glasgow, HMSO, London.

253

Boyle, R.M. (1980), Discussion, Land Assessment in Scotland, Ed. Thomas, M.F. and Coppock, J.T., Aberdeen University Press, Aberdeen.

Braybrooke, D. and Lindblom, C.E. (1963), A Strategy of Decision, The Free Press, New York, USA.

Brennan, Tom (1958), Glasgow's Housing Problem, The Scotsman, 29th April.

Brennan, Tom (1959), Reshaping a City, The House of Grant, Glasgow.

British Transport Commission (1951), Passenger Transport in Glasgow and District, British Transport Commission, Edinburgh.

Bruce, Robert (1945), First Planning Report to the Highways and Planning Committee of the Corporation of Glasgow, Corporation of the City of Glasgow, Glasgow.

Bruce, Robert (1946), Second Planning Report to the Highways and Planning Committee of the Corporation of Glasgow, Corporation of the City of Glasgow, Glasgow.

Butt, John (1971), Working Class Housing in Glasgow 1851-1914, The History of Working Class Housing: A Symposium, Ed. Chapman, S.D, David and Charles, Newton Abbot.

Buttimer, A. and McDonald, Shiela T. (1974), Residential Areas: Planning, Perceptions and Preferences, Studies in Social Science and Planning, Ed. Forbes, J., Scottish Academic Press, Edinburgh.

Campbell, A.D. and Lyddon, W.D.C. (1970), Tayside; Potential for Development, HMSO, Edinburgh.

Campbell, R.H. (1980), The Rise and Fall of Scottish Industry, John Donald, Edinburgh.

Cairncross, A.K. (1954), The Scottish Economy, Cambridge University Press, Cambridge.

Cairncross, A.K. (1958), The Economy of Glasgow, The Glasgow Region, Ed. Miller, R. and Tivy, J., The British Association, Glasgow.

Central Housing Advisory Committee (1944), Design of Dwellings, (The Dudley Report), HMSO, London.

Centre for Agricultural Strategy (1976), Land for Agriculture, CAS Report No. 1, University of Reading, Reading.

Checkland, S. (1976), The Upas Tree Glasgow 1875-1975, University of Glasgow Press, Glasgow.

Cherry, G.E. (1970), Planning and its Social Context, Leonard Hill, London.

Cherry, G.E. (1974), The Evolution of British Town Planning, Leonard Hill Books, London.

Cherry, G.E. (1975), Environmental Planning 1939-1969, Volume 11 National Parks and Recreation in the Countryside, HMSO, London.

Clyde Canal Working Party (January 1980), Forth and Clyde Canal Local (Subject) Plan Vol 11, The Main Issues and Vol 2 Survey Report, Forth and Clyde Working Party, Glasgow.

Clyde Valley Advisory Committee (1963), Achievement of Green
    Belt Provision in Clyde Valley Region, Clyde Valley Advisory
    Committee, Glasgow.
Coleman, A. (1977), Land Use Planning: Success or Failure,
    Architects' Journal, 19th Jan.
Corporation of the City of Glasgow (1954), Development Plan,
    Written Statement 1954, Corporation of Glasgow, Glasgow.
Corporation of the City of Glasgow (1956), Hutchesontown/part
    Gorbals Comprehensive Redevelopment Area: Written Statement,
    Corporation of the City of Glasgow, Glasgow.
Corporation of the City of Glasgow (1957), Report on the
    Clearance of Slum Houses, Redevelopment and Overspill,
    Corporation of Glasgow, Glasgow.
Corporation of the City of Glasgow (1960), Survey Report of the
    City of Glasgow Development Plan, Quinquennial Review 1960,
    City of Glasgow, Glasgow.
Corporation of the City of Glasgow (1968), Annual Report of the
    Housing Management Department, Corporation of the City of
    Glasgow, Glasgow.
Corporation of the City of Glasgow and Scottish Development
    Department (1970), Report of the Glasgow Housing Programme
    Working Party, Corporation of Glasgow, Glasgow.
Countryside Commission for Scotland (1974), A Park System for
    Scotland, Countryside Commission, Perth, Scotland.
Countryside Commission for Scotland (1980), Scotland's Scenic
    Heritage, Countryside Commission for Scotland, Perth,
    Scotland.
Countryside in 1970 Conference (1965), The Countryside in 1970,
    Countryside Planning and Development in Scotland, Report of
    Study Group Nine to Second Countryside Conference 10-12
    November 1965, Royal Society of Arts and Nature Conservancy,
    London.
County of Dunbarton (1952), Part Development Plan - Vale of
    Leven Area, Written Statement, County of Dunbarton,
    Dumbarton.
County of Dunbarton (1968), County of Dunbarton, Countryside
    Map 1968, County of Dunbarton, Dumbarton.
County of Lanark (1953), Development Plan, Part Area 1953,
    Written Statement, County of Lanark, Lanark.
County of Lanark (1962), Central Industrial Area, Part
    Development Plan, County of Lanark, Lanark.
County of Renfrew (1963), First Quinquennial Review, Policy
    Statement 1963, County of Renfrew, Renfrew.
Crane, Jacob (1945), An American Looks at British Housing,
    Journal of Royal Institute of British Architects, Vol. 53,
    No.4.
Cullingworth, J.B. (1974 ed.), Town and Country Planning in
    Britain, 5th ed., George Allen and Unwin, London.

Cullingworth, J.B. (1975), Environmental Planning 1939-1969 Vol.1. Reconstruction and Land-Use Planning 1939-1947, HMSO, London.

Darlington Amenity Research Trust (1978), Scottish Tourism and Recreation Planning Studies, A report prepared for the Countryside Commission, Scottish Tourist Board, Scottish Sports Council and Forestry Commission, Darlington Amenity Research Trust, Edinburgh.

Department of Economic Affairs (1965), The West Midlands, A Regional Study, HMSO, London.

Department of Education and Science (1966), Report of the Land Use Study Group, HMSO, London.

Department of the Environment (1977), Policy for Inner Cities, Cmnd. 6845, HMSO, London.

Department of Health for Scotland (1935a), Working Class Housing on the Continent, HMSO, Edinburgh.

Department of Health for Scotland (1935b), Report by the Scottish Architectural Committee, HMSO, Edinburgh.

Department of Health for Scotland (1944), Distribution of New Houses in Scotland, Cmnd. 6552, HMSO, Edinburgh.

Department of Health for Scotland (1945), National Parks: A Scottish Survey, Report by the Scottish National Parks Survey Committee, Cmnd, 6631, HMSO, Edinburgh.

Department of Health for Scotland (1947a), New Town at East Kilbride, HMSO, Edinburgh.

Department of Health for Scotland (1947b), National Parks and the Conservation of Nature in Scotland: Report by the Scottish National Parks Committee and the Scottish Wildlife Conservation Committee, Cmnd. 7235, HMSO, Edinburgh.

Department of Health for Scotland (1948), Draft New Town (Glenrothes) Designation Order 1948, HMSO, Edinburgh.

Department of Health for Scotland (1949), Nature Reserves in Scotland, Final Report by the Scottish National Parks Committee and the Scottish Wildlife Conservation Committee, Cmnd. 7814, HMSO, Edinburgh.

Department of Health for Scotland (1958), Scottish Housing Handbook: 1 - Housing Layout, HMSO, Edinburgh.

Department of Health for Scotland (1960), Green Belt Circular, No.40, HMSO, Edinburgh.

Department of Health for Scotland (1962), Draft New Town (Livingston) Designation Order, HMSO, Edinburgh.

Dix G. (1981), Patrick Abercrombie 1879-1957, Pioneers of British Planning, Ed. Gordon E. Cherry, The Architectural Press, London.

Edwards, A.M. and Wibberley, G.P. (1971), An Agricultural Land Budget for Britain 1965-2000, University of London, Wye College, Ashford.

Employment Policy, Cmnd. 6527, HMSO, London.

Esher L. (1971), Conservation in Glasgow, The Corporation of Glasgow, Glasgow.

Farmer, Elspeth and Smith, Roger (1975), Overspill Theory, Urban Studies, Vol. 12.

Firn, John R. (1974), Indigenous Growth and Regional Development, Conference on the West Central Scotland Economy, Ed. Cameron, Gordon C., University of Glasgow, Urban and Regional Studies Discussion Paper No.12, Glasgow.

Firn, John R. (1975), External Control and Regional Development: the Case for Scotland, Environment and Planning A, Vol.7.

Firn, John R. (1982), Industrial Regeneration and Regional Policy: The Scottish Perspective and Experience, Industrial Decline and Regeneration, Ed. Collins, Lyndhurst, Department of Geography and Centre for Canadian Studies, University of Edinburgh, Edinburgh.

Fitzpayne, E.R.L. (1948), A Report on the Future Development of Passenger Transport in Glasgow, Corporation of Glasgow, Glasgow.

Foley, D.L. (1963), Controlling London's Growth, University of California Press, California, USA.

General Registrar Office (1942), Current Trends of Population, HMSO, London.

Gibbon, Lewis Grassic (1934), Glasgow, Scottish Scene, Gibbon, Lewis Grassic and MacDiarmid, Hugh, Jarrolds, London.

Gilfillan, J.B.S. (1958), The Historical Setting, The Third Statistical Account of Scotland, Ed. Cunnison, J. and Gilfillan, J.B.S., Collins, Glasgow.

Gillingwater, D. and Hart, D.A. (Eds.)(1978), The Regional Planning Process, Saxon House, Farnborough.

Glass, D.V. (1956), Some Aspects of the Development of Demography, Journal of the Royal Society of Arts, Vol. CIV.

Glass, D.V. (1967), Population Policies and Movements in Europe, Cass, London.

Gomme, A. and Walker, D. (1968), The Architecture of Glasgow, Lund Humphries, London.

Grieve, Robert (1954), The Clyde Valley - A Review. Town and Country Planning Summer School, St. Andrews University, Town Planning Institute, London.

Grieve, Robert (1960), Regional Planning on Clydeside, Town and Country Planning Summer School, St. Andrews University, Town Planning Institute, London.

Grieve, Robert and Robertson, D.J. (1964), The City and the Region, University of Glasgow Social and Economic Studies, Occasional Papers No.2, Oliver and Boyd, Edinburgh.

Hall, Sir A.D. (1942), Statement. Industry and Rural Life, Ed. Newbold, H.B., Faber and Faber, London.

Hall, Peter; Thomas, Roy; Gracey, Harry; Drewett, Roy (1973), The Containment of Urban England, Allen and Unwin, London.

Hall, Peter (1975), Urban and Regional Planning, David and Charles, Newton Abbott.

257

Hanham, H.J. (1969), The Development of the Scottish Office, Government and Nationalism in Scotland, Ed. Wolfe, J.N., Edinburgh University Press, Edinburgh.

Hart, D.A. (1976), Planning as an Iterative Process, Local Government Studies, Vol.2, No.3.

Hallard, D.A. (1976), Farmers and Landowners - Allies or Antagonists, Ed. Travis, A.S. and Veal, A.J., Recreation and the Urban Fringe, University of Birmingham, Birmingham.

Henderson, R.A. (1974), Industrial Overspill from Glasgow 1958-1968, Urban Studies, Vol.11.

Henderson, R.A. (1980), An Analysis of Closures amongst Scottish Manufacturing Plants between 1966 and 1975, Scottish Journal of Political Economy, Vol.27.

Highlands and Islands Development Board (1967), First Annual Report, Highlands and Islands Development Board, Inverness.

Hill, Oliver (1945), A Review of Building Scotland, Journal of Royal Institute of British Architects, Vol.52, No.3.

Hodgen, R. and Cullen, J. (1968), Recent Developments in Highway Planning in Glasgow. Proceedings of the Institute of Civil Engineers, Vol.41, October.

Hollingsworth, T.H. (1970), Migration, University of Glasgow, Social and Economic Studies, Occasional Paper No.12, Oliver and Boyd, Edinburgh.

Hood, Neil and Young, Stephen (1982), Multinationals in Retreat: The Scottish Experience, Edinburgh University Press, Edinburgh.

House of Commons Select Committee on Scottish Affairs, Session 1971-72 (1972), Land Resource Use in Scotland, Vol.1 Report and Proceedings of the Committee, HMSO, London.

Howard, Ebenezer (1902, 1946 ed), Garden Cities of Tomorrow, Faber, London.

Hughes, Michael (1980), The Anatomy of Scottish Capital, Croom Helm, London.

Hume, J.R. and Moss, M.S. (1979), Beardmore: The History of a Scottish Industrial Giant, Heinemann Educational Books, London.

Hurd, R. (1938), Design for Today, Scotland 1938, Oliver and Boyd, Edinburgh.

Jack Holmes Planning Group (1968), The Moray Firth, Highlands and Islands Development Board, Inverness.

Johnston, Thomas (1952), Memories, Collins, London.

Jury, A.G. (1952), Glasgow's Housing Needs, Corporation of Glasgow, Glasgow.

Jury, A.G. (1966), Housing Centenary: A Review of Municipal Housing in Glasgow from 1866 to 1966, Corporation of Glasgow, Glasgow.

Kellas, J.G. (1974), The Scottish Political System, Cambridge University Press, London.

Kirkwood, W.C. (1948), Industrial Estates of Scotland, Glasgow Herald Trade Review, June.

Lea, K.J. (1980), Greater Glasgow, Scottish Geographical Magazine, Vol.96, No.1, April 1980.

Lenman, Bruce (1977), An Economic History of Modern Scotland, Batsford, London.

Lever, W.F. (1974), Regional Multipliers and Demand Leakages at Establishment Level, Scottish Journal of Political Economy, Vol. XXI No.2, June 1974.

Loch Lomond Planning Group (1980), Loch Lomond Local (Subject) Plan for Recreation, Tourism and Landscape Conservation, Consultative Draft, Glasgow.

Lord President of the Council (1975), Our Changing Democracy, Cmnd. 6348, HMSO, London.

Lothians Survey (1966), Lothians Regional Survey and Plan, HMSO, Edinburgh.

Lyall, G.A. (1980), Land Assessment in Scotland, Ed. Thomas M.F. and Coppock, J.T., Aberdeen University Press, Aberdeen.

Lythe, S.G. and Butt, J. (1975), An Economic History of Scotland 1100-1939, Blackie, Glasgow.

McCallum, J. Douglas (1980), Statistical Trends of the British Conurbations, The Future of the British Conurbations: Policies and Prescriptions for Change, Ed. Cameron, Gordon C., Longman, London.

McCrone, Gavin (1965), Scotland's Economic Progress 1951-1960, George Allen and Unwin, London.

McDonald, Shiela T. (1977), The Regional Report in Scotland, Town Planning Review, Vol.48, No.3.

Macfie, A.L. (1955), The Scottish Tradition in Economic Thought, Scottish Journal of Political Economy, Vol.2, No.2.

McIntosh, Angus (1949/50), The Clyde Valley Regional Plan - A Review, Town Planning Review, Vol.XX.

Macmillan, H. (1969), Tides of Fortune, Macmillan, London.

Manson, T.B. (1945), Land Utilisation, Scottish Journal of Agriculture, Vol.XXV.

Mears, Sir Frank (1948), Regional Plan for Central and South East Scotland, HMSO, Edinburgh.

Milne, Sir David (1957), The Scottish Office, George Allen and Unwin, London.

Ministry of Health (1944), Design of Dwellings, HMSO, London.

Ministry of Housing and Local Government (1964), The South-East Study 1961-81, HMSO, London.

Ministry of Labour (1934), Reports of Investigations into the Industrial Conditions in Certain Depressed Areas, IV, Scotland, Cmnd, 4728.

Ministry of Supply (1946), Report by the British Iron and Steel Federation and the Joint Iron Council, Cmnd. 6811, HMSO, London.

Ministry of Town and Country Planning (1945), National Parks in England and Wales, Report by John Dower, Cmnd. 6628, HMSO, London.

Ministry of Town and Country Planning (1947), Report of the National Parks Committee (England and Wales) Cmnd. 7121, HMSO, London.

Ministry of Transport (1963), Traffic in Towns, HMSO, London.

Ministry of Works and Planning (1942), Report of the Committee on Land Utilisation in Rural Areas, (The Scott Report), Cmnd. 6378, HMSO, London.

Mumford, L. (1946), City Development, Secker and Warburg, London.

Morton, H.B. (Ed.)(1973), A Hillhead Album, The Hepburn Trust, Glasgow.

Nairn, I. (1960), Glasgow and Cumbernauld New Town, The Listener, Vol.LXIV, No.1648.

Nicholls, D.C. and Young, A. (1968), Recreation and Tourism in the Loch Lomond Area, Department of Social and Economic Research, University of Glasgow.

Northern Region Strategy Team (1977), Strategic Plan for the Northern Region, Department of the Environment, HMSO, London.

North West Economic Planning Council (1974), Strategic Plan for the North West, HMSO, London.

Notes of Proceedings (1947), Notes of Proceedings at Public Local Inquiry into the Designation of East Kilbride, Typescript, Scottish Office.

Nuttgens, P. (1967), Cumbernauld Town Centre, The Architectural Review, Vol.CXLII, No.850.

Oakley, C.A. (1937), Scottish Industry Today: A Survey Undertaken for the Scottish Development Council, Morey Press, Edinburgh.

Oakley, C.A. (1947), Industry and Commerce, Scotland, Ed. Meikle, Henry W., Thomas Nelson, Edinburgh.

O.E.C.D. (1979), Agriculture in the Planning and Management of Peri-urban Areas, Vol.I, OECD, Paris.

Ormiston, J.H. (1973), Moray Firth: An Agricultural Study, Special Report No.9, Highlands and Islands Development Board, Inverness.

Orr, Sarah C. and Orr James (1958a), Other Engineering, The Third Statistical Account of Scotland, Ed. Cunnison, J. and Gilfillan, J.B.S., Collins, Glasgow.

Orr, James and Orr Sarah (1958b), The Growth of Engineering Industries, The Glasgow Region, Ed. Miller, R. and Tivy, J., The British Association, Glasgow.

Osborn F.J. (1950), Review of the Clyde Valley Regional Plan, The Spectator, 27 January.

Osborn, F.J. and Whittick, A. (1977 3rd Ed.), New Towns, Leonard Hill, London.

Planning Advisory Group (1965), The Future of Development Plans, HMSO, London.

Population Panel (1973), Report of the Population Panel, Cmnd. 5258, HMSO, London.

Potential for Development (1970), Tayside, Potential for Development, HMSO, Edinburgh.

Prentice, R.J. (undated), Conserve and Provide. A Brief History of the National Trust for Scotland, National Trust for Scotland.

Price, Jacob M. (1967), The Rise of Glasgow in the Chesapeake Tobacco Trade 1707-1775, Studies in Scottish Business History, Ed. Payne, Peter L., Frank Cass, London.

Randall, John N. (1980), Central Clydeside - a Case Study of One Conurbation, The Future of the British Conurbations: Policies and Prescriptions for Change, Ed. Cameron, Gordon C., Longman, London.

Regional Planning Committee (1944), Clyde Area Report on Housing Sites, Scottish Record Office, DD 12/35.

Reiach, A. and Hurd R. (1944, 2nd Ed.), Building Scotland, The Saltire Society, Edinburgh.

Reid, J.M. (1960), The Victorians' City, Scottish Art Review, Vol.7, No.4.

Richardson, Harry W. (1969), Regional Economics, Weidenfeld and Nicolson, London

Robb, A.M. (1958), Shipbuilding and Marine Engineering, The Third Statistical Account for Scotland, Ed. Cunnison, J. and Gilfillan, J.B.S., Collins, Glasgow.

Robinson, P. 1980, Community Initiatives in Glasgow - A Case Study, The Planner, Vol.66, No.3.

Ross Young W. (1918), Town Planning in Scotland, Town Planning Review, Vol.VIII.

Royal Commission (1917), Report of the Royal Commission on the Housing of the Industrial Populations of Scotland, Cd. 8731, HMSO, Edinburgh.

Royal Commission (1940), Report of the Royal Commission on the Distribution of the Industrial Population, Cmnd. 6153, HMSO, London.

Royal Commission (1949), Royal Commission on Population in Britain, Cmnd. 7695, HMSO, London.

Royal Commission (1969), Report of the Royal Commission on Local Government for England, Cmnd. 4039, HMSO, London.

Royal Commission (1969), Report of Royal Commission on Local Government in Scotland 1966-69, Cmnd. 4150, HMSO, Edinburgh.

Royal Commission (1973), Report of the Royal Commission on the Constitution, Cmnd. 5460, HMSO, London.

Samuel, Sir John S. (1928), The Local Government and Municipal Enterprises of Glasgow, Ed. Kerr J. G., Glasgow, Sketches by Various Authors, British Association for Advancement of Science, Glasgow University Press, Glasgow.

Scott, John and Hughes, Michael (1980), The Anatomy of Scottish Capital, Croom Helm, London.

Scott, Sir Leslie (1942), Report of the Committee on Land Utilisation in Rural Areas, Cmnd. 6378, HMSO, London.

261

Scott, Wilson, Kirkpatrick and Partners (1962), Interim Report on the Glasgow Inner Ring Road, Corporation of Glasgow, Glasgow.

Scott, Wilson, Kirkpatrick and Partners (1965), A Highway Plan for Glasgow, Corporation of Glasgow, Glasgow.

Scott, Wilson, Kirkpatrick and Partners (1967), Greater Glasgow Transportation Study: Vol.1 - Current Travel Problems, Corporation of Glasgow, Glasgow.

Scott, Wilson, Kirkpatrick and Partners (1968), Greater Glasgow Transportation Study: Vol.2 - Forecasts and Plan, Corporation of Glasgow, Glasgow.

Scottish Council on Industry (1961), Report of the Committee appointed by the Scottish Council (Development and Industry), Inquiry into the Scottish Economy 1960-61, Scottish Council (Development and Industry), Edinburgh.

Scottish Development Agency (1977), Report 1977, Scottish Development Agency, Glasgow.

Scottish Development Agency (1982), Report 82, Scottish Development Agency, Glasgow.

Scottish Development Department (1963a), The Modernisation of Local Government in Scotland, Cmnd. 2067, HMSO, Edinburgh.

Scottish Development Department (1963b), Central Scotland: A Programme for Development and Growth, Cmnd. 2188, HMSO, Edinburgh.

Scottish Development Department (1966a), Draft New Town (Irvine) Designation Order 1966, HMSO, Edinburgh.

Scottish Development Department (1966b), Lothians Regional Survey and Plan, HMSO, Edinburgh.

Scottish Development Department (1968a), Grangemouth-Falkirk Regional Study and Plan, HMSO, Edinburgh.

Scottish Development Department (1968b), Central Borders, Vol.1, HMSO, Edinburgh.

Scottish Development Department (1969), Annual Report 1968, HMSO, Edinburgh.

Scottish Development Department (1970), Report for 1969, Cmnd. 4313, HMSO, Edinburgh.

Scottish Development Department (1972), The Size and Distribution of Scotland's Population, HMSO, Edinburgh.

Scottish Development Department (1973), Land Resource Use in Scotland, Cmnd. 5428, HMSO, Edinburgh.

Scottish Development Department (1977a), Circular 19/1977: National Planning Guidelines, Scottish Development Department, Edinburgh.

Scottish Development Department (1974b), Circular 61/1974: Coastal Planning Guidelines, Scottish Development Department, Edinburgh.

Scottish Development Department (1979), Countryside (Amendment) Scotland) Bill Consultative Paper, Scottish Development Department, Edinburgh.

Scottish Education Department (1947), Planning for Community Centres, HMSO, Edinburgh.
Scottish Home Department (1944), The Report of the Scottish Coalfields Committee, Cmnd. 6575, HMSO, Edinburgh.
Scottish Housing Advisory Committee (1943), Planning our New Homes, HMSO, Edinburgh.
Scottish Housing Advisory Committee (1944), The Distribution of New Houses in Scotland, HMSO, Edinburgh.
Scottish Housing Advisory Committee (1947), Modernising our Homes, HMSO, Edinburgh.
Scottish Office (1966), The Scottish Economy 1965-70, HMSO, London.
Scottish Office (1971), Reform of Local Government in Scotland, Cmnd. 4583, HMSO, Edinburgh.
Scottish Tourist Board (1975), Planning for Tourism in Scotland, A Preliminary National Strategy, Scottish Tourist Board, Edinburgh.
Scottish Tourist Board (1977), Planning for Tourism in Scotland, A report on progress following publication of the Scottish Tourist Board's Preliminary National Strategy, Scottish Tourist Board, Edinburgh.
Select Committee on Scottish Affairs (1971), Minutes of Evidence, Session 1970-71, House of Commons Paper 503-1, Session 1970-71, HMSO, London.
Severnside Study (1970), Severnside Feasibility Study, HMSO, London.
Skinner, David N. (1973), The Countryside of the Antonine Wall, A Survey and Recommended Policy Statement, Countryside Commission for Scotland, Perth.
Skinner David N. (1976), A Situation Report on Green Belts in Scotland, Countryside Commission for Scotland Occasional Paper No. 8, March 1976.
Slaven, A. (1975), The Development of the West of Scotland, Routledge, London.
Smith, Roger (1974a), Multi-Dwelling Building in Scotland, 1750-1970, Multi-Storey Living, Ed. Sutcliffe, Anthony, Croom Helm, London.
Smith, Roger (1974b), The Origins of Scottish New Towns Policy and the Founding of East Kilbride, Public Administration, Vol.52, Summer.
Smith, Roger (1977), The Politics of an Overspill Policy, Public Administration, Spring.
Smith, Roger (1978), Stonehouse - An Obituary for a New Town, Local Government Studies, April.
Smith, Roger (1979), East Kilbride: The Biography of a Scottish New Town, HMSO, London.
Smith, Roger (1980), Barlow, Planning, 25th August.
South East Joint Planning Team (1970), Strategic Plan for the South East, HMSO, London.

South Hampshire Study (1966), South Hampshire Study, HMSO, London.

Spicer, C.C. and Lipworth, L. (1966), Regional and Social Factors in Infant Mortality, General Registrar Office: Studies in Medical and Population Subjects No.19, HMSO, London.

Strathclyde Regional Council (1976a), Regional Report, Strathclyde Regional Council, Glasgow.

Strathclyde Regional Council (1976b), Strategic Issues for Strathclyde, Survey Report, Strathclyde Regional Council, Glasgow.

Strathclyde Regional Council (1977), Main Strategic Issues for Strathclyde, Survey Report 1976, Strathclyde Regional Council, Glasgow.

Strathclyde Regional Council (1978a), The First Three Years, Strathclyde Regional Council, Glasgow.

Strathclyde Regional Council (1978), Strathclyde Structure Plan 1979, Remote Rural Areas, A Discussion Document, Strathclyde Regional Council, Glasgow.

Strathclyde Regional Council (1979), Strathclyde Structure Plan 1979, Written Statement, Strathclyde Regional Council, Glasgow.

Strathclyde Regional Council (1980), Countryside Strategy (Draft), Strathclyde Regional Council, Glasgow.

Storey, David (1982), Entrepreneurship and the New Firm, Croom Helm, London.

Sub Committee of the Scientific Advisory Committee (1943), Report on Infant Mortality in Scotland, HMSO, London.

Swales, J.K. (1979), Entrepreneurship and Regional Development: Implications for Regional Policy, Regional Policy: Past Experience and New Directions, Ed. Maclennan, D. and Parr, J. B., Martin Robertson, London.

Tourism and Recreation Research Unit, Edinburgh University (June 1978), Strathclyde Park 1977, Monitoring the Use of a Country Park, A report sponsored by the Countryside Commission for Scotland, Tourism and Recreation Research Unit, Edinburgh.

Travis, A.S. et al (1970), Recreation Planning for the Clyde, Firth of Clyde Study Phase 2, Scottish Tourist Board, Edinburgh.

Travis, A.S. (1974), A Strategic Appraisal of Scottish Tourism, An assessment of resource potential, Scottish Tourist Board, Edinburgh.

Tripp, H.A. (1942), Town Planning and Road Traffic, Arnold, London.

Treasury (1947), Capital Investment in 1948, Cmnd. 7268, HMSO, London.

Trotman-Dickenson, D.T. (1961), The Scottish Industrial Estates, Scottish Journal of Political Economy, Vol.8.

Uthwatt (1942), Report of the Expert Committee on Compensation and Betterment, Cmnd. 6386, HMSO, London.

Weller, J.D. (1976), Rural Settlement and Landscape, Architects' Journal, 21st Jan.

Weller, J.D. (1979), Land Use and Agricultural Change, (Ed) Lovejoy, D., Land Use and Landscape Planning, 2nd Ed., Leonard Hill, London.

West Central Scotland Plan Team (1974a), Consultative Draft Report, West Central Scotland Plan, Glasgow.

West Central Scotland Plan Team (1974b), West Central Scotland Plan, Supplementary Report 5A The Environment, West Central Scotland Plan, Glasgow.

West Central Scotland Plan Team (1974c), West Central Scotland Plan, Supplementary Report 4 Social Issues, West Central Scotland Plan, Glasgow.

West Central Scotland Plan Team (1974d), West Central Plan, Supplementary Report 1, The Regional Economy, West Central Scotland Plan, Glasgow.

Wilson, L.H. (1960), Cumbernauld - the Design of a High Density New Town. Town and Country Planning Summer School, St. Andrews University, Town Planning Institute, London.

Wilson and Womersley (1969), Teesside Survey and Plan, HMSO, London.

Wise, W.S. and Fell, E. (1978), U.K. Agricultural Productivity and the Land Budget, Journal of Agricultural Economics, Vol. XXIX.

Winch, Donald (1969), Economics and Policy: An Historical Study, Hodder and Stoughton, London.

Worsdall, F. (1979), The Tenement: A Way of Life, Chambers, Edinburgh.

Yorkshire and Humberside Strategy (1970), Yorkshire and Humberside Regional Strategy, HMSO, London.

Index